WITHDRAWN

A Man From Kansas

By David Hinshaw

THE HOME FRONT
A MAN FROM KANSAS

A Man From Kansas

The Story of
WILLIAM ALLEN WHITE

By David Hinshaw

G. P. PUTNAM'S SONS　　NEW YORK

272030

COPYRIGHT, 1945, BY DAVID HINSHAW

All rights reserved. This book, or parts thereof, must
not be reproduced in any form without permission.

Second Impression

PN
4874
W52
H54

MANUFACTURED IN THE UNITED STATES OF AMERICA

ACKNOWLEDGMENTS

I WISH to thank the Macmillan Company for their courtesy in permitting me to quote from Mr. White's books, *Masks in a Pageant*, and *The Changing West, Harper's* magazine for permission to quote from Mr. White's article "The Country Town Newspaper," and the *Atlantic Monthly* for permission to include material from my "Father White" article.

Dr. Everett Rich's able, scholarly biography, *The Man From Emporia*, was most useful to me as a guide and a check. I am deeply indebted to him for so graciously granting me free use of the material it contains. I acknowledge with thanks my appreciation to my old friend Frank C. Clough, one-time city editor of the *Gazette*, for his giving me permission to include herein some material from his book, *William Allen White of Emporia*.

My generous thanks are extended to the *Gazette* staff for their cooperation in making available all bound copies of that newspaper between 1895 and 1943 and for facilitating in every way my work in selecting extracts from Mr. White's editorials over this forty-nine-year period. I am deeply grateful to members of the editorial staff for contributions of incidents concerning Mr. White, especially to my old friends Miss Laura French, former *Gazette* city editor, for reading and checking the first manuscript copy of this book; Calvin H. Lambert, who followed Miss French as city editor, for his contributions; Rolla A. Clymer, a *Gazette* star reporter in the long ago when the world was young; Minnie Yearout, Mr. White's secretary for over twenty years, for the side lights she gave me on him. A host of other old friends of Mr. White's and mine generously renewed and shared their recollections of him.

More than to any other one person I am indebted to Will Irwin for his wise counsel and help in writing this book.

DAVID HINSHAW

Contents

Sixteen pages of photographic illustrations follow page 148

Foreword

Forty-eight years ago, a farm boy near Emporia, I became the Quaker Valley correspondent of the *Emporia Gazette* because I hungrily wanted the paper and there was no other way to get it since my father belonged to the faction and subscribed to the local newspaper which opposed Mr. White's point of view. This work paid no cash, but it brought me the *Gazette* free, subscriptions to magazines, occasional books, a pass to the circus each summer when it came to Emporia, and the friendship of the man whose influence on my life has been greatest.

The freshness and breadth of the young editor awoke an answering echo in my heart. Momentous years, busy, disturbing, glorious years with multitudinous demands and varied interests have come and gone since those far-off days when we were so happy and so poor. But the heart always echoed when he spoke. Neither time nor distance, trouble, misunderstanding, differences, pressing demands, nor any other thing, ever stilled its response.

This book seeks to share with others some of my delights in his joyous spirit, to give the feel of him and thus help others to understand better what made him what he was and thereby gain fresh faith and inspiration with which to tackle their day-to-day problems in this self-crucified, busy, beautiful world of ours.

This impressionistic high-lighting and interpretation of Mr. White's career and personality rests largely on the memories of forty-six years of close friendship, our common background, and his *Gazette* editorials.

In the late spring of 1945, I reread, in bound volumes of the *Gazette,* all of the editorials Mr. White wrote between 1895 and 1943, and selected and recorded by dictaphone portions of many of them for quotation or reference purposes in this book. This task flooded my memory with countless incidents of our long friendship. In all but three or four instances he was "kind and helpful and generous and charitable and forgiving."

The rare exceptions were largely caused by misunderstanding based upon misinformation, and therefore only slightly and briefly affected our relationship. They do enable me, however, to realize that he was not a perfect man. None is on this earth; perhaps that's why God made heaven.

There also is included in the earlier pages of this book some information and description of the settlement of Kansas and its pioneer life which helped to shape the character of her citizens and which flowered so perfectly in her distinguished son.

I have done this first because one must understand Mr. White's environment before fully understanding him, and second because by doing it I will in a slight measure carry out a duty he long had tried to place on me, namely, that I write what he called "a spiritual history of Kansas." It may be, as he insisted, that this book is a *must*. Fearing that I may never write it, I have included in this one a part of the spiritual history of early Kansas because it and the spiritual life of William Allen White are indivisible.

He, more ably than any man I ever knew, bridged the gap between the hard, yet wondrously kind, neighborly pioneer life and today's life of confusion and comfort. Many men were puzzled by this transformation or else lost their way, but not Will White. He clung always to his simple, pioneer faith in man's spark of innate goodness and God's unfolding purpose for man, but he also became a modern of the moderns. He sought for and found the best in men, loved them, and was greatly beloved by them. He sought beauty from life, found and reflected it in all his relationships. There flowed from his deep spiritual wellsprings a continuous stream of understanding, wisdom, tolerance, and justice tempered with mercy. These qualities, combined with great moral courage, wistful idealism, instinctive gentleness, an astounding audacity of the spirit, rare imagination, and a nimble wit, made him uniquely great.

A world peopled with men and women of Mr. White's stature could make the imagination-staggering atomic energy age the golden one of history. The gap between his mental and moral attainments and the sweeping onrush of scientific advance was hardly discernible. His spiritual colleagues, if they are numerous enough and outspoken enough, can turn this newly harnessed gigantic power to constructive social and economic uses, make it lift loads from the backs of men and women, give them more useful leisure, greater comfort, security, and opportunity than heretofore has been dreamed possible.

Undoubtedly I have gilded the lily. Who knows whether or not I have told the truth about him, since no one can say positively whether truth is what should be or what is? Should a man in writing of his friend's life tell the mere facts or should he enlarge upon the bright ideals his friend sought to attain? Is the ideal the truth? It should be, for it alone is real or vital in anything.

Over forty years ago Mr. White said in a *Gazette* editorial:

The picture of life is more real than life. The picture of the sunset or of the ocean or of the meadow is more beautiful, more understandable than the real sunset, the real ocean or the real meadow, and strange as it may seem the picture makes it possible to see the beauty of the real thing more clearly. Because a picture exalts the ideal, omitting ugly details, thereby giving the observer the hint he needs to see things not as they are but as they should be. . . . Truth may thus be said to be not what is but what should be. . . .

If his interpretation of truth was correct the reader will find in the following pages that I have told the truth about William Allen White.

DAVID HINSHAW

August, 1945,
Dunmow Farm,
West Chester,
Pennsylvania.

Part One

THE EARLY YEARS
1868—1900

1. HIS LIFE A PARADOX

THE POSITION William Allen White held in the nation for nearly five decades was unique because he almost perfectly blended provincialism with cosmopolitanism. Because of this blend, together with his wisdom, tolerance, neighborly kindliness, keen sense of justice, clear understanding of the ways of men, and his remarkable ability to describe and interpret them, he became the most quoted editorial writer in the nation and then grew to be a world figure.

Mr. White's kinship with men and women in his community and state made him kin to the men and women of the nation and the whole world. His hatred was for the evil things men do, never for men, and "there was no malice in his heart." The truths he preached and lived were timeless, universal, and noble. His style was clear, concise, and often homely, and he had the knack—or was it genius?—of using always exactly the right word.

These qualities help to explain the paradox he was: the country-town editor who to the end of his life remained primarily that, but who also became and remained the most famous, the most esteemed, and probably the most influential American editor of his day. His death was noted in newspapers throughout the world. The London *Times* commented on his passing with a long, appreciative editorial. Although his newspaper never had a circulation of more than eight thousand copies a day, it nevertheless ranked in influence beside metropolitan dailies with circulations running into the hundreds of thousands. He made Emporia, which never has reached a population of fifteen thousand, the most famous small, *modern* city in the English-speaking world, comparable in a way with Stratford-on-Avon, Lourdes, and Siena in Western world history.

Such remarkable distinction could be given a country town only by a man of exceptional talents, unusual spiritual, moral, and intellectual strengths. Only the most favorable environment could produce such a man—exhorter and prophet that he was

3

—wholesome, courageous, generous, and strong, and dowered with a gorgeous, common-sense Americanism. It has been said of him that his one great urge was to tell the story of the Middle West, to interpret its spirit and purpose to all who would listen. He remained in the state and town of his birth because "I know my life work and I know my limitations—both require that I stay in Emporia."

From the time his salutatory editorial was printed in the *Gazette* on June 3, 1895, until he ceased going to the office at the end of 1943, Mr. White was *the* Emporian of Emporians. This was his town, his home. He was born there. He first attended college there. He found fame, distinction, and great power there. Here were his friends and acquaintances. His children were born and grew up there. All of his dreams came true in Emporia.

More important than all of these things, White belonged in Emporia more completely than he belonged anywhere else in the world. Here he was perfectly cast for the part he was to play on life's stage. Always, with Emporia, Kansas, and the Middle West as his background, his scenery, he was in character. He would have lost his flavor, his lines might have fallen flat had he had a great-city setting. He knew this well, perhaps better than anyone else. And he knew the value to him as a writer, a leader, and a philosopher of keeping in character at all times. Modest and unassuming as he was, no one ever should trifle with the assumption that Mr. White was a shrinking violet. He had an excellent sense of the dramatic, of timing, of when to get on and to get off issues.

He had, too, an especially keen sense of what was news. When he was tipped off by telephone from Topeka that his friend Governor Henry Allen had ordered his arrest in the shopmen's strike in 1922, Mr. White asked the *Gazette* city editor if he had his car downtown. When told that he had, he said: "I'd like to ride into the country. I'm tired of the office this afternoon."

They drove out west of town, up and down country roads for two hours or so. Then he said, "Now let's go back and get me arrested. It will make a better story for the morning papers. If I had been arrested earlier, we would have missed the late afternoon editions."

As a successful journalist he knew how important a "good press" was to him as a writer and as a leader of causes. And able newspaperman that he was, he knew better than most men how to get publicity without seeking it. Thus to the end of his life— although a frequenter of the great cities of the world and known and respected by the great of the world—he continued to be the editor of a country-town newspaper, a rustic philosopher, a man whose "tonsils got sunburned when looking at great city buildings." When standing in line at Columbia University to receive an honorary degree, the man in front of White turned to him and asked where he was from. He replied, "I guess I don't belong here, for I'm just a country editor from Kansas." To this his questioner responded, "I guess I don't belong here either, for I'm only a country doctor from Minnesota." The "country doctor" was William J. Mayo, of Rochester, Minnesota.

White never lost the Emporia touch, never relaxed interest in the town of his life and love. Some Emporians felt that he overplayed the part, but who can judge this? No man ever sees all of another man's soul. The best even the most discerning can do is to catch occasional glimpses of it. Perhaps he did over-idealize Emporia and Emporians. Who knows?

Whatever the case may be, Mr. White's love of Emporia and Emporia neighbors found constant expression in words and actions. Once in a *Gazette* editorial he commented on a fire at his home, and told how, within an hour after the water was turned into the house, every stick of furniture, every book, every picture, every rug and carpet—everything was out of that house but the wallpaper; had been moved out by the Whites' neighbors. "Not a glass in a picture was cracked, not a paper lost and no articles of any value disappeared," he said. The damage to the house and furniture was negligible, he wrote, because of good neighbors who came quickly, worked methodically, and used their heads.

The neighborhood around Tenth and Exchange [he wrote] may not have the social distinction that graces other environs, but by George, the neighborhood around Tenth and Exchange is equipped with heads and hands that work like clocks and the neighbors have hearts of pure gold! And a good neighborhood is rather to be chosen than great social qualities. It's not a pedigreed neighborhood: it's not perhaps a good beef breed of folks; rather it's Holstein—some black and some white. But they are good grade folk and we're all for 'em against all comers!

He knew, too, with that remarkable sixth sense of his, that Emporia and Kansas, aside from satisfying his genuine liking for life in a country town, furnished him, as a social, economic, and political philosopher, with exactly the right setting for what he had to say about men and movements. There he belonged. He remained at heart, to the end of his life, a Kansas pioneer in neighborliness, in public interest, in hopefulness. This was inevitable because the pioneer life of this keenly observant, acutely sensitive boy put its brand on his soul and its romance fired his imagination.

2. WHAT MADE KANSANS PECULIAR

Buffalo still roamed the prairies when Mr. White was a boy, and buffalo hunting was still a major sport. As the railroads pushed westward during these early years, each new terminal became a shipping center for the great herds of cattle which were driven north over the Chisholm Trail from the plains of Texas to graze and fatten on the lush blue-stem grass of the Kansas prairies and later to be shipped to eastern markets. Each one in turn was for a while the headquarters of gamblers, fancy women, and two-gun men who shot from the hip at the slightest provocation—or none. Violent and sudden death were commonplaces. Abilene was the first of these wild and woolly headquarters. Later Dodge City became equally infamous when the Santa Fe Railroad reached there and it in turn became the shipping point for the Texas eastward-bound cattle. In both of these and in many other similar Kansas communities mob law ruled. "Boot Hill" cemeteries required more and more space in all these places as cowboys, after months or even years away from communities, used their revolvers to drill holes in each other or in the night sky above. As she matured, Kansas outgrew these uncurbed practices, but they left a residue which gave her people a touch of the frank, confident, and humorous manners of the old wild West.

The "mover wagon" was a familiar sight to young Will White as it wormed slowly across the plains, carrying hopes rather than worldly goods. Even to the turn of the century these white canvas specks, during periods of reasonable prosperity and good crops, continued to move west and south in an unending flow to the "promised land." During the years of crop failure in the Middle West or periods of economic depression throughout the nation most of them moved eastward, starved out. On their way west some of the canvases would carry the painted words: "Pike's Peak or Bust" or "Kansas or Bust." Some months or years later these same wagons on the way east would carry under those

7

words another line: "Busted, by God!" or "Busted—Back East to My Wife's Folks!"

These prairie schooners, or "mover wagons" as we children called them, were lumber wagons with sideboards, over which a canvas top was stretched on hoops. The front end was open, the back end closed with a pucker-rope.

In all seasons except winter countless numbers of them singly or in groups passed and repassed my boyhood farm home four miles east of Emporia. A corner of my father's farm lay across a bend of the Neosho River from our house, a few acres of second-bottom timberland which had not been fenced and was not farmed because it was so often flooded. This made a perfect camping place for these hordes of aspiring poor people who were looking for better opportunities. Most of the men were tall, gaunt, and tobacco-chewing, and were dressed in faded overalls. Most of the women, equally gaunt, wore calico dresses and sunbonnets. All of them had bronzed, strained faces.

I came to know the type well. Their wagons were filled with bedding, cooking utensils, dishes, clothing, perhaps a cook-stove, frequently lengths of rusted stovepipe tied to the wagon bows, and always children. A crate of chickens usually was fastened to the back end of the wagon. Frequently a sore-footed cow or two trailed along at the end of a rope, and usually one or more hound dogs brought up the rear. With barely an exception the phrase "poor but honest" might have been coined to describe them. They were desperately poor, nearly all of them, poor but honest, and proud men who paid their way. They hunted with bony fingers in their deep, gaunt, leather pocketbooks for the nickel, dime, or quarter with which to pay for whatever supplies they bought.

Too often the men, and even more the women and children, seemed as tired and uninspired as their worn-out horses and their bony cows. As a general rule the men and boys walked to lighten the load. In dry weather they slept in the open; when it rained they pitched tents or lay in their wagons. Sometimes, as frequently happened at our place, they would bed down in haymows. Few of them had more cash than the trip cost, and most of them lived on the slender hope that they would be able to find the place of their hearts' desire. I do not remember of a single family of this kind settling in our neighborhood, where the soil was rich. Nor can I recall more than three families from our community who took to the road in this manner for another place—and those who did came from the less stable, less industrious and thrifty group.

All such wandering families helped to keep the frontier population fluid. Many of them succeeded in the communities where they settled at the end of their trail; all served as object lessons for those who remained behind, made them a bit more determined to make a go of it where they were.

Another factor which helped mold the character and fix the habits of these early Kansans was the lack of any organized medical care. There were few doctors, no hospitals, and no community nursing services. Children were born with the help of neighbor women. There were no undertakers in the modern sense. Relatives or friends prepared the body of the deceased for burial. All were put to rest in rough coffins and hauled in lumber wagons or long spring wagons to the little cemeteries near by. If a farmer became sick or died his neighbors cultivated and harvested his crops without charge. These neighborly services created an easy intimacy and contributed to the spirit of give and take which still marks Kansas manners. People had to help and be helped or perish. Otherwise they would lose their fight for a great cause. In an early magazine article, "Emporia– New York," one of the reasons Mr. White gave for preferring Emporia was the fact that in no metropolis could one have such range or intensity of intimate friendships as in a small Kansas town. "Our affairs become common with one another, our joys become mutual and we are not alone in our sorrows," he wrote.

Coupled with this warmth of feeling for men and women individually was his desire to report from day to day in a small-town newspaper the record of their interests and activities, because "we who read them read in their lines, the sweet, intimate story of life . . . makes us wondrous kind . . . reveals us to ourselves, and keeps our country hearts quick and our country minds open and our country faith strong."

He knew this to be true because he grew up in a small frontier town where life had few refinements. Homes were simple, candles or oil lamps provided light, dirt roads or prairie trails con-

stituted the highways, railroads were barely known, and food
had little variety. The life these frontiersmen lived differed but
slightly from that which men had lived for centuries before.
The men and women were sturdy and self-reliant. They had to
be to survive. Each one stood on his own feet. Existence on this
frontier was especially precarious because nature in Kansas was
either abundantly generous or despairingly miserly. Always
in those days it was either feast or famine. Life was hard and
rough but kind and hopeful—especially hopeful. Tomorrow's
clouds would bring rain to the parched ground, revive the wilt-
ing crops. Next year there would be plenty. Next year the house
would be repaired. Next year or the year after, the railroad
would come to town. These conditions helped to make Mr.
White an optimist, as is revealed by the constantly recurring
phrase in *Gazette* editorials over a forty-eight-year period: "But
times will be better in the spring." In fact, all other Kansans of
that day constituted a race of optimists—the pessimists returned
to their old homes to live off their wives' relatives, and the
weaklings died. The spiritual qualities of most early settlers
made them idealists also. Hard conditions channeled their
efforts toward what Theodore Roosevelt called "realizable
ideals." The clear blue distant skies and the far-off gray horizons colored their idealism with wistfulness.

The indelible imprint these conditions made on the mind
and heart of the boy were expressed in later years by the man,
who believed that:

. . . there are higher gods who always smile—and wait. Tomorrow
also is a day. So behold, gentle reader, the cat out of the bag. You
are now forewarned that these chapters are written by an optimist;
alas, by an idealist. Pause, turn back, or expect the worst. It will be
a vague, wistful idealism. All idealism is that if it is sane. The materialistic view of life is simple because it is at any time easy to
demonstrate the thesis of materialism, even its pragmatic reality,
statistically, or actually by any rule of thumb. The materialistic
philosophy holds dogmatically that things are bad; so probably will
be worse. The premise is unassailable, the conclusion may not be
logically gainsaid. "And yet"—in these two words lies the idealist's
creed. For in that nebulous, indefinable hope he is convinced with
Job that his redeemer liveth, that life is worth while, that dreams
come true, that man's visions are God's reality.

These pioneers, as Mr. White described them in *The Changing West,* were unimpeded by economic inequalities or any
others inherent in the qualities of men. "There for the first time
on earth a free people worked at their own political and social
salvation." They were free to think and speak as they pleased
and to demand what they earned as their own. "Growing out of
these freedoms, spiritual and economic, were two other typical
and deeply symbolic institutions" that appeared in every settlement of the new country. These were the schoolhouse and the
church. They were built ahead of even city halls and court-
houses. "The morals of these communities grew out of a yearning for justice." The aspiration in their hearts embodied those
things which they felt made for righteousness. So in their "little
box-like churches they set up the gods who incarnated their
ethical ideals, and on those ideals of human conduct they wrote
their laws and achieved those ideals as they could tolerably
comprehend." They did not expect too much from God in a
material way, even when plagued with insects or suffering from
terrible droughts. One summer when crops in the Emporia
region were burning up and creeks and rivers were running
dry, some Emporians asked an elder to call a meeting for the
purpose of praying for rain. "What's the use?" he answered.
"When the wind is in the southwest it never brings rain."

Regardless of their human shortcomings they sought liberty
above all else, something a man cannot have unless he gives it
to others, which man does not strive to get "unless he has faith
in his fellow men." Thus their religion rested on an abiding
"faith in others that implied the acceptance of the Golden
Rule." Their religion was the spiritual structure on which their
laws were based, from which their institutions grew. "The ethics
of the Christian religion are essentially hopeful. They require
faith in man because Christ taught men that the good neighbor
cannot achieve happiness in the possession of worldly goods
alone. The religion of the people in these pioneer communities,
in its more significant manifestations, was essentially one of
optimism combined with a deep faith that kindness pays in the
lasting satisfactions of the human heart."

Alongside the churches they built their little schoolhouses,
crude one-room affairs. Wherever half a dozen families gathered

in a community the schoolhouse appeared, and "because it represented the pioneer's contact with reality it became in a faintly perceptible way his temple of research." It was a challenge to moral, political, and economic stagnation.

Mr. White was a true product of Kansas, perhaps the most typically American of the forty-eight states. It is the only state west of the Alleghenies whose pioneers acted not on the impulse for bettering a man's condition, but almost solely on political or moral motives. Of the eastern states, Massachusetts, Rhode Island, Pennsylvania and Maryland were founded by men who sought in a new world freedom from spiritual oppression. Their founders, however, came not to use the sword but to find peace. The settlers of Kansas, on the other hand, conducted a kind of double crusade which was the prelude to a civil war. The Kansas-Nebraska Act of 1854 laid down the principle of "popular sovereignty." The vote of the majority in this new territory would determine whether Kansas should be slave or free. Thus the early settlers of Kansas were the extremists of the nation, men from the North and East who flocked there to incorporate their conviction into law. In Whittier's words—

> They crossed the prairies as of old
> Our fathers crossed the sea
> To make the West as they the East
> The homestead of the free.

Those fighting abolitionists did not get their own way easily, because extremists from the South flocked to Kansas in great numbers, determined on their part to make Kansas a slave state. These proslavery settlers in turn were supported, in the bitter struggle to settle the fate of the state that was to be, by the "Border Ruffians" from Missouri, whose destructive raids gave the new territory the name of "Bleeding Kansas." All of them were men and women of conviction who felt and lived deeply and dangerously.

The result was that a white man's Kansas was born in a struggle which, no matter how hideous some of the details, was regarded by the free-soil immigrants as a holy war for human rights and by their Southern adversaries as defense against an immoral attack on property rights. Many of the Southerners held with the pious Stonewall Jackson that—as **Fletcher Pratt** has formulated it—"God ordained slavery as the portion of the Negro race; let the world be sown with corpses sobeit His will be done." But some groups of that Northern element which was destined to prevail in this struggle were the more fanatical. After John Brown and his band at Pottawatomie Creek murdered five proslavery men, Brown did not repent, even when he stood on the gallows. He slew in the spirit of a Joshua or a Gideon—smote the sons of Anak, exterminated the servants of Baal whom the Lord had doomed for their idolatries.

Two of the writer's great-grandparents and his four grandparents, all Quakers and strongly opposed to human slavery, settled in the future Emporia in 1855 to cast their lot with freedom's cause, to use their influence through peaceful means to help make it a free state. Thousands of other settlers went there hoping to help determine the outcome with ballots instead of bullets.

Among these early Kansas settlers who went to abolish or promote slavery there were also adventurers of every kind—get-rich-quick town-lot promoters, plain thieves, murderers, adulterers, hypocrites, liars, and others of unsavory reputations and practices. They leavened the pure loaf, creating a social admixture not too far above the national average.

Through this meeting and living together of people with many-sided ideas and notions there flourished a distinct growth of prejudices. No one, in Mr. White's opinion, should ever apologize for the prejudices of Kansans, because they have been "a compelling force in the history of the states"; democracy grew out of them; "Kansas is Kansas today by logic of prairie environment . . . It was the Kansas prejudice that did the work." To White, Kansas was hardly a state; "It is a kind of prophecy."

Another time, in a *Gazette* editorial entitled "Kansas a Dream State," Mr. White wrote:

". . . Kansas is a spiritual tuning fork. Upon it the events of contemporary history fall and Kansas gives key to the tune that runs through the world.

"Kansas probably does not lead; Kansas originates only deeds. Kansas acts after the spirit of the country has sought long and become restive because no action has culminated from the multitude of counsel."

Mr. White went on to say that for centuries before John Brown hundreds of men had cried out against slavery, but John Brown struck out against slavery and the institution fell. He led nothing, but he followed gloriously. On prohibition, he said, Kansas acted only after the nation had frittered away half a century in idle talk about the useless waste of saloons. He then pointed out that in the long line of social, political, and economic reforms, comprised in that old Populist program which had become respectable in the first decade of the century, Kansas had worked out things which others had merely thought out.

"Kansas never broods over things, never spins fine theories, Kansas is no lean and hungry Cassius."

Kansas sees what others see, he wrote, the common-sense thing, and then performs her plain duty; she has worked out a dream state, "a commonwealth where justice is more nearly done to man in all relations of life than is done in any other place in the world." She has done nothing more than replace human wrongs with human rights.

"Kansas is a child of a race of pioneers, not a race of dreamers. The 'dream state' we have erected on the visions of other minds, other generations . . . is no house of refuge for theorists but when a two-fisted practical man with a workable plan to produce justice and good will comes ambling up the Kaw Valley, he is met by a brass band. Nothing is too good for him."

To which the *Kansas City Star* replied editorially: "Kansas is a dream state. William Allen White is its alarm clock. Mr. White says Kansas is practical and knows when to go to work. Almost everybody does when wakened with a rope's end."

Colonel William R. Nelson, publisher of the *Kansas City Star,* once expressed his belief that:

"Kansas is the greatest state in the Union. It thinks. It produces things. Among other things, it produces crazy people. It's a great thing to have a few crazy people around! Roosevelt is crazy! Oomph! So were the men who started the Revolution to break away from England.

"Most of the people in the United States don't think. They are indifferent and apathetic. They don't want to work."

Another factor was introduced into the Kansas situation when, following the war between the states, a larger number of emigrating Union soldiers, who had faced the alternatives of life and death in the cause of human freedom, settled there than in any other state. This occurred because the federal government threw open tens of millions of acres of public lands on extremely favorable terms for settlement by Union soldiers. The great majority of these veterans were members of the Republican party. They, like the earlier settlers in the territory, all had been places, seen things, lived adventurously, and developed opinions and convictions on public questions. Even unto the present generation if you scratch a Kansan you will find a politician. The crusading spirit of the people persisted in this tense atmosphere, this confusion of religion and politics—which explains such phenomena as Carrie Nation, Mary Elizabeth Lease, and Senator Wm. A. Peffer on the light end of the scale of common sense, and William Allen White on the heavy end. But here comes an anomaly: For a quarter of a century this spirit expressed itself in an almost fanatical adherence to the Republican party, which by the end of the '60's had ceased to crusade nationally and became temporarily a congeries of hidebound reactionaries. Kansas finally revolted and turned for a brief period to the Populist movement with all the old vigor and religion-like ardor. The Populist revolt notwithstanding, Kansans clung to their Republican party moorings. In the twenty-two presidential elections since admission into the union, the electoral vote has been cast for sixteen Republican nominees, and in forty-four state campaigns the G.O.P. has elected thirty-nine governors.

This steadfast loyalty of a majority of voters to the Republican party is in no way indicative of submissiveness or sheeplike tendencies. No whip can be successfully cracked over the heads of Kansans, no goat can lead them to Democratic slaughter. Members of the Republican party usually make their fights family ones, with no holds barred; and these contests within the party are always more savage than are those of Republicans

versus Democrats. This situation helps explain the appraisal of
Kansas which Mr. White made two decades ago:

Kansas is a state of the union, but it is also a state of mind, a
neurotic condition, a psychological phase, a symptom, indeed, something undreamt of in your philosophy, an inferiority complex against
the tricks and manners of plutocracy—social, political and economic.

Kansas is the Mother Shipton, the Madam Thebes, the Witch of
Endor, and the low barometer of the nation. When anything is
going to happen in this country it happens first in Kansas. Abolition,
Prohibition, Populism, the Bull Moose, the exit of the roller towel,
the appearance of the bank guarantee, the blue sky law, the adjudi-
cation of industrial disputes as distinguished from the arbitration
of industrial differences—these things came popping out of Kansas
like bats out of hell. Sooner or later other states take up these things,
and then Kansas goes on breeding other troubles. Why, no one seems
to know, Kansas . . . is the nation's tenth muse, the muse of prophecy. . . .

3. WHITE'S ANCESTRY

OTHER THREADS, strange to life today, contributed to the pattern of life which was William Allen White's background. His ancestry had a touch of paradox. His father, Dr. Allen White, was of pure New England stock. After an imperfect training at one of the primitive medical schools of the day, he had hung out his shingle. He practiced medicine—of sorts—to the end; but after he came to Kansas the spirit of his Yankee forebears rose up in him and he became mainly a trader in lands and goods. In Kansas he met and married Mary Ann Hatton, the daughter of Frank Hatton, a stonemason, and Annie Kelly "that was" —Irish immigrants. Sweethearts from their childhood, they had eloped for fear of paternal opposition, got married in a little church at Longford, Ireland, and sailed from Liverpool to Canada. There they made themselves a home in the primeval wilderness and there, on January 3, 1830, Mary Ann Hatton was born. In 1909, with her son and his family, she journeyed to Ireland, saw the house in which her mother was born, the church in which her parents were married, and the entry in the parish books which recorded this event. Eventually, the elder Hattons moved to Oswego, New York. There, when Mary Ann was sixteen years old, they both died. Fate, and the necessity of caring for a younger brother and sister, took Mary Ann to pioneer Chicago.

She was a most unusual woman—mothers of great men usually are. Superficially, at least, she resembled one of those typical New England women of whom Mary Wilkins wrote. She was repressed and somewhat restrained in manner, rigid in her beliefs, strict in morals and manners, high-minded, frugal. She had above all that mania for culture which marked the Yankee in the days when the Concord school flourished and the mill girls of Lowell were listening to Emerson and publishing their own magazine. There was an odd contradiction in this Celtic woman with the puritan character: The typical Irishwoman is witty, the typical Yankee has a gentle but biting humor; but she, like Lucy

Stone, the beautiful, serious-minded feminist of her day, must have wished that "when she got to Heaven she would be brought to understand jokes." Mary White never did on earth; her son has testified to that. She had two passions of the spirit: good literature and music. She began reading to her son as soon as he could put words together. As Will grew toward school age the elder White used to complain that the boy never would learn to read for himself if she kept that up. He need not have worried. Will absorbed with his pores "the tedious meaning of the alphabet," as he always did anything which interested him. His mother took time from a busy life to keep up this custom until Will was twelve years old and she was on the verge of widowhood. Long before that she had read him the standard works of the Concord school with especial emphasis on Emerson, the greater English poets, Dickens, Thackeray, Scott, Wilkie Collins, and even George Sand. He must have liked to absorb his literature in that way, for he never rebelled as he did in the case of piano lessons.

More important than teaching her son the love of good literature and good music, Mary Hatton White infused in him her own strict ideals of morality and fair dealing, together with a religious faith which emphasized love at the expense of hell to a degree regarded as barely Christian in those days. She did this with the conviction that a man owed service to the best there was in his generation. These teachings, which lay hold on the eternal, remained fixed for life in his mind and soul.

Mary Hatton White, strong-willed and independent, changed from Catholicism to the militant evangelical Protestantism of her times. By industry and persistence she managed to matriculate and spend two years at Knox College, Galesburg, Illinois; she was probably among the first thousand women in the United States to have the benefit of a higher education. She came crusading to Kansas just after the close of the war between the states, to teach Negro children.

She was a pioneer Kansan of the unionist variety, and one temporal corollary to this teaching was her firm adherence to all that the Republican party was and was to be. Even before the war between the states she had regarded slavery as downright wickedness, had sympathized unreservedly with the Kansas

squatters who fought the good fight, had known and adored
Mother Bickerdyke, who was a rough angel of mercy to Sher-
man's army. A touch of persecution sharpened these beliefs, for
when she came to Kansas as a teacher she insisted that black
children should not be segregated from white ones in her school.
She chose the wrong town, Council Grove, for this experiment
and lost her job. Another paradox in that family was the fact
that Dr. White, a Democrat in a violently Republican community, had known his own touch of persecution. She never persuaded her husband to accept her convictions, but young Will,
almost wholly under her influence in his early years, absorbed
his mother's rigid political creed and held to it strictly far too
long, as he afterward admitted.

Dr. Allen White, a brilliant, expansive, enterprising, mer-
curial man, a good mixer and a Jeffersonian Democrat, exercised a powerful influence on his son's life, even though he died
before young Will had entered his teens. There was about him
a bit of impishness, impudence, and prankishness which he bequeathed to his son.

Once in commenting upon something that had been printed
about his father's activities in El Dorado, Will White recounted
an incident in the county-seat war between that town and Augusta.

These county-seat wars between the towns of early-day Kansas
were bitter affairs. El Dorado had stolen a march on the rural
Augusta by building a courthouse. Following the practice of
the times, the residents of Augusta went to El Dorado with fire-
arms, prepared to storm the courthouse by force. The El Dora-
doans, having been forewarned, manned the courthouse; their
rifles stuck out of the windows and doors and bristled from the
roof like "quills upon the fretful porcupine." But Old Doc
White—he was called "Old Doc" though he was only in his fifties
—his son wrote, "was a shining target in white nankeen pants,
white pleated shirt and white Panama hat. He paraded the
streets around the courthouse, the only unarmed man in the
town, in order to greet the invaders with gay and festive persiflage. His wife begged him to put on his black Sunday suit to
be less conspicuous, but he was ribald in his reply that if they
hit him they wouldn't hit the courthouse!" Will White wrote

that the Augustans went home and burned the "Old Doc" in effigy, and added, "it gave him delight to his dying days for he was so built that he enjoyed better than the applause of the multitude, the impotent, cackling rage of his enemies. At that he could chuckle. He smiled at the memory of that hour on his deathbed." How like the father was the son to become!

Dr. Allen White further revealed this elfin, prankish streak in his nature by an advertisement which he ran in the *Emporia News* in October, 1867. This curiosity of commercial literature, presented here in type as nearly comparable to the original as possible, belongs to the neolithic age of advertising. As Will White once said, in this day of clearer psychological knowledge it would be a dead loss. Dr. White was calling attention to his store rather than to his stock and his prices. Announcement of bargains did not find its way into advertising until about the turn of the century, and definite statement of prices, as a general custom, came even later. Today, however, there is a slight drift backward to "institutional advertising"—information about the store itself, its reputation for low prices and high quality of goods, its standing in the community. The opposite page displays Dr. White's offering in full.

Will White also inherited or acquired from his father a quickened interest in public affairs, generosity, and a keen sense of civic responsibility. During his life in El Dorado Dr. Allen White headed every subscription list. In addition he gave free medical service to every ex-soldier and his family and in other ways created a working model from which his son shaped his career in Emporia during the long stretch of years between 1895 and 1944.

Dr. Allen White and his wife were not typical specimens of the races which produced them. However, heredity, as biologists know, goes not by individuals but by strains, and "we inherit from our uncles." William Allen White, their only child, was, as stockmen say, a "true cross" between these breeds, inheritor of the best qualities in both stocks—Irish wit and Yankee humor, Irish fighting quality and Yankee steadfastness, Irish mysticism and Yankee eagerness of intellect, Irish sensitiveness and Yankee common sense.

Great Excitement!

IN EMPORIA

Extensive Stock Of

Dry Goods

GROCERIES
BOOTS AND SHOES, HATS & CAPS
CLOTHING

Also to every other

MAN

woman and child that can be

FOUND

in this country! I am bound not to be undersold; my clerks are always
on hand and you will not find them

IN BED

I am willing to work hard and contented

WITH

large sales and small profits. I have no disposition to run down

ANOTHER MAN'S

business. I am only aiming to build up my own; but do not intend to
get so excited that I cannot keep my

SHIRT ON

If I do not get my share of the Public Patronage, it will not be

FOR

want of sufficient inducement being offered in quality and quantity of
goods. Should the incredulous desire any further

PARTICULARS

in regard to my extensive stock of goods and my manner of doing a
cash and ready pay business, please

CALL ON

me at No. 159 Commercial Street.

ALLEN WHITE

October 8th, 1867.

Something else vital to Mr. White's character, life, and works
came out of this marriage of opposites. In that home of two
strong-willed parents who held deep and widely divergent
convictions on the slavery issue, the youth began to reconcile
the irreconcilable, learned to understand and sympathize with
the proponents of each side of the bitter struggle which brought

freedom to the Negro. Respecting and caring for his parents, recognizing the honesty of their convictions as he did, he learned for himself that the people on neither side of a question have a monopoly on the horns, tails, and cloven hoofs with which human beings are prone to furnish their opponents. Such an experience helped to bring out that faculty which he shared with others beloved of the gods: the ability to assay the gold in every character; to disregard its alloy; to discover the common ideals of minds otherwise antagonistic.

This early training in tolerance and the use he made of it throughout a long, busy, useful life would alone have made of him a man of unusual distinction. Coupled as it was with his native warmth of heart, it helped make him unique. What other public figure could have been acceptable, as he was, to his fellow trustees of both the Roosevelt (Theodore) Memorial Association and the Woodrow Wilson Memorial Association? All who knew him well saw nothing inconsistent in this; rather they took pride in his breadth.

His sympathies knew no bounds. Even the devil was a misguided soul who occasionally, it was true, had to be fought with hot pitch—and he always had some ready for use. Nowhere in literature outside of Mr. White's writings and two poems of James Stephens, "The Fullness of Time" and "What the Devil Said," has the writer ever discovered expressions of boundless sympathy.

Hundreds, if indeed not thousands, of men and women contributed to the making of the man he became, a man who was trusted, admired, or loved by literally millions of our citizens during the last quarter-century of his life. But aside from his father only four people, two women and two men, exercised really profound influence on his life, thinking, and outlook. They were his mother, Mary Hatton White, his wife, Sallie Lindsay White, his boss, William Rockhill Nelson, publisher of the *Kansas City Star,* and Theodore Roosevelt, twenty-fifth president of the United States. The brilliant staff of *McClure's* magazine, as a group, also contributed mightily to the growth of his social consciousness at the turn of the century. Each of these four individuals and the *McClure* group will be treated at

length later, but their influence on his life deserves a word
here.

His mother must have realized in his early boyhood that she
had given the world a genius, else how could she so gallantly
and with such persistence and able understanding have cultivated his tastes, stimulated his curiosity, fired his imagination?

As for Sallie White, after their marriage his every act and relationship in life revolved around her. She and he were truly
one in outlook, ideals, interests, and friendships. Their perfect
union brought all of his talents into full blossom.

Colonel Nelson taught Mr. White to create and weld a newspaper staff into a co-operative, harmonious unit; how and why
an editor should regard as his first duty that of trying to make
his community better and more attractive for the people who
lived in it. He learned from Nelson what courageous fighting
could do for a town, what power for good a man of independence could wield in it, what opportunities an enterprising editor with initiative could create for it.

Theodore Roosevelt had a tremendous influence on White's
political and social outlook. So great was it that T.R., almost
singlehanded, made a crusading liberal out of the thirty-year-
old laissez-faire conservative. Other personalities and factors, of
course, had their part in this transformation, but the credit and
glory for it belongs largely to T.R., may the Lord love him always and give his great soul peaceful rest.

Mr. White was born February 10, 1868, in Emporia. His
mother was in her thirties, his father in his late forties. Dr. Allen White's second and only other child, Frederick Hatton
White, was born March 7, 1870, and died August 19, 1870. His
father, feeling the need for more elbow room, left the growing
metropolis of Emporia when Will White was still a child and
moved to El Dorado, some seventy miles away. There he practiced medicine, bought and sold land, built and ran a hotel,
and served as a county official. He made, for that time and
place, a great deal of money easily, but his death came at a low
period in his fortunes. Kansas was visited by one of its many in-
sect plagues in the same year as that of a blighting drought. The
ensuing hard times brought a sudden deflation, bank failures,

financial disaster. Before he died Dr. White had lost a substantial part of his liquid assets and real estate. Just after his death another bank failed, sweeping away $1,000 that he had deposited in it for his son's higher education. Some lands remained, but they had no great value during this financial stringency. At that time Will White was halfway through high school. Mary Hatton White resolved that her son, the absorbing interest in her life, should go to college. By means such as only the poor know, by saving and scrimping, teaching private pupils and keeping boarders, she was able to carry him through high school in El Dorado and to send him to the College of Emporia for two years. Here he worked on a newspaper in his spare time, first as compositor and then as a reporter. In later years Mr. White related in a *Gazette* editorial that he was able quickly to graduate forever from compositor to reporter because his roommate and friend, Ewing Herbert, who was a reporter for the same paper, entered the state oratorical contest. White took over the job when Herbert went to Topeka to deliver his masterpiece. The young orator, White wrote later, "walked on the stage at Topeka, struck an attitude, opened his mouth, spoke his first line, and stood there silent and beautiful. He kept standing there more silent, more beautiful, before an audience aghast. Then he turned and walked off the stage, grand, gloomy and peculiar. He could not come back to face Emporia, and so his printer student roommate got his first regular reportorial job."

At the end of his second year in college at Emporia, Will White, just turned seventeen, set his foot down and for the first time defied his mother. He did not propose to have her work herself to death for him. He would leave school and support himself and then as soon as possible support her. He wrote applying for a job to three El Dorado men, a dry-goods merchant, a grocer, and an editor. The editor was the only one who replied. He published a struggling Democratic newspaper. And so White became a newspaperman.

This was a seeming accident, but in the long view it was only destiny manifesting itself more promptly than usual. This was the work he was born to do.

4. ORGANIZED PROPAGANDA BORN

Because the early settlers of both Northern and Southern factions went to Kansas as crusaders, they appreciated a half-century in advance of the European powers that propaganda is an integral part of war. They took with them to Kansas type and presses, along with their rifles, bowie knives, and Bibles, and in buildings many of which yet lacked either doors or windows they began shooting forth newspapers which smote the Philistines hip and thigh.

Even in the 1880's when Will White entered the profession, Kansas journalism was still a child of the pioneer background. It was partisan to the point of religious mania and as rough and flamboyant, occasionally as humorous as the Tombstone *Epitaph*. Editors usually were graduates or half-graduates of the printer's case. And when help was short or a tramp printer drunk they would compose their copy "on the stick"—set it up in type without the preliminary of writing it out. Most of them wrote in the highfalutin style peculiar to the old West and akin to its oratory—a style which in the hands of Brann, the Iconoclast, became almost good. In descriptive passages it ran to pink clouds and purple sunsets, and in references to political opponents to the invidious adjectives of the Bible or the vocabulary bequeathed by the Union army. It was sometimes ungrammatical but always highly rhetorical, and more likely than not it was witty. It was personal often in the most intimate sense of the word. Sometimes it went the limit in revealing town scandal or denouncing town nuisances. There were libel laws in Kansas then, but both the editor and his victim ignored them. Only a sissy brought a libel suit. A he-man settled such personal affairs in a personal way. He either responded in kind through the rival newspaper, grinned and bore it, or attended to the matter with his sidearm. Even Will, far milder during his apprentice days than most of his contemporaries, once in Kansas City looked into the yawning muzzle of a Colt's 45, once in El Dorado ran away from the horsewhip of an offended trav-

eling saleslady who peddled corsets, and once in Emporia
dodged the blacksnake of a bootlegger's wife. Again in Emporia he outsprinted the rawhide-carrying wife of a "doctor,"
and another time took a crack across the head from a heavy
cane.

In a *Gazette* editorial, written in 1901, Mr. White wrote
about the old crowd of Kansas editors whose work was finished,
"good work, well done."

He described how they "had fought the devil in his various
forms, boomed the state, builded the towns, stood by their
friends, vanquished their enemies and helped to promote 'reason and will of God' as an inspiration by example to their successors."

He then proceeded to ask, "What is the editor's office?"
Certainly, he replied, the editor is not a preacher, for the sheriff
will close him out if he preaches too much, and if he is too
much of a teacher the mob will close him out. Nor is he a
giver of law or ruler of the people, for if he tries to be an autocrat in either of these fields there will be "an atmospheric
uneasiness and places that knew him will know him no more."

The editor, he said, nevertheless was something of a preacher,
teacher, and autocrat, even though his main business was to
print the news, to be "judge of his news, of how it is told, what
is recited and what is omitted."

It was his expressed belief that an editor must take a "side"
in everything, because "nothing fails so rapidly as a cowardly
paper, unless it is a paper that confuses courage with noise."
Moreover, "an editor must not expect political preferment or
worldly power." He must be "guide philosopher and friend to
all . . . executioner and undertaker, promoter and herald . . .
following the light given him, only remembered . . . by what
he has done."

Neither Mr. White nor the editors of his nor of the previous
generation ever cloaked themselves in anonymity. Their papers
mirrored their own personalities, boldly presented their convictions. It was inevitable, therefore, with their almost unique type
of reader and their forthright presentation of convictions, that
those earlier editors should wield great political power, occupy
high places in government in the state. It is unlikely that dur-

ing a seventy-five-year period, between 1861 and 1936, the people of any other state have elected six editors as governors, eight editors as United States senators, and at least eight editors as congressmen, to say nothing of the hundreds if not thousands of Kansas editors who have been elected state legislators or county officers.

Noble Prentis, in his fascinating *History of Kansas,* remarked that "Napoleon said that every French soldier carried a Marshal's baton in his knapsack"; the printer's rule in the Kansas editor's pocket became his Marshal's baton, enabled many of them to enter to high public office. Once in an editorial entitled "Ask of the Wind" Mr. White stated that the question had been raised why there was such an exceptionally large number of clean, decent, well-edited newspapers in Kansas, and replied:

"Most of the Kansas newspapers whose reputations are statewide, are owned and edited, either by native Kansans, or by men who have grown up in Kansas from boyhood—men whose parents were of the pioneer stock. They are thoroughbreds."

Mr. White once explained that two things, early in his newspaper career, encouraged him to shift from flamboyant to simple, clear writing. The first was that, when as a reporter on the *El Dorado Democrat,* he composed his news items in his head as he set them to type with his hands. Because he was an extremely lazy boy, he quickly learned to shun verbosity and long words, thereby reducing the number of pieces of type he would have to set.

The second thing that caused him to change his style was an episode which occurred not long after he took his job with the *El Dorado Democrat,* with a two years' college education mostly in Latin, Greek, and what American teachers called French in those days. He hustled for local news items on this job, and wrote a few editorials. One of the latter dealt with the death of his father's hero, Samuel J. Tilden. Young Will, mixing his metaphors, wrote with flamboyant grandeur that:

"His name will be carved in the hearts of his countrymen and carved deep in the tablets of fame after the echo of other names will have died away and are lost forever."

Soon after the issue of the *Democrat* was off the press young White went to the *Republican* office to borrow some type.

There he found Mr. and Mrs. Murdock reading his piece.
Years later he wrote of the incident in the *Gazette:*

"Its grandiloquence must have been very amusing, for I remember they were laughing at it, and reading the vain, pompous phrases with great delight. I have never had the courage
to read the piece since, but it taught me a lesson, and that was
that Mr. Murdock's style, simple, direct, and above all, understandable, is the only kind of writing that really pays."

One purely commercial factor made journalism flourish like
a green bay tree in Kansas during those days: It took little
money to start a newspaper. Even in 1895 when Mr. White
bought the *Emporia Gazette*—type, press, good will, job business, and all—he paid only $3,000 for it. Every cent of this was
borrowed. Intense political rivalry made it possible for a printer
with a gift of gab or artistry with a lead pencil to talk some
leader or leaders of a faction into supplementing his own sav-
ings, if any, with loans. Such loans, White wrote afterward,
were sometimes as low as $700. The practice of untrammeled
journalism in Kansas during that period thus consisted in playing the game of the political leader until the borrower could
pay up. Only then could he call himself a free man, be able to
speak his own mind. The growing communities naturally were
always overnewspapered, and so the competition for subscribers, for advertising both private and public, and for job printing business was torrid and cutthroat. Newspapers would fall
on the town like the snows of winter and vanish like the spring
thaw. A quarter-century after White bought the *Gazette* he
wrote:

"Fourteen men have come joyously into Emporia to fill a
long-felt want with another paper—'a bright, snappy paper that
will print all the news'—in the twenty-five years and they've all
walked sadly out or ridden to Maplewood cemetery."

Yet in spite of all this—perhaps even because of it—Kansas
small-town newspapers in the generation that followed the Civil
War were probably the best of their kind in the United States
or anywhere else. Her type of citizenry made Kansas a paradise
for newspaper editors because an uprising was always in the
making. If given a moral twist it quickly became an army with
banners. The public interest in Kansas in such movements

caused editors in other states constantly to chant the prayer, "Please, God, when I die, don't take me to Heaven right away. Let me do a hitch in Kansas first."

This perfect seedbed for editors grew an amazing crop. High in this group was Ed Howe of the *Atchison Globe*. He made his paper a model for the editors of newspapers in small towns throughout the nation. There were the two Murdocks, Bent of El Dorado and his brother Marsh, and Marsh's son, the late Victor Murdock, whose brother now publishes the newspaper their father founded, the *Wichita Eagle*. Also in this group are Henry J. Allen, owner and publisher of papers in Manhattan, Ottawa, Wichita, and Topeka, who was later governor and senator; Arthur Capper of the Capper publications of Topeka, and Clyde Reed of the *Parsons Sun*. Capper and Reed are the present United States senators from Kansas.

There were literally scores of others of equal or nearly equal rank. These men were all able editorial writers. Because the settlement of Kansas was inspired by an ideal rather than by a desire to better conditions of life, the people of the state were more interested in philosophies than in facts.

Another factor which caused the editors to stress editorial excellence was the fact that politicians, who backed such a large number of the newspapers, had little interest in news as such. What they wanted was good propaganda for themselves, their factions, or their parties. Further, the Associated Press, the sole news bureau, was as yet a luxury which only the larger newspapers could afford. Various "pony" services flashed skeleton sentences of the more important national news items, such as election results or the murder of President Garfield in 1881. The editors either used boiler-plate, waited for the exchanges from Kansas City or Denver, or else depended upon a mail news service from Kansas City. For the rest the editor himself, in the intervals he could snatch from other work, or a young reporter who more likely than not was also the printer's devil, hurried around picking up local items. When there was any notable local news such as a murder or one of those out-of-doors hangings in which the public of those days had such a morbid interest, either the editor or the reporter had to take a day off from his regular job.

The editorial writer in Kansas in that period was not re-stricted as he now is to formal editorials. Many of them would be classified today as columnists. In his ten years of apprentice-ship, young Will White wrote for the papers he served not only news reports, editorials, and feature stories, but verse, humor-ous essays, fantasies, character sketches, and enough full-fledged short stories to make in the end a published book.

Mr. White's record at the *El Dorado Democrat* showed such promise that Bent Murdock, publisher of the *El Dorado Repub-lican,* gave him a job. He worked on the *Republican* for more than a year, developing his talents along with a growing fasci-nation for his profession. Then, as he once explained to me, he decided that perhaps he did have enough sense to justify going to a university. He wanted to learn more about such subjects as economics and sociology, which would bring him into closer touch with modern life. Having a trade and the rudiments of a profession, he was able to earn a substantial part of his expenses at the University of Kansas in Lawrence by working on news-papers in that city.

5. INFLUENCES AT HOME AND COLLEGE

Until he went to the College of Emporia Will White never had been separated from his mother for more than a few days. Even at Emporia he was only seventy miles away from El Dorado, so they could still see each other frequently. But Lawrence was more than eighty miles still farther away from El Dorado. So they both went to Lawrence. His mother sublet her house in El Dorado, rented a cottage, and made a home there for her son and his friends.

In a sense he was tied to his mother's apron strings—then and all his life. She followed him to Kansas City, where she made a home for him and continued to live with him after he was married. After his success with the *Gazette* he established her in a house of her own next door to his, and when he was in town he went to see her every day until her death at the age of ninety-four.

His relations with his mother could be interpreted by exaggerators of Freud as proof of the "mother complex," with the disagreeable inferences which they always pin to that tag. This, however, in Mr. White's case, would be a wholly false inference. His attitude toward women, whom he liked enormously, was masculine and normal. He already had been in and out of love several times when he went to Lawrence. This was to happen again and again before he met, in Sallie Lindsay, the love of his life.

Also the apron strings which tied him to his mother were so elastic that upon coming to the age when boys feel a social urge he joined a "gang" of which he became the leader. Judging by the passages in his reminiscent stories gathered under the title "The King of Boyville," he and his friends were not innocent of such boyish delinquencies as raiding orchards, fighting among themselves, getting into trouble at school. His main interest, nevertheless, was "playing band" with any instruments at hand, from a Jew's-harp and a tin whistle on up to a battered brass trumpet which was the boy White's most precious pos-

session. Most of his "gang," including Will himself, were gradu-
ated from these concerts to the town band.

Perhaps because of his close association with his mother, perhaps because like almost all artists he had a touch of the feminine in his make-up, he who was afterward to play a man's part
in many a fight retained all his life certain feminine interests
and tastes, or deficiencies in taste. A minor illustration of what
might be considered femininity, not conclusive (for many other
hairy-chested he-men have the same peculiarity) but indicative,
was the fact that he was likely to faint at the sight of blood.
When a boy in El Dorado he once bloodied another boy's
nose in a fight, and then fainted. In later years he went to
Frank Foncannon, the family doctor in Emporia, to get an in-
growing toe nail treated, and asked if he might sit up and watch
the job. The Doctor agreed. It wasn't long before he drew
blood. Mr. White said, "Excuse me, I'm going to faint," and
did.

Mr. White had a natural ear for music, a natural liking for it
which was to grow into a passion, because there was music in
his heart and harmony dwelt in his soul. Once in a *Gazette* editorial entitled "Power of Music," he wrote:

> The grip that music has upon the hearts and minds of the people
> is evidenced in the millions of concert and opera goers of the civi-
> lized world. But it is still more surely evidenced in the homes of
> tens of millions of families. The musical homes, and the homes in
> which music in some shape or form is a home amusement, are le-
> gion. And the explanation is easily found in the incomparable
> power of music to provide one of the common interests which draw
> the members of the family together for common pleasure.

Mr. White's mother actively encouraged his taste for music
and started to cultivate it. He sang alto in a church choir until
his voice changed. Then at about the age when a country boy
discovers the outdoors and its delights—the swimming hole in
summer, sliding downhill and snowballing in winter, making
thrilling botanical and biological discoveries in all seasons—she
began giving him piano lessons. He never continued them far
enough to be able to read music. The drudgery of scales and
five-finger exercises bored him insufferably. He saw little sense

in reading tunes from sheet music when he could learn them
by ear: So he simply refused to practice and his wise mother did
not insist on his keeping on with it. Probably she refrained because she realized that forcing him was the best way to make
him hate music forever. But he kept on with the piano in his
own way, fixing in his remarkable musical memory tunes or bits
of harmony which he had heard and liked, even improvising.

Rolla Clymer, now editor of the *El Dorado Times,* has written of one of Mr. White's musical performances which took
place in Emporia when Clymer was a reporter on the *Gazette:*

Once, at the end of a swank musicale in Emporia on whose program numerous outstanding artists had appeared, Mr. White drifted
to the instrument and began to play some of his favorite selections.
Astonishment among the musicians themselves knew no bounds.
Miss Florence Hobart, who was a piano instructor at the State
Teachers College, exclaimed, "Why Mr. White, I never dreamed
you could do anything like that." He grinned at her impishly,
snapped out, "Oh you kid," and kept right on playing.

To the end of his life he refined and sharpened his musical
taste. Upon his return from a trip to Europe a decade before
his death, the New York newspapers told in front-page stories
how he and the late Cardinal O'Connell, of Boston, spent many
hours together around the piano in the salon of the great
Italian liner on which they crossed. According to these stories,
Cardinal O'Connell sang and Mr. White played the accompani-
ment on the piano.

A few days later Mr. White and I were together in a taxicab
driven by a man who made the Players–National Arts Club
stand his operating base. He knew both of us as regular cus-
tomers. I remained in the cab while Mr. White got out somewhere for a quick errand. The driver, who had read one of the
news stories, turned to me and remarked, "And him thinking
he could sing and play with the Cardinal!"

Alcohol did not tempt him at all, at least not after he met
Sallie Lindsay and decided that she was the one woman for
him. At that time he was a "gay young blade" who enjoyed
drinking with his friends. But wise and understanding Sallie
Lindsay, knowing that his ebullient spirits needed no stimulus,

promised to marry him only on condition that he give up liquor. Realizing that he gained so much for yielding so little, he agreed and thereafter scrupulously kept the bargain. He never smoked, at least after his boyhood days. His only incipient vice was the love of good eating, and he curbed that at times only short of gluttony. He liked to cook and he did it with the artist's touch. Through the years his editorials on cooking, his constant publication of recipes and editorials condemning the boardinghouse fare of hard fried beef, and his apostrophe to pork and beans, all testify to this. Time after time he gave his women readers detailed information on how not to parboil a goose, how to make this or that raw material into an inviting dish.

Mr. White had no rigid aversion to gambling, but he never played cards nor any other game, parlor or athletic. All sport seemed to be a blank to him. One of his teachers in later years remembered that as a child he merely looked on, generally amused, at the rough games the other boys were playing. No record exists that he ever played baseball. However, there crops up from time to time in his writings some mention of the joy of fishing, and biographers have mentioned that he did indulge in this activity as a boy. Although he began to take his summer vacations at Estes Park in 1889 when the Rockies still were advertised as the hunter's paradise, he neither hunted nor fished there. He made his first trip to this summer vacation home of his with a group of undergraduate friends from the University of Kansas. When during the summer of 1906 he offered me a job soliciting *Gazette* subscriptions on the rural delivery routes out of Emporia and adjoining towns, he emphasized that this would be a good experience, and told how once when an undergraduate at K. U. he had solicited subscriptions for Colonel Oscar E. Leanard, owner of the Lawrence, Kansas, *Journal,* for one month in 1889 in exchange for a round-trip railroad pass to Estes Park, where he spent his vacation with some undergraduate friends who had induced Dr. F. H. Snow, professor of physical science, later chancellor of the University of Kansas, to take them on a field tour for the study of natural history. The group included Henry E. Riggs, who was later professor of civil engineering at the University of Michigan; Frank Craig, banker, one-time president of the Oklahoma Bankers Association; Herbert S. Hadley, later attorney general and governor of Missouri, and finally chancellor of Washington University at St. Louis; William S. Franklin, later professor of physics at the Massachusetts Institute of Technology; Vernon Kellogg, also of Emporia; Edward C. Franklin, later professor of chemistry in Stanford University, and once president of the American Chemical Society; and Frederick Funston, later a major general in the United States Army.

At Estes Park the young men camped, fished, and hiked over the mountains. Young White, who once said that his legs served him as do a frog's—to propel him forward—was a natural, easy walker. This was the only form of exercise he ever took. Some of his friends hunted on these vacations, Funston among them. He has told me of Funston's daring even as a youth. For instance, he said, once the boys chased a mountain lion into a cave. Thereupon young Funston, with foolhardy courage, attempted to crawl into the cave unarmed to drive the beast out. But Funston's companions grabbed his legs, pulled him out, and sat on the kicking, volubly protesting young daredevil.

At the University of Kansas young Will "sat under" some strong men. The faculty members who greatly influenced young White's thinking included Dr. Arthur Richmond Marsh, professor of English literature, a militant liberal who made converts of his students.

Dr. E. Miller, professor of mathematics, taught White little mathematics, but a great deal about life and living. His advice to youth was:

"Keep cool, a hard thing to do in Kansas sometimes; take good care of your body, think pure thoughts, read the best kind of literature, be at peace with all men, and do your whole duty as a man among men regardless of what envious people may say of you; serve God and your country with all the powers of your being, and as decade after decade passes, don't dry up."

Dr. James H. Canfield, professor of history, made a tremendous impression on White. Canfield had three good mottos:

"All at it and all the time at it; that is what wins."

"What you can do, or dream you can do, begin it. Boldness hath genius, power and magic in it."

"The public business of America is the private business of every citizen."

At the time of the professor's death in 1909, Mr. White declared editorially that Dr. Canfield (father of the distinguished writer, Dorothy Canfield Fisher) had "left his endurable impress upon the character of the young generation . . . one of the great teachers and scholars of his time . . . [his] example remains an inspiration and encouragement to all who would do their work well."

Vernon Kellogg, one of White's undergraduate friends, whose father had traveled to Kansas in 1867 in the same stage with Mary Ann Hatton White, merits more than a passing mention. He and Will White entered the University of Kansas in September, 1886, together and were inseparable until White left the university in January, 1890. Together they joined the local chapter of Phi Delta Theta. This group was a normally gamesome set of young men, addicted to the old-fashioned Western practical joke of "snipe hunting"; but they all had minds and were learning to use them. The friendships he made in the fraternity gave him his first experience with conversation on an intellectual plane.

At this period of his life, Vernon Kellogg probably had more influence in forming White's mind and character than did any of the faculty members listed above. Vernon Kellogg's father, Lyman Beecher Kellogg, was one of the forces of light in pioneer Kansas. He served not only as the president of the State Normal School (Teacher's College) but as a builder of the state's educational system. He was a little man, Chesterfieldian in manner and dress, with an engaging personality, and wherever he lived his home was a kind of salon where mind met mind. As a farm boy I knew him slightly and always thought of him as the finished gentleman. It was in such an atmosphere, bookish but not pedantic, that Vernon Kellogg grew into an all-round man with a wide variety of developed talents. In the course of his busy life he did fundamental work in entomology and biology, wrote books that contributed generously to popular knowledge of evolution, sociology, and world politics, and published under a pseudonym charming studies of Florence and Florentine art. When Herbert Hoover assumed the task of feeding Belgium in the First World War, Mr. Kellogg got a leave of absence from the faculty of Stanford University, joined the Commission for Relief in Belgium, served as its "ambassador" at German headquarters, and by judgment and prompt action more than once forestalled demands by the extreme German militarist faction to throw the commission out of Belgium and let the inhabitants starve or accept German nationality. When this work was finished, Kellogg wrote *Headquarters Nights, A Study of German Will to Power,* as true to the perverted psychology of that people in the Second World War as in the first. The rest of his fruitful life he spent as the driving force of the National Research Council in co-ordinating research in the United States and in educating the public on modern scientific developments.

He was physically a well-built miniature of a man, but unlike so many other little men, he never showed any signs of a complex of inferiority and the protective mechanisms which go with it. Even in late middle age he had a surprisingly young face. The sophomores who took him for a freshman and started to haze him—that was a standing university joke during his professorship at Stanford.

Vernon Kellogg was a little older than Will White and his early environment had made him more mature. Although he did not lack a sense of humor, he seemed serious-minded beside his lively and witty chum; but their minds met and clicked and they had a bond of youthful idealism which they never lost. Will White learned from Vernon Kellogg to face without flinching the daring conception that the world and all that it contains were not created, as recorded in Genesis I, at a single stroke, but had evolved majestically from star dust and pond scum to man; learned too that this need not contradict the faith in a benevolent God for Whose purposes evolution is one instrument. The discovery of this concept was important in White's mental and spiritual growth. When at last he found himself he saw politics, government, society in that light—as living institutions, as sentient beings struggling upward, not as machinery. He viewed men as frail human creatures who in their highest and best moments approached the godhead.

In sharp contrast was Funston, who touched other facets of

White's complex nature. Funston, the son of a former Kansas congressman, lived an adventurous life without rating as an adventurer. He was a conductor on the Santa Fe Railroad, a guerrilla leader with the Cuban insurgents before our war with Spain, and a general of our army during the Philippine insurrection. He had a touch of the showman in him, but with all this he was hardheaded, realistic, and courageous. Many legends grew up about him. One concerned an incident when he was a railroad conductor collecting tickets from passengers. When he asked a tough cowboy for his ticket the cowboy pulled out his revolver and remarked, "I ride on this." Funston replied, "That's good, that's good," and went about his business, only to return later with a large-bore rifle which he pointed at the cowboy, saying, "I came back to punch that ticket."

At the time of General Funston's death in 1917, Mr. White wrote for his *Gazette* readers the following tribute to him:

. . . He lived a full, useful, cheery life. He lived life as we planned he should live it in our boyhood dreams a generation ago. He held that rarest of all God's precious gifts—the joy of seeing every dream he dreamed come true, and beautifully true. He went into youth with the gay serenity of childhood, looking with eager pleasure at everything about him, tasting of every form of nectar that the Fates hold fine and worthy. He went into maturity with the zest of youth always in his blood. He served his country, he was loved of friends, and beloved of those nearest to him. Life never staled for him. It was a long and happy day of merry adventure. And with the cup of joy laden to the brim with its richness, he drank its best and never knew the dregs.

"How beautiful it is!" he cried as he heard the music; then the angel touched him, beckoned him, and he went into death, life's grandest adventure of all—with youth still warm in him. He lived and he died the eternal boy. When years and their chains would have bound him he ran to hide from them in immortality.

Another one of Will White's undergraduate friends at the university was William E. Borah. Shortly after Senator Borah's death, Mr. White in a *Gazette* editorial in January, 1940, wrote that he first met Borah fifty-four happy years before at Kansas University, and that they both attended the classes of Dr. James

H. Canfield, who taught economics and sociology, political science and European history. His classes, wrote Mr. White, sat around a U-shaped pine table covered with brown calico, with Canfield at the head between the two prongs. Canfield did not ask questions but let his students discuss the topics of the day's session. With White and Borah sat Vernon Kellogg, Herbert Hadley, the two Franklin brothers, and Funston. White described Borah as a thick-necked, starry-eyed boy with an Irish twitch when he smiled with his loose-lipped mouth, a twitch which looked as though he were scaring away a fly with his nose and lower jaw; but it was a good smile, he added, "with a twinkle in the top of his nose, and emphasized by a clear charming voice when he spoke. That voice was one of his most precious gifts."

Mr. White added that God had given Borah another gift, the capacity to argue, and that Professor Canfield encouraged this. Although Borah joined a fraternity, "he was not a fraternity success nor was he a college leader. He got good grades, but he wasn't a grind." Borah, White wrote, never ganged up much with his fraternity brothers nor anyone else, never attended dances nor interfraternity parties; never sang with the boys when they went out with their mandolins, guitars, and banjos. Borah "was older than the other boys and seemed to have no time for the gayer, more frivolous phases of college life—poker with matches and hard cider, girls and baseball."

"I," said White, "who was everybody's dog like a shepherd pup, his complete antithesis as a student, couldn't make up with him, much—though I tried."

Mr. White added that he and Borah used to walk up the hill to the university together at odd times and talk seriously, for Borah the student was always a "serious cuss"; he had little humor then or thereafter. The last time they saw each other was at the Republican convention in Cleveland at which Landon was nominated. White had gone as an emissary for a small subcommitee which was writing the Republican platform to find out what Borah wanted.

"I went into his room at midday, where he was in bed," he wrote. "He was sheltered by nurses in a darkened room, back of a barricade against the army of seeking reporters. He was undressed, wearing a striped gown, but someway it emphasized the gaunt lines of his figure. He sat on the bed and I sat on the edge of a chair, two old gentlemen—one in the twilight of his late sixties, the other nearing the middle of his seventies. We talked about trivial things for awhile; then got down to business, agreed on two or three points, and as I got up to leave he walked along beside me with his arm around my shoulder, we stood for a moment at the doorway and he said to me: 'Well goodbye Will; I am glad you came,' held my hand affectionately for a moment and then he smiled that old quizzical smile and said something about the busy years that had passed and the ways we had walked to find ourselves there. And for a moment, clasping hands, we said nothing and I said, 'Funny isn't it?' and he answered 'It certainly is!' Then we both sighed and I turned and went to the committee's grind. It was all we could do and all we could say to express the meaning of the strange ways of fate that had kept us together through our long and busy lives, two old inarticulate gentlemen who had once walked together tiptoeing along the path of youth with our heads in the stars.''

The faculty of Kansas University when White was there probably would have called him a browser rather than a serious student. Once in writing of his mother and her passion for education he referred to himself as a "naturally unstudious son." Without that "purpose in life" which, especially in those days, members of the teaching profession always mention favorably in commencement addresses, he seemed to have made reasonably respectable marks in economics, sociology, English, history, literature, and the humanities, because he was interested in these subjects. His scholastic work required only part of his energies; he also became a full-time newspaper reporter. But despite the demands of these two activities, a new fact or a new idea was more than likely to set him off on a self-prescribed course of unrequired reading. He took less than no interest in higher mathematics, largely perhaps because he found the subject an unfathomable, mysterious one. Moreover, he probably did not need higher mathematics. Certainly, unless a man is educating himself to create and cultivate an orderly mind, he does not need training in this field, and White's mind was born orderly. But he could get nowhere, positively no-where, with solid geometry. Three times he failed in this course, which then was a requirement for graduation, and failed disastrously. Thus he never received a degree from his be-loved alma mater. When thirty years or so ago the University of Kansas voted to give him an honorary degree, he declined on the grounds that such degrees had become meaningless because colleges and universities had conferred them on so many unde-serving men. As a result of his refusal the University of Kansas has never since that date conferred an honorary degree upon any individual.

His failure to pass the examinations in solid geometry was doubtless due to a lack of visual imagination. To understand solid geometry one must be able to see in his mind's eye what the pieces of the cube or sphere or cone, cut up in some regular but freakish way, will look like. This is precisely the faculty that any graphic artist or good mechanic must have; it figures largely in the aptitude tests for army recruits. But Will White, with all his passion for music and his response to beauty in literature, had a blind side for painting and sculpture.

Writing to the *Gazette* from Europe on his first trip abroad in 1909—he had a fictitious character "Omaha" describe his visits to the art galleries in Rome and other notable art centers. Mr. White quoted "Omaha" as saying, "I didn't get much educa-tion in higher art. I'd already seen all the naked women in all those galleries in the saloons of America . . . and as for the various venuses and bathing nymphs and other marble Maudes and Mabels, I'm getting too old for them."

In Florence, he was tremendously impressed with a painting of Michelangelo's face, "the strongest, most heart-breaking face" he ever had seen. As we all tend to do in similar circum-stances, he related it to his own background: "that was the face of old John Brown—fanatic, prophet and crusader . . . heart lines of unrealized hopes . . . infinite pity and great vision and unchecked faith are so marvelously like the face of John Brown that the two might have been brothers—or the same soul molded in different ages in one immortal mold. Great souls are all akin."

In Munich, he seemed most impressed by the fact that

Rubens and other Dutch masters, unlike the Italian painters, sent "all the sylphs and woodnymphs to glory and the fat people elsewhere," and added:

"It probably has nothing to do with art, and is pure personal opinion, but it does seem bad taste to fill hell with fat people. They aren't so bad. They mean well. They are sinners, of course, but they're sorry. And to give the skinny people the exclusive use of Heaven is going to make it a mighty dull place. But then probably Rubens knows as little about the real population of Heaven and hell as the rest of us—which is precious little."

The painting in Munich which seemed most to interest him was Albrecht Dürer's canvas of John the Baptist. When his eye caught it he exclaimed to Mrs. White, "There's Old Stubbs! There's Old Red Stubbs!" (He was referring to W. R. Stubbs, then governor of Kansas.) Mr. White wrote: "The likeness is more than marvelous; it is creepy. Here is a tall, awkward, red-haired, one-sided man—curly hair at that—with the face of a fanatic and the frame of a giant; blue-eyed, fine-featured, the spitten image of Stubbs . . . a man full of man's weaknesses and full of faults but a rabble-rouser and a crusader . . . Did Dürer imagine Stubbs four hundred years ago?"

Only these two paintings by the masters, of all that he saw, touched Mr. White deeply, and each of these attracted him because in them he saw not great art so much as he saw the mirrored souls of two men from Kansas.

By the same token, in contrast to most Americans he was ineffably bored by machinery. He never learned to drive an automobile; tried once and wrecked it, then quit. When he bought his first rotary press and his first linotype machine for the *Gazette* he liked to watch them flooding out papers and blocks of type, but the newspaper's mechanical force learned early that when they explained to him, American fashion, how the "durn things" worked, then they caught that characteristic faraway look in his eyes which suggested that he was off in another world. So he did not have a mind that could grasp the fundamentals of solid geometry, he who went out into the world after some profitable years at the young University of Kansas.

He had enjoyed every minute of his time at the university. Then and always, to the end of his life, that was his reaction to this world. Tomorrow was another day, full of enticing experiences. His chums in the fraternity, those who gathered in his mother's home, and his incidental friends outside of their charmed circle, vaguely tagged him in their minds as an able fellow who probably would get somewhere. Otherwise they remembered him only as a "good fellow." The faculty seemed to take his departure calmly. If they noticed it at all it was probably to wonder that a young man so long exposed to their influence could be so allergic to it. What Mary Ann White thought of his failure to file up onto the platform with his class on commencement day we do not know; neither probably did her son. Like another Mary, she kept these things in her heart.

6. UNDERGRADUATE NEWSPAPER
EXPERIENCES

THE FACULTIES of those days, even so able a lot as taught at the University of Kansas in the 1880's, looked askance at those "extracurricular activities" from which students with an original turn of mind often gleaned more education than from Greek composition or lectures on philosophy. White was in these "extracurricular activities" up to his neck. Student politics, of course, was meat and drink to him—the delight of the students and the bane of the faculty. In the atmosphere of the frontier small towns in which he had lived, music, presumably, had soared little higher than "Silver Threads among the Gold," "Juanita," the Strauss "Blue Danube" waltz, and the standard hymns—although church choirs might render a little Bach or Handel on special occasions such as Christmas and Easter. Everett Rich records in his able biography of White that at Lawrence, almost by chance, he came across a string quartet playing the classics and immediately registered for a course in music. He was assigned to the piano, the only musical instrument he handled with authority. He went at it in his own way —getting his part into his head, that is, learning by ear. Then when he struck a sour note a heart-to-heart talk with the professor followed. Finally the professor extracted the astonishing confession that his promising pupil was musically illiterate. He dropped the course by request but kept on with his music. He played for fraternity dances; he picked up a few dollars now and then by playing at social occasions among the townspeople. The indications are that otherwise he did little toward earning a living for himself during his first year at Lawrence. Kansas was prosperous in the late 1880's and it is probable that Mary Ann White's income had been supplemented by the sale of some lands which she had inherited from her husband.

But by his second year at the university he was able to earn what seemed to him real money. Lawrence and the university, true to the Kansas pattern, were both overnewspapered. The town, with less than ten thousand inhabitants, had two established newspapers, another one trying to break in, and a weekly. The university had two dailies and a weekly. The latter were strictly private enterprises. The boys who ran them divided the profits, if any. White, who had had behind him a year or so of practical newspaper experience, inevitably drifted toward university journalism and as inevitably took command. He began, however, as business manager of the *Review* (where he played a trick with an advertiser, to be mentioned in more detail later) but he wrote for it also—"squibs," news, even verse modeled on James Whitcomb Riley, and not bad of its kind. Next term he took over the *Times* as editor and made it, according to general opinion, the liveliest college publication in Kansas.

The nonacademic Lawrence newspapers, like those of any college town, economized on salaries by employing, intermittently or regularly, inexpensive university talent. The versatile Kellogg, more advanced and experienced in cultural training than his lively chum, was already doing this kind of work. When the next summer he became managing editor of the *Daily Journal,* one of the town's newspapers, he gave White a job as city editor, in which capacity he served until he left the university. Just how he managed to get in any academic work after the fall term opened is not clear. It is possible that his blindness to solid geometry was not the only reason why he was unable to earn a degree. In this newspaper job he plunged into an orgy of old-time, exuberant, fighting, Western journalism —although the judicious Kellogg did his best to smooth down these edges. White did not confine himself to sitting at a desk, planning the treatment of the day's news and assigning the reporters. He was his own star reporter. Moreover, his mental energy spilled over into editorials, brief wisecracks after the fashion of modern columnists, even rhymes.

When, in that time and clime, there were two or more newspapers in a community, the editors were expected by their readers to fight each other tooth and nail. The subscribers opened their newspapers with eager anticipation, not so much of thrilling news as of the billingsgate which Smith would spit that day at Jones or Jones at Smith. Fortunately for White the *Journal* was Republican in politics while the *Democrat,* a newly established rival, lived up to its name. White turned his guns loose not only on this paper's politics but on Foley, its editor, personally. Foley was far, far too sensitive for a Kansas Democrat of those days. According to one of White's reminiscent editorials in the *Gazette,* Foley once got drunk and "came to call with a large feverish ball bat, and remained to pray." White seemed to be careless of his life when he treated of local politics, which Kellogg left entirely to him.

His partisan creed then was a clear cut, simple one: It was the equivalent of "all Democrats may not be s.o.b.'s but all s.o.b.'s are Democrats." Conversely to him "all Republicans are exemplary citizens." This creed colored his treatment of local politics despite the physical risks it involved. An offended Lawrence Democrat sent word that he would shoot White on sight. One such incident actually did bring him close to bodily harm.

Some years before, a mob had disgraced that passionate Union town, Lawrence, by lynching from a bridge three Negroes accused of murder. It was the rubber stamp of lynchings in that period. The mob marched to the jail, where the sheriff, with only a faint show of resistance, gave up the keys. He was now prominent in the opposition, and a county election was in the offing. White raked up the old story—then trouble started. In the bitter war that followed there were threats of shooting, and for the first time in his life, perhaps even the only one, White carried a gun.

His war with the established Democratic newspaper was more formal and here he gave one of his early and best illustrations of that prankish Celtic spirit with which he spiced so much of his mature journalism. The rival journalist, whose organ was an evening paper, fell ill. Following the newspaper code—"all fighting off in a crisis"—White, whose *Journal* came out in the morning, carried on both jobs. He diverted himself by starting a bitter, insulting war between the two papers, and when his rival came back to the job he contributed this to the local weekly:

We have been much amused, and some days not a little disgusted, by the recent bickerings indulged in by the editors of our two daily contemporaries. Precisely what the caterwauling is all about we will not presume to say, but the gist of it seems to be that each thinks the other is a mixture of fool and knave, equal parts. No doubt each has blundered on the truth; but as there is no novelty for the readers of either sheet in the discovery we cannot see the reason for devoting so much space to it. The better class of people are coming more and more to realize the shallowness of daily journalism in this city and turn to the . . . [weekly] for intelligent comment on current events.

In a *Gazette* editorial in 1918, White recited some of his Lawrence journalistic experiences:

. . . we have winged many a gay mile down Massachusetts Street before irate citizens, and have faced many a furious mob of Democrats in the office, coming in to stop subscriptions and order out advertising. . . . The only flash of light that illumines those Lawrence literary days in our memory was the friendship of Nash Walker, a colored porter in the Eldridge House, who afterward became famous as an actor and once, in New York, let us touch the hem of his fame and stand in the reflected glory of our association. Nash never tried to kill us. But he sat at the reporter's desk and grinned that incandescent smile of his while a drunken printer with a long-bladed knife came in one midnight and chased us all over the room, out into the business office and through the stock room. Nash certainly had a sense of humor, and the thought of a printer killing us who had no special grievance other than that we had asked him for a quarter he had borrowed, while good and virtuous burglars whom we had libeled and slandered had failed to wing us—the subtle humor of that situation certainly did give Nash a few merry moments.
. . . Yet, as we are facing fifty, we look back from these placid heights without much regret. We are more circumspect than we used to be; words are weighed more carefully than they were in our teens and twenties and thirties, when we tossed language gayly about like the dews of heaven, letting it fall upon the just and the unjust.

But these facts and these confessions do show that the young Will White had still only an imperfect conception of newspaper ethics. His political ethics were definite and simple. They could be expressed in one sentence of six words, plagiarized fifty years later by the Germans: "The Republican party is always right." In the episode of his "lynching" editorial, his motive was the defeat of two candidates who, failing to get the Republican nomination, were running on an independent ticket. That action, according to his lights, constituted black, unpardonable treason. On the other hand, in those boyhood days when it came to drawing the thin line between what one should and should not do to keep his private desire and advantage out of the picture, he failed to make the connection with his well-developed personal integrity in such matters as paying his debts, keeping his promises, and standing by his friends. One little transaction when he was business manager of the *Review* just barely skirts the margin of blackmail. It concerned a Jewish tailor and presser by the name of Isaac who was dependent on the college trade for a living. The tailor had refused flatly to advertise. Mr. White wrote and published a fictitious news item:

"Urbanasky Flashowiski, a Russian Jew, who keeps a junk shop in Messopotamia, don't advertise in the *Review* and one of his clerks died from the effects of solitary confinement the other day. Ah there Isaac."

In the subsequent rumpus White maintained with perfect sincerity that a merchant who lived by and largely off the university, and would not help support its publications by spending a little money in advertising in them, deserved all he got. The students seemed to take the same view. The tailor lost business. He settled for a $50 advertisement which was cheerfully accepted.

The case of the saleslady who chased him with a horsewhip in El Dorado, mentioned earlier, was inspired by a local merchant who did advertise in his paper. Later in life he sympathized with her. She had come to the town peddling corsets and, having no overhead, undersold the local merchants. He agreed with the retailer that this constituted a vicious assault on the advertisers who were the support of his newspaper, and denounced her in print. The lady bought a keen rawhide from a harness shop and spent two days looking for White, who while covering his regular beat traveled the alleys and peered into the stores from the back door before entering.

He has told how he wrote his copy on the back stairs and sent it in by the devil, who, enjoying excitement, whispered this fact to the lady. And a fine foot race resulted. He ridiculed the

Farmers' Alliance and they rode him in effigy through the streets and boycotted his paper, while the candidate for county attorney bought a gun with which to answer White's charges. At another time in El Dorado he "roasted a circus that didn't advertise enough to suit our nice tastes in those matters and if the circus had sent a sober man to do its fighting he might have caught us." Also at about the same period he found himself much attracted by a young woman of El Dorado. However, he had a rival, a professional gambler, who drove her around in a buggy with red wheels. White knew that the man was running a gambling joint contrary to law. He knew also that the police had ignored the gambler's activities. Moved by jealousy, he exposed the gambler in the *Republican* and brought the police down on the joint. "That gambler," White wrote in later years, "sat up for four long days trying to get a chance to kick our base of supplies into our subconsciousness and only a fleet and earnest pair of young feet kept the gambler from achieving this end. Incidentally, he got the girl. Which taught us a lesson about the gratitude of republics." To these last two performances he himself bore testimony, but he never wrote of the affair of the Jewish tailor. Probably it was one of those early peccadillos that he, who in later, wiser years broke the power of the Ku Klux Klan in Kansas and the nation, preferred to forget.

7. A WORKING NEWSPAPERMAN AND THE *KANSAS CITY STAR*

Mr. WHITE was just past voting age when he left the university and returned to El Dorado, much better equipped and trained to follow his profession than when he left home. As one who belonged there, he settled down on the *El Dorado Republican* as city editor and substitute for Thomas Benton Murdock, the editor and proprietor, when the latter, who was also a state senator, was campaigning or attending legislative sessions in Topeka. He was much more happily placed there than in the office of the *Democrat* four years before. In later years Mr. White said: "Bent Murdock was the best editorial writer I ever knew." His style was "simple, strong, built upon the commonest words of the language, put together with short, direct sentences."

Mr. White, who in his reminiscent moods loved to make fun of the callow young cub that he was at that period, paints himself as a frivolous rounder, or as much of a rounder as was possible for a man of his nature who had no major vices, who attended Congregational church services on Sunday, and whose relations with women were proper. But he did indulge himself a little in the matter of dress. "A Prince Albert coat and grey pants, patent leather shoes and white spats and a broad black Stetson hat"—this, probably exaggerated for humorous effect, is his own description of his array when he took the El Dorado girls buggy riding.

During this period of service on the *El Dorado Republican,* he served as a combination of city editor and executive editor, and, when Mr. Murdock was away, editorial writer and manager of the entire newspaper. These duties seemingly would leave him little time for gallivanting, but during this time he fell in and out of love more than once. Moreover, during this period, as he has testified, at night or on days off he wrote his early short stories and undertook other experiments in literature. He was mixing with people all the time, and long be-

fore he reached voting age was taking an active part in politics—making speeches, attending county conventions as a
delegate, serving as a worker both during campaigns and at the
polls, renewing his old acquaintances, making new ones. In
addition to these activities, during his trips to Topeka, the state
capital, he met state political leaders, became acquainted with
their philosophies, outlooks, and mental reach or lack of it. In
all this work he was polishing that faculty which he retained
through his life of making instant and pleasant mental contact,
and on exactly the same terms, with all kinds of men, humble
and great.

More even than being his own boss much of the time, free
to publish any copy that his nimble, penetrating mind fancied,
he enjoyed occupying the driver's seat on the local political
bandwagon. In this position he could lambaste to his heart's
content what he then considered the insane vagaries of the
Farmers' Alliance and the Populist party. He held their theories
up to scorn in a variety of ways. His efforts were so successful
that the leaders of these radical movements came to consider
him as their number one public enemy.

Unless a man has lived in the midst of a political crusade
such as the Farmers' Alliance or the Populist movements, he
cannot possibly visualize the intensity, the frenzy even, of its
members. The upheaval was preceded by something like a
strange madness which swept over the prairies. Men, women,
and children everywhere seemed to catch the infection from
the very air. It was bred in crop failures, in past-due mortgages
which carried high interest rates and were held by moneyed
people and institutions in the East. Almost every schoolhouse
in the country districts served as a meeting place where, under
kerosene lamps which "twinkled back vain hope to the stars
. . . they sang crude hymns which glorified their cause with a
fanaticism not unlike that which moved the crusaders. . . .
They listened to emotional speakers who with catchphrases
and half-truths made them believe that capital and wealth were
diabolical, that the devil himself lived in Wall Street and had
forced men and women of the prairies, to sell their bodies for
the necessities of life.

"The remarkable thing was not that these people were susceptible to the madness which swept over the prairies; it was that they confined their protests to a biting denunciation of capitalists" and to broken ties with the established political parties. Existence was difficult. During those years of poor crops in Kansas, combined with a national depression, life was extremely hard, with no luxuries and few necessities. Money was almost unknown. The farmers paid their land and school taxes by grading the dirt roads, as I can personally testify. Many country schools were closed, especially those not fortunate enough to have a railroad crossing their district boundaries, for the railroads paid their school taxes in cash. Clothes made over and handed down were worn with pride and thankfulness. In ordinary times, food of a kind was plentiful. Sugar came from the bottom of the sorghum molasses barrel, chickens, hogs, and steers provided meat for those farmers fortunate enough to own any, flour for bread was ground from their wheat, if any, by the local miller. Corn bread usually graced the farmers' tables twice if not three times a day. And there also was a limited supply of canned or dried fruit and vegetables, or potatoes and turnips kept buried under a cover of straw deep in the ground. During the worst years much of this simple fare became scarce. There was no use in leaving the farm, for there was no gainful work to be had. The shiftless and improvident fringe actually approached starvation. Over the centuries similar conditions have brought vigorous protests, even violent uprisings—the *Jacquerie* in France, Wat Tyler's rebellion in England, Shays' rebellion in Massachusetts. But Kansas still pinned her faith on the magic of the ballot.

The men and women in our community were no less susceptible to this curiously contagious fever than were those in the rest of Kansas. Every man in it, save only my father and perhaps my grandfather (I never was certain about the latter, for he had periods of grave doubt about the rightness of the established order), left the Republican party, first for the Farmers' Alliance and later for the Populist ranks. While the madness was on them these neighbors held meetings year in and year out in the Quaker Valley schoolhouse. When we went to school on the mornings after their meetings we would find the walls decorated with great banners which proclaimed "Equal Rights for

All, Special Privileges to None." The pages of their little blue paper-backed songbooks lying scattered around over our desks clearly revealed both the intensity and the sincerity of their feelings. The devil was to pay and they were getting the pitch hot.

This fever grew progressively worse during those years in the early 1890's when crops were poor and prices low. Then, as financial conditions eased throughout the nation, as nature, which seemingly had forgotten our existence and tragic need, smiled again and gave us bountiful crops, the plague lifted as suddenly and as mysteriously as it had descended. "Kansans forgot their slogans and shibboleths, their hatred and anger. For years afterward many of them seemed to be a bit ashamed of having followed after such strange gods."

Despite the low esteem in which the radical leaders held him, White had unlimited confidence in himself during this period; it may indeed have risen to conceit. If it did, he lived that down. No man ever was more modest than he in his days of greatness.

The pertinent fact about his two years on the *Republican,* however, is that his experience with writing for the news page and for such space as the *Republican* afforded for features were his to command. Although Mr. Murdock advised or criticized now and then, he did not censor. White had in this apprenticeship one advantage denied to most beginners; he was his own publisher. He did not have to face the discouragement which follows the receipt of pink slips from unknown editors, or piles of rejected manuscript. Bad as some of his copy undoubtedly was, he saw it in print. No editor nor teacher is one-half as effective an instructor as is the copy which one writes and later reads in cold type. Inaccurate phraseology, bad structure, half-baked and poorly expressed ideas, or faulty judgment have a way of jumping out of the copy, biting the writer, and making him so uncomfortable that he learns to better his ways.

Then only twenty-two years old, he wrote a regular column in the guise of the superannuated village philosopher "Elder Twiggs"—invaluable training in making characters talk in the Kansas manner and the Kansas dialect. He also trifled a bit with purely humorous writings and did editorials or paragraphs of comment in an Addisonian style, fruit of his years at the University of Kansas. Some critic of his time spoke of Addison's style as "intimate but not familiar." This, however, was not true of Will White's. It was conspicuously familiar.

In addition to this writing, and for variety, he produced a great deal of copy of a personal nature in the flamboyant, breezy, old Western style with which many are still familiar. While Murdock was away in Topeka he wrote editorials in imitation of his employer's severely eloquent style and finally turned out a score of short stories far better than his Kansas readers realized at the time, for they broke virgin soil. With few exceptions, American popular literature had not yet come down to earth. Virtually no one at that time had written of the small town as it was instead of as the author felt that it might be and should be. To get accepted by any of the standard Eastern magazines, young Will White would have had to warp his own sincere conception of Western life into a pattern. The best of his stories of this period dealt with a woman who was little better than the town's strumpet and her affection for her father —a theme which literature of that day sternly barred. However, it is not recorded that White ever submitted any of these earlier stories to the established magazines. They had to wait for a larger audience until he had leaped into national fame. Then the best of them were published under the title *The Real Issue*.

Yet oddly it was one of the worst of them that showed him the way to promotion and pay. "The Regeneration of Colonel Hucks," published in the *Republican* just when the Populist movement had begun to break and twist all party lines, was a political story. Colonel Hucks, who has been reared a regular Republican, grows sour on the party and declares his independence. But an old friend, handling him gently, tactfully, understandingly, lures him to a Republican state convention. Gradually the Colonel comes to see the light. He returns home and rejoins his party. Translated from political to theological terms, it would have made a very sweet story for a Sunday-school library. But it had interesting, realistic details. Like any other good Kansan of that day, White knew his politics intimately and at firsthand. Also he knew his politicians, both Democrat and Republican. This was evident in his writings even from his first stumbling efforts, for no matter how bad they were, what he had to say in them was interesting. If you started one of them, you had to read it through.

Subsequent events constitute an amusing footnote to the story of his life during that period. "The Regeneration" filled a long-felt want for editors fighting the Populist movement and for politicians trying desperately to check desertions from the G.O.P. It gave a touch of warm emotion and inspiration to their campaign. Newspaper after newspaper—always Republican ones—reprinted it. It even attracted attention outside of Kansas. Colonel William R. Nelson, of the *Kansas City* (Missouri) *Star*, read it, and although he could not bring himself to approve its sentiments, he saw that the young editor could write, had him looked up, and offered him a job on his paper. Unfortunately, for the time being at least, Nelson's rival, the *Kansas City Journal*, a Republican paper, saw the article. The *Journal* reprinted it and made an offer of its own. White knew that the *Star* was independent Democratic and the *Journal* all-out Republican. This knowledge settled the question for him.

He played the wrong horse, because the *Star* was on its way toward that eminence among American newspapers which it maintains even to this day. The *Journal* was then frankly an intermittent strumpet whose soul was its own only when there was no demand for it from a corporation. Moreover, competing with a man like Nelson was almost a hopeless task, for Nelson was a genius and a splendid citizen.

Will White was not happy in the *Journal* office, particularly at the start, when they set him to the job of writing advertisements. He served next as political reporter with his principal task that of covering Kansas politics from headquarters in Topeka. While there he had an excellent opportunity to learn for himself what made the legislative wheels go round. Nevertheless, a newspaper such as the *Journal* did not afford an atmosphere in which a man of his kind could breathe. However, the crisis which brought his resignation was not created by the *Journal's* unethical practices. The staff of any kept newspaper always loses interest and slacks its work. White and another reporter were covering the Populist party's state convention in Topeka. One night he learned from an unimpeachable source that the "boys" had reached an agreement in a smoke-filled back room and were going to name a dark horse—L. D. Lewelling—which they did. White wrote an exclusive story and hurried it to the *Journal*. It did not appear in print. He and the other reporter rushed back to Kansas City to find that the telegraph editor, not believing him, had simply tossed his copy into the wastebasket. The two reporters told the telegraph editor what they thought of him in hot, intemperate language in a vain effort to prod him into a fight. Then they resigned. This is notable as the only record of White's courting a physical encounter after his boyhood days. He walked over to the *Star* and saw Colonel Nelson, who still held the old offer open and welcomed him as a brand from the burning. There he stayed for three fruitful years.

The *Kansas City Star* was a "happy shop," as decent, successful newspapers usually are. Noble L. Prentis was the editor when Mr. White joined the staff. Mr. Prentis would occasionally beamingly say to his brilliant young assistant, "Well, son, you certainly writ' a piece, a good and great piece." In an editorial of July, 1900, entitled "The Influence of Prentis," Mr. White wrote:

He was democratic in his kindness. He gave with almost prodigal generosity the best things in his heart to all who touched his life. The office boy knew his loving kindness as surely and as well as the man who owned the paper. In all his life he was never a toady, never a snob. He was a fine, courteous Christian gentleman and scholar, who loved his books to the end of his busy happy life.

But when all this is said the real worth of Prentis remains unrevealed. He was valuable to the world as an influence. He was a good influence. He stood preeminently for decency. That, more than the sweet gentleness of his nature, will be the bright gem for his crown. He wrote charmingly and with an incomparable style—but that was not the best part of it—for he preached decency, manhood, courage and Christian chivalry in every line. The men around him, especially the younger men, breathed the spirit of Prentis in what he wrote, in what he said, in what he did. He helped. Whatever of dog hair there was on them Prentis tried to remove. Hundreds of young men in Kansas owe much of whatever good is in them to the precepts and example of Noble Prentis. In these good works, even to the third and fourth generations, will Prentis find his immortality. He will be remembered not for what he wrote—though it is sweeter than honey in the honeycomb—but for what he was, a brave fine soul, who lived a gentleman and died beloved.

He has rested from his loved employ. May his rest be peaceful and his dreams come true.

Alex Butts, another able newspaperman, chief editorial writer of the *Star* at that time, did his level best—but unsuccessfully—to trim the exuberance out of White's copy. Ralph Stout, a name to conjure with in Middle Western journalism in that period, was the *Star's* city editor in those days. These men and successors trained under them run the *Star* today, and keep the high standards he set for it, and demonstrate that Colonel Nelson, the publisher and owner of the *Star*, had an uncanny ability to pick able men. Thus it is entirely reasonable to suppose that he appreciated the possibilities in this young man with a small-town Kansas background.

Colonel Nelson deserves some special mention here both because of his influence on Will White's life and because of the standards he set and maintained for journalism in the nation.

He moved to Kansas City, Missouri, about 1880 from Indiana, where he had lived during the war between the states. Although a Northerner, he was a Southern sympathizer and a Democrat. He never was a great admirer of Lincoln's. Once he asked me to try to get T.R. to stop praising Lincoln and quoting from him so frequently in his speeches. "Some of us don't think too much of Lincoln," he said. I replied that I'd do almost anything in the world for him except that, for I knew my Theodore Roosevelt and what he thought of the Liberator.

The foregoing is of value only because it helps fill in Colonel Nelson's background. Perhaps a belated tribute, after more than forty years, in the form of personal testimony will give some sidelights on the character of the man, the kind and quality of the newspaper he published, its service to its subscribers, and its influence on them.

My formal education, until I was nearly a grown man, consisted of what the Quaker Valley School, conducted in a one-room schoolhouse in a farm community east of Emporia, had to offer and the few books we had on the farm. The *Star* was my only interesting and important contact with the great world beyond Lyon County. It presented and interpreted news events in an able, interesting way. But it did far more, as witnessed by the fact that when I entered preparatory school I had a broad though superficial acquaintance with the best literature of the ages. I first discovered Robert Browning, Robert Louis Stevenson, Finley Peter Dunne and his "Mr. Dooley," George Ade's "Fables in Slang," and a host of other classic and popular writers in the *Star*. To Nelson, "noble thoughts were news." Instead of filling his paper with trash, Colonel Nelson, who had a high regard for his subscribers' intelligence and tastes, scattered throughout the paper or in special departments poems, paragraphs from classical essays, bits of philosophy from the great writers of all time. Many of these verses or paragraphs, even single sentences, he had set in type for use as column fillers. This practice enabled him to give his readers more than a good, well-written newspaper, for they received in addition the equivalent of all the McGuffey Readers and the material usually included in the best anthologies. Thus he fed them culture with a spoon, helped them learn to like it and ask for more, cultivated their tastes, fired their imaginations, stimulated their curiosity, and lifted up their vision—without which a people perish.

He was, moreover, a man of the highest integrity and great foresight. These qualities, coupled with that sincere regard of his for the intelligence of his subscribers, laid the foundation for what was to become and continues to be one of the dozen really great newspapers of the world.

Colonel Nelson never permitted advertisers to intimidate the *Star*. He was perhaps arbitrary, even unjust at times. But always he was honest, always he tried to give his subscribers the truth as he saw it about men and events, for he sought to build an empire on the great principles of justice and honesty.

In time his Missouri valley public understood and supported him in his efforts, accepted his paper's shifts from one political camp to another without protest, because they felt that he was activated by what he believed was for the public good and knew in their hearts that these shifts were never motivated by expediency.

At the time of Colonel Nelson's death in 1915, Mr. White wrote appreciatively of his contributions in a *Gazette* editorial:

. . . . When he took a position, it was tenable not only the day he took it, but ever after. He saw far, because he saw justly. Yesterday's fights never arose to defeat today's, because yesterday's fight was righteous. That is genius. But he had more than genius, he had a sweet and beautiful soul filled with a love of men, a passion for the welfare of humanity. That was the motive of his life. Such a life, when it is expressed through a strong medium, is vastly immortal. It cannot die, no matter what happens to the body or the soul after death. . . . The Kansas City *Star* was printed for the hour it left the press. Its future and its fate are of no great consequence. But it is of first importance to this generation and to the next in this world that there lived and wrought here with tools of ink and paper a fine free soul with a trained mind, who fashioned out of the world about him every day he lived, the reality of a great dream of democracy.

Colonel Nelson was not devoid of humor, but he was a little too serious-minded to let it run away with his paper, as it eventually did with Dana's *New York Sun.* And so he probably missed some of that elfin humor with which this brilliant cub was later to sharpen his own crusader sword. As for White, in spite of an admiration for Nelson that amounted to reverence, he seemed to have been not wholly happy. The reason, probably, was that he was dreaming, even then, of owning and running his own paper in a Kansas college town. He preferred Emporia, the town of his birth, in which were located a denominational college and a state training school for teachers. He knew then what he wanted, was determined to get it if he could: a home where he could put his roots down deep, his own native soil, a newspaper that would make him a living, choice of the subjects he would write about, freedom to write what he honestly believed.

Mr. White frequently discussed with his friends this dream newspaper of his. Such talk, his surviving friends of this period remember, mostly revolved around the men and women of his dream town—their activities and how he would report them, what his newspaper could do to develop the community. He was by instinct a booster of both material and spiritual things, but he was much more interested in spiritual things; hence his determination to select as his base a college town rather than a country manufacturing or business center.

8. SALLIE LINDSAY, EMPORIA, AND HOME

However, the most important event of his three years on the *Star,* more important even than knowing that gallant, courageous, valiant old crusader, Colonel Nelson, had nothing to do with the newspaper. It was in Kansas City that he met and married Sallie Lindsay, and this woman had as much to do with the blossoming of his spirit as Mary Ann Hatton had with its budding. Once in a *Gazette* editorial he wrote that he had made probably not more than a half-dozen major decisions in his life. The first one of these, he said, was when he decided to marry Sallie Lindsay—"and she says I had nothing to do with it. She says that she took a look at me, a gay young buck from the country come to Kansas City with a come hither eye, and saw that I was a marrying young man. She says she spread her apron and kicked the tree and I fell in it. She was there and she knows. I thought I pursued her. But probably not. Anyway, that was the smartest thing I ever did in my life, to have sense enough to know that this was the girl I needed, that I had to have to develop what qualities I had. I have never made even a secondary decision that we have not canvassed it carefully and agreed before the decision was made."

Whatever the facts of the case may be, this is certain: Sallie Lindsay, a charming, beautiful, and highly intelligent young schoolteacher, the daughter of distinguished parents born and reared in Kentucky, went to the party the night they met, knowing that Mr. White would be there. She had admired him from a distance for some time through his poems which the *Star* reprinted from the *El Dorado Republican*. They practically "slew" her. She went to the party to meet a brilliant young man, who turned out to be her hero for life. They were married in 1893.

The love for the rugged, massive grandeur of the immortal Rockies which youth time vacations had engendered in him lasted throughout his life. There he and his bride went in 1893 to spend a part of their honeymoon in a cabin, where without beds they slept on pine boughs which they cut themselves. While there he lost his job on the *Kansas City Star,* as a result of a staff curtailment during the panic of that year. Years afterward he told me, "I talked fast by telegraph and got my job back, and having only enough money for one ticket to Kansas City and a little to spare for Mrs. White's food, I hurried back to the job to earn her return fare."

There he built a cabin for summer vacations on the side of a gently sloping mountain, which across a valley faced Long's Peak. His favorite pastime was to sit in an easy chair on the porch, with his feet up on the rail, hat pulled low over his eyes, and absorb the inspiring grandeur of Long's Peak and its satellites, all the while carrying on an intermittent, easy, but sparkling conversation on any subject of little or great moment.

It was here, too, that he and Sallie White and their children returned summer after summer for rest or work. Here in another cabin, somewhat up the steep mountainside above his home, he worked on his first major book, *A Certain Rich Man.* This work cabin was a wonder to behold. It consisted of a single large room with fireplace, desk, chairs, and practically the largest bed in the whole world—so large that mattresses, sheets, and blankets had to be made specially for it. There also was a bathroom, whose water supply was piped into it by gravity. Mr. White rigged up unique arrangements for heating the water. They consisted of a copper wash boiler, with a spigot, resting on two small electric plates set on a shelf above the tub. Turning on a faucet filled the boiler with cold mountain water. After it had been heated and turned into the tub, enough cold water was added to suit the bather's taste.

The friends of Will and Sallie White are legion and every one of them has noted and remarked upon the unusual relationship that existed between them. It could not have been otherwise, for here was a marriage not only of "true minds" but of hearts and spirits. Fully her husband's wife, nevertheless Mrs. White maintained her scintillating personality—no mean achievement. The good fairy who left beauty in her cradle, with rare indulgence, held back the hand of time, softening instead of withering the olive skin, the lovely eyes, the raven hair. Through the years the charm of the exuberant young woman deepened as she grew into an incomparable hostess. She, too, had abilities as a writer, and she had also Will's acute perception—call it intuition if you wish—to a remarkable degree. The correspondence of their purposes and ideals, and their attitude toward each other, were an inspiration to all who ever had the rare privilege of being with them.

No married man, other than a clod, could watch his eager, constant devotion to her without wanting and trying to be a better husband. No married woman would witness Mrs. White's responses to his remarks and his attentions, her method of expressing her opinion when they happened to disagree, without wanting to take her as a model in her relationship with her own husband. No happily married couple could see Will and Sallie White together without wanting and trying to follow the example they set. I have heard him telephone her from the office and say, "I haven't anything on my mind, I just wanted to hear your voice," and then chat away for a while about everything in general and nothing in particular.

His marriage whipped to the point of action his urge to get established as his own man. But added to that was the fact that some of the stories he had written for the *Star* got the paper into trouble.

In his scattered reminiscences he made light—as usual—of his reasons for quitting the *Star:*

. . . life grew gradually dull and monotonous. A glance into the howitzer carried by Joe Davenport, who came to whip the editor of the *Star* and a leap from the second story of the building to a desk in the business office of the *Star* on the first floor, to escape the gun, was the most considerable episode that came to relieve the drab life. A delegation from the stock yards once came to fight, but we were out and they ignobly let the matter drop. A leading citizen named Owsley and a gentleman named Blitz obligingly threatened to kill us, but without satisfactory and lasting results. So we left Kansas City for Emporia, where for a few years business did pick up.

And for a minor—or was it a major—motive, he longed for the intimacy of life in a small town. Kansas City had become too metropolitan for him, even though the combined population of the Kansas Cities of Missouri and Kansas, really one town although in two states, was probably less than 150,000 at that time. It was, nevertheless, metropolitan for the area between St. Louis and Denver, and it had all the appurtenances of a metropolitan community from theater and opera, cathedrals and symphony orchestras, to political gangs and slums. The spirit and the quiet of a small Kansas town had gripped White's heart with an unshakable hold. It held the atmosphere he loved and longed for and clung to throughout his life.

Here he was now on the threshold of his twenty-seventh year with two tries at getting a college education, with the experience of having been his own boss in running a newspaper in three different small Kansas towns, with a term on a kept newspaper and with nearly three years of association with one of the finest groups of newspapermen and under one of the greatest editors that the nation has ever produced. Since his boyhood he had been up to his neck in politics of the serious, seething Kansas variety. He had covered the legislature for his newspapers; he knew most of the political leaders and newspapermen of the state; now he was married and ready to strike out on his own.

This background of varied and remarkable experience had given Mr. White enough skill and craftsmanship, enough understanding of human nature, enough experience with people, to run his own newspaper. These years had all been fruitful in one way or another; with his mother's early training they fixed the course of his life. Someone has called attention to the fact that Abraham Lincoln and Huey Long sprang from the same element, the poor dispossessed whites of the south. Do not scorn Long's intellect. It is not at all improbable that he would have beaten Lincoln badly on an IQ test. They both started poor and ambitious. What then was the difference between Long, the loud-mouthed demagogue, and Lincoln, the liberator? It was that from whatever environment surrounded him, Lincoln chose the best and Long the worst. It shows even in their public expressions, their style: Lincoln upward from his awkward announcement as a candidate from Sangamon County to the Gettysburg Address, Long downward from his early, able legal briefs to the cheap insincerity of his "share-the-wealth" orations. Will White had the same instincts as Lincoln. He chose the best, and what he chose from his previous newspaper work and especially from his service at the *Star* finished off his overrealistic education. It waked in him a sense of responsibility far wider than party allegiance, the responsibility of a newspaper to its community, inspired him to work for its highest interests. It taught him where to draw the line between the fair and the unfair, the decent and the shameful in the publication of news. From the *Star,* which of course means Colonel Nelson, he learned, too, that a fighting newspaper has other and better weapons than blatant denunciation. And the intelligent copyreaders and directing editors of the *Star* had sandpapered some of the raw edges from his youthful style without snuffing out the light of originality in him.

He was ready now to make the break, prepared as he was in heart and mind and buttressed with friendships all over the state. One friendship perhaps should be mentioned here because it is so directly connected with his first taste of fame—with Eugene Ware, a Connecticut-born, Iowa-reared veteran of the Union Army, a self-educated but sound scholar who knew intimately the works of the great Latin poets. Ware served a turn as a newspaper editor, studied law, and, during a long period of years previous to his becoming commissioner of pensions under President Theodore Roosevelt, was a leader, if not *the* leader, of the Kansas bar. He came of "undiluted Yankee strain," and had its virtues of "thrift, punctuality and realistic appraisal." He was an uncompromising and undeviating Republican. Along with his other qualities and traits he had a rare gift of expression. He gained considerable distinction by his poetry, published under the pseudonym of "Ironquill." It was natural that he and Will White should become cronies, that Will during his service as a reporter of legislative activity in Topeka should come to know him intimately, to admire him greatly. In later years he wrote of Ware, "There was no malice in his voice nor in his life. His capacity for hate was directed at causes, not men." The editorial which gave Will White national fame in 1896 was inspired by Ware.

All unheralded the man who was to give it world-wide fame descended upon Emporia. The *Gazette,* an evening daily newspaper, was for sale. It had a circulation of less than five hundred copies and advertising patronage of next to nothing. W. Y. Morgan, who had bought it from its founder, J. R. Graham, wanted to move to a larger town, so he offered it lock, stock, and barrel to White for $3,000 cash. White had saved no money but he had learned that leaders of a Republican faction in Emporia headed by Major Calvin Hood, president of the Emporia National Bank, wanted an organ because the other local Republican newspaper, the *Republican,* was the mouthpiece of a rival faction, the First National Bank group. Knowing Major Hood and his crowd and the ways of men, he borrowed from them the balance of the purchase price of $3,000 on his note—he had fortified himself before going to Emporia by getting a loan of $1,000, also on his note, from Governor E. N. Morrill. This $3,000 was, if anything, an overpayment. The worn type, the senile flat-bed press, the office tools and furniture probably wouldn't have brought $1,000 at public auction. The rest was "good will." The only item of good will worth mentioning was the fact that the *Gazette* was already a Republican newspaper in a community which was normally Republican. To balance that, however, the only real competition he had in an already overcrowded field was from a newspaper which also was Republican. Division in the local party concerned patronage rather than policy, so White had no decision to make as to whether his policy should be liberal or conservative.

On June 1, 1895, having traveled from Kansas City on the conventional railroad pass with less than two dollars in his pocket, he got off the train at Emporia, took a hack to the dilapidated office of the struggling *Gazette,* made the deal, and sat down in the editor's chair. A long-nursed dream had come true.

9. GROWTH THROUGH COMPETITION

WILL WHITE was to occupy that chair for forty-nine years and to glorify that corner of the *Gazette* office even as the rainbow round the throne which St. John saw in the Apocalypse. Although neither he nor Emporia knew it, even then he "had everything." In later years he could have gone as a directing journalist wherever he chose—to the editorship of a New York or Chicago daily, even to the lordship of such a great domain, such dazzling wealth, as Hearst possessed at his peak. But he had no interest in power for its own sake and wealth did not tempt him then or ever. Then and always he did want to live comfortably and decently, perhaps amply, to have some extra money to give away or to spend in those friendly hospitalities which always marked the White establishment. As for social position, the last infirmity of ignoble minds, he knew with his own mind that such a thing existed but he never knew it in his heart, and neither—perhaps more to the point—did Sallie White.

In spite of the fact that he once was offered $400,000 for the Emporia *Gazette,* he never was what would be considered a great moneymaker. After he got it finally established, he paid himself a salary of $3,000 a year. He stuck to this sum even when the cost of living inched upward. At the end of each year he collected the margin of profit, if any. He did, however, add substantially to his income by his stories, magazine articles and books. However, during the first years much of this revenue went into new *Gazette* equipment, to buying and improving Emporia real estate, or to helping, financially, scores if not hundreds of individuals and causes. When he was fully established, when he finally came fully to his social consciousness, he installed a profit-sharing plan for his employees, much before most other business concerns. This left him with small margin of profit, even in the good years of the *Gazette.*

On June 3, 1895, the next day but one after he took over, he published a salutatory editorial setting forth his intentions and purposes. It is worth reprinting because of its prophecy of his career, because of the statements of his intentions.

ENTIRELY PERSONAL

To the gentle reader who may, through the coming years during which we are spared to one another, follow the course of this paper, a word of personal address from the new editor of *The Gazette* is due. In the first place, the new editor hopes to live here until he is the old editor, until some of the visions which rise before him as he dreams shall have come true. He hopes always to sign 'from Emporia' after his name, when he is abroad, and he trusts that he may so endear himself to the people that they will be as proud of the first words of the signature as he is of the last words. He expects to perform all the kind offices of the country editor in this community for a generation to come. It is likely that he will write the wedding notices of the boys and girls in the schools; that he will announce the birth of the children who will some day honor Emporia, and that he will say the final words over those of middle age who read these lines. His relations with the people of this town and country are to be close and personal. He hopes that they may be kindly and just. The new editor of *The Gazette* is a young man now, full of high purposes and high ideals. But he needs the close touch of older hands. His endeavor will be to make a paper for the best people of the city. But to do that he must have their help. They must counsel with him, be his friends, often show him what their sentiment is. On them rests the responsibility somewhat. The 'other fellows' will be around. They will give advice. They will attempt to show what the public sentiment is. They will try to work their schemes, which might dishonor the town. If the best people stay away from the editor's office, if they neglect to stand by the editor, they must not blame him for mistakes. An editor is not all-wise. He judges only by what he sees and hears. Public sentiment is the only sentiment that prevails. Good sentiment, so long as it does not assert itself, so long as it is a silent majority, is only private sentiment. If the good, honest, upright, God-fearing, law-abiding people of any community desire to be reflected to the world, they must see that their private opinion is public opinion. They must stand by the editors who believe as they do.

It is a plain business proposition. The new editor of *The Gazette* desires to make a clean, honest local paper. He is a Republican and will support Republican nominees first, last, and all the time. There will be no bolting, no sulking, no "holier than thou" business about his politics—but politics is so little. Not one man in ten cares for politics more than two weeks in a year. In this paper, while the politics will be straight, it will not be obtrusive. It will be confined to the editorial page—where the gentle reader may venture at his peril. The main thing is to have this paper represent the average thought of the best people of Emporia and Lyon County in all their varied interests. The editor will do his best. He has no axes to grind. He is not running the paper for a political pull. If he could get an office he wouldn't have it. He is in the newspaper business as he would be in the drygoods business—to make an honest living and to leave an honest name behind. If the good people care for a fair, honest home paper, that will stand for the best that is in the town—here it is.

In the meantime, I shall hustle advertising, job work and subscriptions, and write editorials and "telegraph" twelve hours a day in spite of my ideals. The path of glory is barred hog tight for the man who does not labor while he waits.

White, it will be observed, began his editorial career and his leadership of the *Gazette* with humble homage to the Republican party and its immortal principles. That excessive loyalty was strengthened, perhaps, by his resistance to the atmosphere created by the Farmer's Alliance and the Populist movements in which he had lived for the past three years. Otherwise this editorial should be taught in every school of journalism, framed in the office of every honest newspaper.

Four years after he wrote it, party loyalty, as he interpreted it, brought the last physical violence of his career. It happened in this wise: Colonel Luther Severy, an old-line Republican leader and Union soldier, sought his party's nomination for mayor. He lost. He then ran as an independent candidate. White roasted him as a traitor to his party and pointed out that any man who would place office above principle wasn't worthy of public support. The two men met on the street. White spoke to the Colonel, who cut him cold. Then, just after they had passed, Colonel Severy whirled and swung his heavy cane down on the back of the editor's head. White fell; the Colonel hit him again. Stunned momentarily, Will rose and began brushing off his clothes. A spectator called him a coward. White knocked the man down and the crowd separated them. The next day in court White pleaded not guilty and went free. Colo-

nel Severy pleaded guilty and paid a fine. The episode ended
when a new gold-headed cane, purchased by popular subscription, was presented to Severy in the office of the *Emporia Republican,* the rival paper.

The *Republican* was owned and published by a man of considerable ability, a former lieutenant governor of the state, C. V.
Eskridge. He was a solemn-faced, smallish, dignified, scholarly-
looking gentleman of the old school and an ardent Republican,
contemptuous and perhaps a bit afraid of the *Gazette's* young
and virile editor. Governor Eskridge's paper was as dignified
and aloof as he himself. You had to belong to the elite or else
herd with the police-court crowd to get your name into it.
Even then the name appeared with only the most skeleton-
like information about you or the news concerning you. Still,
the *Republican,* rather than the feeble Democratic *Times,* was
the *Gazette's* real rival. This rivalry was natural, not only because of the poles-apart differences in temperament and outlook
of the two rival editors, but because they were competing for
pretty much the same clientele in a small community. Three
months after White set up shop he was able to get the county
printing and advertising away from the *Republican.* This was
possible because the Hood bank and the faction it represented
in the Republican party was dominant at the moment, while
the Cross–Martindale–First National Bank faction was temporarily out of control of the party locally. In the Middle West,
county advertising and printing was the backbone of a country
newspaper's revenue.

Shortly before Mr. White took over the *Gazette,* the *Republican* ran the following editorial note:

"It is reported that W. A. White has purchased the *Gazette,*
a paper published in this city, and will take charge the 1st of
June. Next!"

In the forty-nine years following that June 1st the *Gazette*
had had no *next,* whereas the *Republican* passed out of existence a few years after printing that item. But before it did the
rival editors carried on a verbal war after the best old-fashioned
Western model, with quarter neither given nor asked. Kansas
still clung to the belief that the quarrels of rival editors were a
good thing because they stirred up interest. This idea is related

to the theory that fleas are good for a dog because they keep
him from thinking too much about being a dog, as Mark Twain
put it.

Mr. White also carried on guerrilla warfare with the editor
of the Democratic *Times,* P. F. Yearout, whom he at times
called Mr. "Polly-Fox" Yearout, or the Honorable "Peter Free-
Coinage" Yearout.

Once, when referring to some generous remarks that had
been made about Mr. Yearout's fine qualities, Mr. White wrote
in the *Gazette:*

"The sight of those budding wings upon the shoulders of
Pete Yearout has jabbed the seething irons of jealousy into the
proud flesh of the editor who indites these lines. The hint that
this good man is a trickster is revolting."

During this period, White was not yet able to cover a quip
or a bit of sarcasm with a sugar coating of apparent flattery. His
chief asset in a fight was still his sharp good humor.

Whatever the merits of that old tempest in a small teapot,
Eskridge was as completely unqualified to match wits with Will
White as he would have been to have a battle with James J.
Corbett, current champion of the world. It also goes without
saying that as soon as White really got the *Gazette* brightened
up, the more because he did most of the writing, the inhabitants
began to buy it. My own family provides as good an illustration
as any. After seeing an occasional copy of his paper, perhaps
about 1896, I began to want it, but my father, as a follower of
the Cross-Martindale-Eskridge faction, subscribed to the *Republican,* and two papers were beyond our means. Thus I was
unable to become a regular reader of the *Gazette* until I became
its Quaker Valley correspondent. White selected correspondents in all communities of the county to gather local news
items, and implored us to "write them on Sunday and send
them in on Monday, for Tuesday is everlastingly too late."
(The weekly *Gazette* was published on Thursdays.)

The *Gazette's* circulation doubled, then quadrupled; private
advertising followed. Early in this century the *Republican*
folded up. The Democrat paper lasted a decade or so longer as
a daily, then became a weekly.

As recorded earlier, other men bought the secondhand plants

of these rival Emporia newspapers after they had failed, and tried to outshine the sun, and in turn also flickered out. Then came the period when the swollen costs of publishing a newspaper made it impossible for more than one daily newspaper to exist in a community as small as Emporia, and for the last twenty years of his life White had virtually no competition.

Although he did some splendid bits of reporting in his time, he was by desire and instinct primarily an editorial writer, a commentator upon the passing show, an interpreter of the ways and waywardness of man. Regardless of how high a star reporter soars, there is bound to be a certain amount of leg work and of idling around while he waits for the brass hat to summon him to the presence. White was so averse to physical exertion that he limited his exercise to walking from home to office and back, and in later years he did this only when the family car was otherwise engaged. By contrast, he had intense mental energy. The amount, variety, and high quality of the work he did in the course of his life proves that. He thought best on paper. His ideas flowed freely only when he was writing them down. It was always an inspiration to me as a boy to see him sitting humped over his old, double-keyboard, blind Smith typewriter, making the keys hum and from a rear view looking for all the world like a fat man riding a bicycle up a steep hill.

Since his métier was editorial comment and interpretation, he chafed at the limitations of reporting. The sound theory of American and British journalism—in contrast to the Continental European variety—is that the news columns, no matter how vividly written, should be as free as possible from all bias and expression of opinion. American journalists have operated under the belief that the reader, having absorbed the fact, may then turn to the editorial column and learn what the editor thinks of it. But a middle ground has developed since White's education in journalism—the writer who deals as his fancy dictates with affairs of the day, whether the facts be already revealed to the reader or whether he is publishing them for the first time. We call such writers columnists. They are now the popular favorites of American journalism, just as the star reporter was at the beginning of this century—and was to be again temporarily during our two great wars. If it were possible exactly to classify a phenomenon so original as Will White, we should have to call him a columnist rather than an editorial writer. This statement probably would disturb him because his opinion of columnists generally was very low. This opinion, expressed privately, rested largely on his belief that they subtracted a vital factor from the editor's responsibilities.

From his first days on the *Gazette* Will White began to make good his declaration of principles; to try, according to his lights at the time, to make a better and more civilized town. "This world is made better," he wrote, "by every man improving his own conduct—no reform is accomplished wholesale." In the news columns and in his editorials he began tilting—still in his exuberant and somewhat violent early style—at things which were wrong with Emporia and her people, and pinning roses on things which were right. Once he wrote: "An ex-nun is raising a literal and exact counterpart of hell in Topeka by delivering a 'ladies only' lecture against Catholics. Anyone who would attend such a lecture should be shunned by decent people." From his first day in the editor's chair he put new clothes on old truths and made them attractive; preached and practiced friendliness, neighborliness, and helpfulness. He was a man of the people, as was Lincoln, and his way of life, like Lincoln's, was perfected in an age and region where people lived in a neighborly way, as had their forebears for centuries.

Once, nearly fifty years ago, I filled a bad chuck hole in the road near our farm, solely because travelers were severely jolted as they drove over it. Only my father's hired men had seen me do it, and they ridiculed me. Then a *Gazette* editorial said that the man was a good citizen who on his own initiative took a shovel and filled holes in the road. Within ten minutes after reading that editorial I had grown six inches in mental and moral stature. In filling that hole, I was only being neighborly. But when Editor White, who did not know of my action, called such deeds evidences of good citizenship, he opened a new world for me.

A genius he certainly was; and being such he saw things differently from the vast majority of his fellow Emporians. Moreover, he was far ahead of his times, and so occasionally voiced opinions or made proposals which to the minds of that solemn, God-fearing generation seemed absurd, even wild.

I remember listening one night when a boy to a long discussion in my grandfather's home about Mr. White. My grandfather, a Unionist who had moved to Kansas from eastern Tennessee, was a college-trained man of positive convictions. He had been a lieutenant of Andrew Johnson's in the struggle to keep Tennessee on the Union side, then hurried to Kansas to help keep it a free state. He never was uncertain about his beliefs, and he expressed them freely and ably. His visitor that night, a member of the Kansas State Supreme Court, was also able and expressive. Both of them discussed the young upstart White at length and in detail—his style of writing, his proposals, his outlook on life. Their unanimous verdict, their last word, was: "The man is crazy."

Editor Eskridge added what faggots he could to keep the fires burning. There was, for instance, this gem from his paper regarding that "lunatic, Silly Willie":

"Hot bricks to his feet to create proper circulation of blood and a wet rag pinned around his head to reduce the swelling might be beneficial for a time but there is no hope for a permanent cure."

In his running war on sham and pretense, the young editor created fictitious families in Emporia and panned the life out of them. These included the Lystander J. Appleton and the Colonel Alphabet Morrison families. The daughters of the latter family, lazy, incompetent, gadabout creatures, White said, would come sailing down Commercial Street with their silk petticoats making more noise than a threshing machine going full blast. Outwardly they were perfectly gowned Venuses, and yet the poor, lowly heathen in Africa would be ashamed to be caught dead in the underwear they wore. In one way or another he used these nonexistent families to drive home every truth of living and being that he held fair, lovely, and of good report.

During his first few years in Emporia the young editor, an excellent reporter, and a hustler, filled every job on the paper —covering local news, writing editorials, proofreading, editing telegraph, soliciting advertisements, even writing them, setting type in a pinch, kicking the "Gordon Jobber," building up his country correspondence, and acting as chief booster for the town and the surrounding countryside. His own business manager as well, a few months after he bought the *Gazette* he talked a merchant into using the first full-page advertisement that ever appeared in an Emporia newspaper. As he told the story later, he breezed into the A. O. Rorabaugh store one day and made his proposition. The terms were: Nothing, with no discount for cash. The ad was to run two days. It seemed reasonable to the merchant but on further thought he tried to get out of it because he never before had thought in terms of a full-page ad. But, as Mr. White later said, "we were fast talkers in those days." The results were astonishing. "The crowd broke into the store on the third day," according to Mr. White, "and about put him out of business. He couldn't afford to take an advertisement before that day. He has never been able to afford a month without one since."

In 1898 White promoted a "street fair," with many novel attractions. He had brought in real Indians whom no hotel would accommodate, so he bedded them in hay at a livery stable. The first automobile ever seen in Emporia was shipped there from Chicago for this occasion. There was a "Little Brown Brother" cakewalk (this was at the time of new and heightened interest in the Philippines) which he and Mrs. White organized. For one dollar each they induced ten small pickaninnies to strip, don white loin cloths, and cakewalk to band music, each carrying a long stalk of kaffir corn. All went well until some town cutup slipped Mike Grady, local bandmaster, a dollar bill with the request that he play "All Coons Look Alike to Me." Irish Mike performed. Indignant Negro mothers who, previous to seeing their nearly naked offspring performing, had known nothing about the affair, rushed in. Each grabbed her child and yanked him out of line, and so broke up the show. But the crowd was so gratified that old-timers in Emporia still chuckle over the incident.

The "street fair" had many other thrilling attractions. I saw my first moving picture there, a crude, flickering, jumpy thing, shown in a black canvas tent.

Thousands of men and women and children from miles

around filled the town and spread the holiday spirit everywhere except in the columns of the *Republican,* as revealed by an item in the *Kansas City Times* which said: "If you don't want to read about Will White's street fair in Emporia read the *Emporia Republican.*"

10. "WHAT'S THE MATTER WITH KANSAS?"

BUT THE STORY of his early years with the *Gazette* as I have told it so far is *Hamlet* without Hamlet. Fourteen months after he took over the paper he jumped into national notoriety which was to grow into national fame. On August 3, 1896, when Bryan's free-silver campaign was getting up speed, White published in the *Gazette* a long editorial entitled "What's the Matter with Kansas?"

Concerning the genesis and inspiration of this editorial there have been many printed accounts. All of them save his own, written as a preface to *The Rhymes of Ironquill,* a book of collected poems by Eugene Ware, state that he met some Populists on the street, had a hot argument with them, went back to the office in a blaze of intellectual fury and wrote this masterpiece of invective before he cooled off.

As he told the story himself, the campaign of 1896 was the first one since the war between the states when an economic issue was disturbing the people of the entire nation. This was currency inflation. Since the introduction of machinery endangered our political economy, Bryan was the first man to take up the cudgels for this old favorite of the Jacksonian Democrats. Eugene Ware, that wise, scholarly New Englander, Union soldier, able, loyal, and undeviating Republican, was indignant. A month or so before the publication of "What's the Matter with Kansas?" White had been in Ware's office when Ware began a monologue, a diatribe against Kansas Populists. He recited to his pupil all of the disagreeable things they had done, picturing their incompetence in glowing, lyric terms. This diatribe set Will White's blood afire. When Ware had finished, White said, "With your permission, sometime I'm going to use these facts and give them your slant." Ware replied, "Take them with my blessing." The idea gestated in White's brain for a month or two. After his argument with the Populists he went to the office and poured his indignation and Ware's facts onto paper. White had taken no notes, but as he said later, Ware had "laid hands on me spiritually and out of his heart, in his rage and shame over Populist defamation of Kansas, I wrote it."

White also told how he and Ware often talked afterward of that editorial and its aftermath, and added, "he was happy that I took it, over the fame it brought me and he shared the joy over its wide use with me."

In his maturity White was decidedly ashamed of most of the sentiments in this outburst, and especially of his biting scorn for the judge who declared that production should be for *use, not profit.* He even came almost to despise it as a piece of literature. From the week he took over the *Gazette* he had been fighting that Populist movement which had now annexed itself to the militant column of the magnetic boy-orator of the Platte. "A lot of my earlier editorials on this subject were better stuff," he later wrote. Some academic critics have agreed with him, some others call his sudden success just an accident. The editorial came, they say, at a fortunate moment.

The writer must disagree as to its literary merit. That editorial was written in a white heat which flowed into its lines. It is as though he had said to himself, as did Robert Louis Stevenson when in a similar mood he sat down to polish off the defamer of Father Damien, "This is what I learned to write for." It goes with a breathless rush that carries the reader along with it. Not one writer in a hundred ever knows his best work when he sees it.

Nevertheless, the time *was* ripe. Political historians have said that if we had held the election of 1896 in August instead of November, Bryan would have won. Hard-pressed Republican editors not only of Kansas but of neighboring Colorado and Missouri fairly tore the editorial from the exchange copies of the *Gazette* and rushed it to print. It was as though a battleship had suddenly come out of the mist and aligned itself beside a squadron of cruisers. Its subject was local but its application national. Mark Hanna, the chairman of the Republican National Committee, printed and distributed more than a million copies of it. Thus the tide rolled on to both coasts. If it had been sent over the Associated Press wires it could scarcely have got a wider publication.

Immediately after writing the editorial and putting it on the copy hook, White left Emporia with Mrs. White for their vacation in Colorado. The current shop foreman of the *Gazette*, a Democrat, took it off the hook and was so incensed and outraged that he refused to set it up in type. He was convinced, moreover, that its publication would put the *Gazette* out of business. But run it he must, so he turned the copy over to Miss Laura French, his assistant compositor. Miss French, also a Democrat, seethed with rage, but she went through with it. She, too, believed that the editorial was so full of dynamite that it would destroy the paper.

Before the Whites returned from their vacation, the great newspapers of the nation were wiring to Kansas for biographical sketches of this obscure, twenty-eight-year-old country editor. Publishers were writing to explore him as a possibility for books and magazine articles, the exalted heads of the Republican party were gloating over him as a new and rich asset.

All of this was to seem strangely anomalous before long. By the queer workings of destiny, this blow for conservatism opened for William Allen White the gates to liberalism.

Part Two

THE MIDDLE YEARS
1900—1916

1. EDITOR AND WRITER

Wᴵʟʟ Wʜɪᴛᴇ had the true newspaperman's mania for experience—that is, experience within the range of his interests. Never before that sudden, unexpected hit of his "What's the Matter with Kansas?" had he traveled beyond Kansas, Colorado, and Missouri. Until the summer of 1896 Kansas City was the largest city he had ever seen; then he went to St. Louis to cover the Republican National Convention for his own newspaper and the *St. Louis World,* but he didn't like St. Louis at all. A few months after his famous editorial was printed, that and another fortunate coincidence started him on his travels, which before he died took him to Europe several times, to the Orient, Mexico, the West Indies, and all over the United States.

Up to that time he still cherished the illusion that there was a definite line between "literature" published in the magazines or between book covers, and journalism, which appears in newspapers. Already he and Albert Bigelow Paine, afterward Mark Twain's biographer, had privately published a slim volume of verse which, for its rarity rather than its merits, is now a collector's item. When, about the same time, he shifted from Kansas City to Emporia, he gathered the best of his early short stories into a book entitled *The Real Issue,* which Way and Williams of Chicago accepted for publication. A few months after "What's the Matter with Kansas?" made him famous they persuaded him to come to Chicago to take part in the ensuing ballyhoo. The publishers showed him off to Chicago's literary set. He returned to Emporia with unswelled head and continued with his job of getting out a good newspaper.

The sales of *The Real Issue* were going very well. In those days the newspapers compiled no best-selling lists, but within a week it was among the three best sellers in Chicago—which was doing extremely well, considering that then as now most people read their short stories in the magazines and are inclined to scorn them between book covers.

More to the eventual benefit of the author, the fact that this small-town newspaperman who wrote "What's the Matter with Kansas?" could also write good fiction constituted news. Eastern reviewers, who ordinarily would toss aside a book from this comparatively obscure (to them) Chicago publishing firm, took up the book. It was too advanced for some of them and they poured vitriol over this crude Western upstart. Others heard in it the familiar "new note," gave it most favorable reviews.

In another way the times worked favorably for the budding young author. In 1893, S. S. McClure, owner of a pioneer newspaper syndicate which controlled its field, founded *McClure's* magazine, one of the pioneer "ten-centers," and began carrying it to the heights. This magazine flourished for the next ten or fifteen years. It is now remembered mostly because it opened the muckraking era in popular American literature, but today few know its influence in bringing our literature down to the soil of the earth. A little before "What's the Matter with Kansas?" set critical as well as political leaders to talking about young White of Kansas, *McClure's* had begun to give Viola Roseboro her head. As Will Irwin has noted in the *Saturday Review of Literature*, she was the extraordinary manuscript reader who maintained that American fictionists had been neglecting ten thousand aspects of our rich, complex American life. At once she set forth to fill the gap with stories which arrived in the mail from unknown and unappreciated young American authors. The popular success of the first stories that she chose proved her point. The "Olympian Trio," *Harper's, Scribner's,* and *Century,* and the classic *Atlantic* ruled the roost. Their fiction still imitated the best models of an earlier period. American realism was not wanted, so they sat waiting for manuscripts of just the right, refined, highly literary tone to come in of themselves. The young McClure was not the man to wait for anything. Either he or his editorial scouts ranged the country looking for promising young authors, encouraging them, even coaching them. They saw *The Real Issue* the moment it appeared; *McClure's* violated all precedent by publishing, as though they were newly printed, two stories from it. And Mr. McClure clamored for more stories from the Kansas grass roots.

McClure's at that time had not begun to print those exposés of financial juggling in high places, of corruption and graft in municipal and state governments, which created a new pattern for reform, but the *McClure* group was alert and intellectually stimulating. Ida Tarbell was then working on her life of Lincoln, a subject on which White was an enthusiast. They found common ground there and began a friendship which was to last until her death. She was already gathering material for her history of the Standard Oil Company, the first big gun in the barrage of exposures which the popular magazines fired in the first decade of this century. It is likely that she discussed this work with him; and if so, she gave him a few glimpses of the shortcomings of the laissez-faire theory of government. Ray Stannard Baker was still working hard as manager of the McClure Syndicate; Lincoln Steffens had not yet joined the staff. As for S. S. McClure, the enterprising, imaginative young go-getter whom Robert Louis Stevenson used as the original for his character of Pinkerton in *The Wrecker,* he had no vivid interest then or thereafter in reform for its own sake. What McClure wanted was a readable, salable magazine. His interest in White was to get more good copy.

White's next excursion after his Chicago visit in the fall of 1896 took him to a political banquet in Ohio early in 1897, and following this he went to New York to see publishers—an occasional necessity for a provincial author in a generation that knew not the literary agent. Short as he probably was on ready funds, he made these trips pay for themselves. The railroads still gave passes to bona fide newspapermen. And he could always pick up a bit of correspondence from some newspaper or syndicate to pay for food and lodging. In addition to this, his impressions gained while making the trips and written for the *Gazette* in the language and mental attitude of Emporia enriched that editorial page for which he did his daily stint.

Wherever he traveled and whatever else he did, he came back from the New York trip with an embarrassing load of orders for magazine articles and short stories, virtually accepted sight unseen; and he had a loose, yet binding, arrangement for a regular run of copy to the McClure Syndicate.

His "Court of Boyville" stories, which first appeared in *McClure's* and were published in 1898 as a book, were followed by scores of magazine articles and personality sketches dealing with politics and life in the Western towns and in remote farm homes. There was a whimsical touch in his writings of those days, as there was, even to the end, in his conversation. Astonishingly, in view of the fact that some of his first articles appeared in a despised ten-cent magazine, *Scribner's* noted him and solicited copy from him. He wrote for them a batch of political stories, realistic studies of backstage political jugglery, both in an unnamed Western capital which everyone recognized as Topeka and in Washington, which also was clearly recognized. In the literary slang of the times, again he struck a new note. Five of the stories he wrote for *Scribner's,* some of novelette length, were gathered into a book and published by that firm under the title of *Stratagems and Spoils;* and when William Dean Howells, then the arbiter of American literature, gave them enthusiastic reviews, White had a right to feel that he was made as an author.

Magazine prices, of course, were then low by present standards. Three hundred dollars was about the top price for any American short story, and two hundred was very good pay. But the checks he received from the large number of magazine stories and articles which he wrote so swiftly grew to a substantial sum. The first of this money went to pay his debt for purchase of the *Gazette*. He bought the present site of the *Gazette* in 1899, and in 1903 erected a new building and moved in. On the tenth anniversary of his editorship, he wrote that he had not only paid off the original debt but had bought new mechanical equipment including a rotary press, a linotype machine, and a dress of job and display type, and established his family in a good unmortgaged house. He did not mention the money he had given away, although he was already doing that lavishly, albeit judiciously.

In telling his readers about new dress of type he wrote:

. . . The old types, used to print the *Gazette* from the beginning, have been turned into the type foundry. They have told of many a town comedy, and of many a town tragedy; their black bodies have stood up for Emporia, and, when the occasion came, they have marshaled their lines for the right—against sham and pretense. They have been found on the side of upright living and manly worth. May the new types tell of more happiness in this town, more prosperity, more Christian living and the growth of more moral courage among the people. When they shall have stories of tragedy to tell, and such stories must fall to the lot of types, may they not tell it gloatingly, but with a humility and in sorrow; may they laugh with those who laugh and mourn with them that mourn.

All of this, at least nearly all, came from magazine and syndicate writing or from royalties on his books. His salary as publisher and editor of the *Gazette* and profits during these ten years were for the most part used to support his family. But his financial independence was being made constantly more secure because he was piling up a substantial reserve in the continually increasing value of his newspaper.

During this period he came to more than one parting of the ways. Metropolitan editors were continually offering him jobs. That great publisher, Joseph Pulitzer, of the *New York World,* dangled $10,000 a year before his eyes. He was not dazzled. "Whoever would leave tree-lined Emporia for New York would murder his own grandmother with her crutches," he replied. A few years later he dismissed with the same humorous contempt an offer of $25,000 a year from the *Chicago Tribune.*

To a different man the same choice might have been harder, especially when literary success offered the prospect of an easy life with four or five hours' work a day and an office under his hat, with periods for gorgeous loafing in between. But White had made this choice long before, even before he returned to Emporia in 1895. In 1911 or thereabouts, he and I were discussing the *Gazette* and the amount of time it took. When I asked him why he did not turn the management over to someone else, so that he could devote more time to the greater national field of writing, to politics, and to public movements in which he was so much interested, he dismissed the idea quickly and completely on the grounds that the *Gazette* really was his life—without it he would be separated from the people, get lost.

These other activities, this bigger field, he said, represented occasional sorties for him. The inspiration and urge to undertake them grew out of his work as editor. And he needed Emporia as a home base from which to work, because he was so happy in his life there, happier than he possibly could be anywhere else.

He had, of course, tremendous inner energy, and with his physical inertness and his total want of interest in all games and sports, there was no way to blow off some of his excess steam except through the channels of the mind and soul. His recreations were intellectual and spiritual. A social being, he genuinely liked people both in the mass and as individuals. To humanity in groups he brought a tolerant understanding, to his friends deep personal interest and warm affection. He was most at his ease about a congenial dinner table doing his part—but no more—in good talk. This talk did not have to be serious to interest him; in fact, it could be charmingly trivial. He preferred it wise, and if wittily wise all the better.

Once in the *Gazette* he wrote that he supposed that "really the best thing men do in the world from the standpoint of human satisfaction is to talk. A time comes when a human being gets to that point in life where horses, poker, politics and the ladies-god-bless-'em have been sloughed off and one's mind turns naturally to things of the spirit. Good talk is worth all that it costs—even to live three score years and ten. And if it be four score, still it is a swell show."

When he first went East he had his fill of good music for the first time, and he sampled the theater also. These two expressions of the arts fascinated, stimulated, and interested him throughout his life. Going to the opera or a symphony concert with him was an experience. That was an occasion when he didn't care for good conversation, no matter how wise or witty. It was like a boy's going fishing with his father; you were not supposed to say a word for fear of driving the fish away. A single word seemed to bring his spirit back to earth from a distant sphere in which harmony opened great vistas of beauty that kindled his mind with noble inspirations and ideas, put him into closer communion with our unfathomable, mysterious, awesome universe.

Life on those terms—running his newspaper, living comfortably in his own home, surrounded by old friends and good neighbors, working off the excess of his tremendous energy by writing for magazines and book publishers, mixing in state as well as national politics, having a brief period once or twice a year with Mrs. White in New York, where they could hear the finest music, see the best plays, and commune with some of the best intelligences in the country—that was the life for him.

Even in his later years he testified how he woke every morning "raring" to go; feeling that the day would bring him glorious adventure; and few days disappointed him.

Only a man who lived on such terms could have turned out the volume of work that he performed between 1896, the year of his first success, and about 1904, when his all-round duties at the *Gazette* became lighter as a result of its increasing financial stability and the able functioning of the staff he had assembled. The business of writing editorials for the *Gazette* in the morning, broken with directing the staff, laying out the make-up, making decisions for the business office, dictating letters, taking time out to be courteous to callers, who, with or without business to transact, would walk through his always open door, filled his day. Subscribers and advertisers invariably went to him instead of to the business office, and without exception he pleasantly directed them to the right department. Leading citizens with causes, people wanting favors, kickers—all came to him; none was made to feel that he should not have done so. Occasionally when these interruptions came thick and fast he would say to his stenographer: "The devil is hot on my trail today."

During his first two years on the *Gazette,* life was so crowded for the Whites and their small staff that none of them retained any orderly memory of events. White was the Pooh Bah of his own newspaper. He wrote the editorials and anything else of local or public interest that came under his observation or into his mind. He and Mrs. White jointly served as managing editor, city editor, business manager, and advertising solicitor. He would have been tied to his desk at Emporia but for two things. First was the fact that his writing in the spirit of a columnist was the chief asset of the *Gazette,* and he could write anywhere. Wherever he went he followed the rule set down by the ancient Latin author, "No day without a line." In his case, however, the line might swell into a column or a page. Every day while he was away from home he did his stint: editorials, fantastic little paragraphs, scraps of reporting—his aversion to the smells in St. Louis, his estimate of interesting people he met here and there, his first sight of New York—all flavored to the taste of the people who lived in an interior town.

When she didn't accompany him, Mrs. White slipped into his seat at the *Gazette* and carried on—writing, editing, deciding questions of policy, and otherwise filling the editor's job most capably. She went to the office even when young Bill was a tiny baby, and kept him tucked away in a big wastebasket, which had started in life as a clothes basket. White had not yet developed from the staff Walter Hughes, who a few years later became business manager, nor Laura French, who for sixteen years was to serve the *Gazette* as a most capable managing editor. Miss French had learned the printer's trade in the back shop of the *Gazette*, starting to work there one month after Mr. White took possession of the paper. Hughes had been a boy in the shop, learned there to set type, went on to the mechanical department. Later he developed into an able business manager and Mr. White's "no" man in the *Gazette* office and the community. Without Hughes's conservatism to check his own ebullience, Mr. White probably would have made many costly moves which he would have regretted later.

Even after Mr. White had his editorial and business staffs well organized, he continued to take on such relatively unimportant work as reading and editing the weekly news items of his correspondents in rural communities. These reports, which related neighborhood activities, triumphs and tragedies, joys and sorrows, told simply the story of rural life. Best of all to him, they carried the names of many men, women, and children. I know that he edited the country correspondence himself, because about 1898 he told a *Gazette* employee that I was the *Gazette's* best rural correspondent. This was the first accolade of my life.

Mr. White strove always to have the *Gazette's* columns filled with news stories about people; to seek and print every item of interest to the people of that district. In 1915 he stated that a *Gazette* reporter recently had counted the names which appeared in one day's issue of the *Gazette*. This count did not include country correspondence, nor the Associated Press reports. The reporter's count revealed that the *Gazette* that day ran 210 names of Emporia people and their friends, and Mr.

White added, "This was a dull day in a quiet month too." He went on to say that the name of almost every citizen of Emporia and Lyon County appeared in the *Gazette* at some time in the course of every year, hundreds of them frequently; and then he observed: "These stories of the home people constitute the real news in the paper."

One other activity at the office to which he devoted considerable time was that of reading exchanges, particularly the editorial pages of the Kansas newspapers. He would sit in his easy chair with the exchanges in wrappers piled on a chair in front of him, slit the wrapper with one of his little fingers, unfold the paper, scan the editorial page, glance at the make-up and the advertising columns. If he read something that generated an idea, he would put that paper aside and write an editorial on the subject. Often these were bantering, joshing editorials such as the publishers of the papers in Kansas at that time were wont to write, poking fun at each other's ideas or towns.

He did most of his magazine writing at night, on days off, or in odd moments stolen from the office. Until writer's cramp began to trouble him about 1920, he did all of his *Gazette*, magazine, and book writing either with pen or typewriter. After that, he dictated all his enormous output of copy and then chopped it to pieces after it was typewritten. Yet that copy was of such quantity and quality that the average "hard-paper" professional writer who did nothing else would have called himself overworked.

As for his writing for the *Gazette*, he had two styles. He used the more finished one when he wrote of state or national affairs. This never was heavy, stodgy, or self-important. The swing, the rush, the simplicity of those nationally important *Gazette* editorials made them run like mercury through the press of the United States. The other one, the one in which he treated local issues or wrote about his people, was informal and clothed in the Kansas idiom, drawing no lines between words and phrases recognized in Webster's unabridged dictionary and the idiom of the corner drugstore and the livery stable—such as "kick in the pants," "keep your shirt on," "love of Mike."

I remember once, during that early period when Mr. White was an especial hero of mine, discussing him with a friend of the family. This man, a highly cultured member of an extremely brilliant family and a graduate of an Eastern college, spoke in rapt terms of White as a writer and thinker as revealed by the copy he produced for magazines and books. But he dismissed with disdain what he considered White's commonplace *Gazette* editorials. The *Kansas City Star* held a contrary view. About this time it declared that "The best writing that Mr. White does is in the editorials for the *Gazette*. There is in them a quality of audacity, tempered with a well-considered verbal extravagance, that always makes the piece hit the mark without leaving a scar."

White's editorial comments covered the entire range of human thinking and human experience. In 1903 he commented editorially on a ten-line news item in the previous issue, which had announced the death from scarlet fever of a little girl, the daughter of an engineer on the Santa Fe railroad. He said that Emporians had poured on the desolate home the benediction of their sympathies. "Because," he said, "child love is the one universal emotion of the soul, and child death is the saddest thing in the world.

". . . A child's soul is such a small thing, and the world and the systems of worlds and the infinite stretches of illimitable space are so wide for a child's soul to wander in, that sane as we may be, stolid as we may try to be, we think in imagery, and the figure of little feet setting off on the far track to the end of things, hunting God, wrings our heartstrings and makes our throats grip and our eyelids quiver . . ."

In 1902 he wrote that envy is the first and best sign that a man is losing his sense. It was his belief that the more sense a man has, the surer his recognition that every other man also carries heavy burdens; and the more important the man is, the heavier his burdens become. And he added, "The more sense a man gets the surer he is to bestow charity on the rich and the poor alike and to envy no one. Charity is the essence of philosophy and religion and happiness . . ."

During Mr. White's nearly half-century as editor of the *Gazette* he constantly described and interpreted for his readers the beauties of nature. He loved flowers. Once in expressing the opinion that a house with a flower garden indicated that the people who planted it were trying to give pleasure to others, he wrote:

"Flowers are planted and grown to make beauty out of doors where every one may see them, may enjoy them and share in the joy that comes with seeing beautiful things. Flowers about a house are a sign of kind hearts inside. Flowers about a house are the sign that the house is a neighborly house. Flowers are the insignia of generous folks trying to reach their neighbors by mute tokens of good will . . ."

Another time, this in 1901, he told his readers that some people will run all over the world to find beauty but only those who stay at home find it; that spring in Emporia held more beauty than did all the crags and peaks of Colorado, because Emporia was "a town of wide lawns and bluegrass and flowers and fairest of all, blossom-like children fluttering about. Today the peach trees and the pear trees and the apple trees are out and dandelions, the golden carpet tacks of sunshine that nature drives in the edges of the sward, and Johnny-jump-ups, are in bloom: and old-fashioned purple flags add color to the shady places . . ."

Mr. White's joyous appreciation of life was not confined to the mysterious beauties of nature: people came first. The qualities which he found or saw in individuals or groups he used as texts of editorial sermons. One such was devoted to the splendid qualities of Emporia's large Welsh population, which he said were "the best single strain of blood in our Emporia life." Although Americanized, they had "retained their strong qualities of thrift, of honesty, of industry, of deep moral qualities. Also they are the basis of the best artistic feeling in the community. More than the Americans of several generations, these newer Americans have the sense that money is not all of life, that there is something better than hard cash, and they have given Emporia much of its best tone, its steady-going homely purpose and its wholesome detail."

Once he told editorially how a contemporary had asked him to abandon his war on the fruit salad and to get into the fight against mince pie. Emphasizing his reluctance to take on too many fights because a man who spreads himself too thin gets nowhere, he added nevertheless:

This much is eternally true: Mince pie may not be the source of moral intelligence and stamina in this country. But it is a fact which should challenge the wise curiosity of trained scientists that whenever a community is found in which mince pie is made and served with temperate profusion, there is found the courage and vision of the republic. And in such communities, investigation will demonstrate the fact that in those homes where mince pie is honestly built and judiciously eaten, the backbone or moral courage that sways the community is found. And to go still further, those members of the mince-pie eating family who are most copiously addicted to mince pie, both hot and cold, may be depended upon for that cantankerous persistence in the defense of sheer right, as such, for which the embattled farmers fought at Lexington and John Brown died at Harper's Ferry. This may be coincidence. And then again it may be cause and effect. We know not . . .

Once in response to a correspondent's query as to when a visitor ceases to be company, he pointed out that this was a close question on which courts had differed, and added that even the United States Supreme Court had reversed itself several times on the subject. Mr. White, however, held in a general way that:

". . . company becomes kin when he or she quits getting the tenderloin and gets the tail of the porterhouse for supper. However, excellent authorities claim that company merges into the family when clean towels are not kept in the bathroom every morning. And recent Federal opinions tend toward the theory that a man is no longer company when they change sheets on his bed only once in two weeks . . ."

One subject about which he always enjoyed writing was criticism of himself by others. Always he agreed with the critic and then joyously built up an even worse case against himself. One time he wrote that:

"A heart searching young gentleman correspondent for a Stafford County paper in Topeka writes to his paper that the editor of the *Gazette* is 'badly overestimated'. Perhaps that may be in Topeka and in Stafford County, but here in Lyon County, in Emporia and in the Fourth Ward in particular, they have the person in question cut down to an equitable basis, with all the water, air and fizz squeezed out . . . and he is used as a doormat whenever the fellows feel that they should clean their feet."

One rare quality of Mr. White's, perhaps his most beloved one, was warmth of heart and sentiment without stickiness. He was able to see, understand, and write simply about the inexpressibly simple, beautiful human experiences which sweeten the lot of men and women. Never was he more understandably tender than when he wrote of young newlyweds. In 1907 in an editorial, "God Bless 'Em," he wrote:

They came in on the Howard Branch [a Santa Fe Railroad branch line which served Emporia] this morning—he in his best Sunday suit and she in her white cloth suit, with her white hat and shoes, and they went past the courthouse three times and he was four hours getting her to go in. They walked up and down Commercial Street half a dozen times, saw all the store windows, and bought some oranges at Ireland's and stood in the cold, raw March wind at noon eating them in front of the Mit-Way. The crowd of drummers inside made up a purse of two dollars to get them the best dinner in the house and then sent a cigar drummer out to ask them in. But he lost his nerve and the purse was dissolved.

Then they walked to the courthouse and after that vanished from the street. They went straight up. They were too happy for this world, and no one has seen them since the ascension.

Once in commenting on the impatience of reformers, Mr. White said that the first thing a man has to learn when he desires to accomplish anything in politics is "to keep his shirt on"; second, never get tired; and third, that "he doesn't amount to much anyway." Reformers needed faith too, he said, because "the world is growing better and the reformer who has no faith should get out of business . . ."

In 1902 he told his readers that it pays to be decent in politics, "to be fair, honest and above board . . . in business, and in religion and in family relations . . . sooner or later destruction overtakes the man who cheats . . . history proves that nothing pays—not smartness, not industry, not agility, not intelligence—as character pays. It is the great thing in life. A strong, honest, wise character can never fail . . ."

Later in 1902 Mr. White discussed "Pilate's Question." He wanted to know whether truth is what should be or is:

". . . The picture of life is more real than life," he wrote.
". . . There is no beauty in the world for the eye untrained.
To the savage, nature reveals little. Only after a poet has come
is the land really discovered. Only after a reporter has come, is
a people or a community found to be worthy.

"Truth may thus be said to be not what is but what should
be. And when the *Gazette* says good things of Emporia don't
laugh. The reporter is merely telling the truth."

In 1900 Mr. White, writing on "Grub 'n Things," said that
he had been abused for two weeks because he had insisted that
it was as much a girl's duty to learn to cook as it was to spell and
parse. These complaints objected to his placing the human
stomach before the human mind. He disclaimed being a slave
to his stomach, but, he said, he did believe "that sound bodies
are more important than crammed minds" and that "wholesome scientifically cooked foods save souls just as much as
preachers and hymn books, for dyspepsia is the devil's strongest
weapon. It breeds melancholy. It makes men hate their neighbors. It makes hell on earth . . . This matter is more serious
. . . than the liver or the tariff, for the American people are
becoming nervous, emotional and erratic . . ."

This editorial was shortly followed with another, "concerning country girls." Mr. White wrote that a young woman had
asked him for an opinion on this large topic. He replied that
it was too deep for him; that all he knew of country girls was
limited to one in Butler County who had "pulled his beautiful alabaster leg for a fifty-dollar livery bill and brought the
entire family out to laugh at him when he tried to hitch up
. . . and shook him for a drummer." He concluded, "Because
the country girl learns to work she is bound to be happy in the
long run. It is the way things even up in this world. Merit wins.
There is no sense in taking any other view. Work is the only
key to success."

In October, 1901, he advised his readers to "Saw wood and
save the sawdust," because, he said, prosperity is not "here forever." And if you aren't saving money in good times, "don't cry
when hard times come. The man who can't save money now
will always be poor and it won't be his wife's fault either."

Once in an editorial item he noted that an office boy had

been whistling "Juanita" around the *Gazette* office that day, and with mock lamentation he told how "for twenty-five long, weary years" he had heard youth admonishing "Juanita" to "ask thy soul if we must part," and added, "But never a word from sister Juanita. Anyone knowing what she did say will confer a favor on an anxious listener by sending a reply to this office in a plain sealed envelope."

The *Chanute Tribune* once printed an advertisement which offered "men's dawn-gray spats for sale." Mr. White's editorial comment, headed "Spatsies," called upon the "Willie boys" to step up, "all you male sopranos, and you too, you big mincing she-pansies with a sensitive shank. Drag Kansas' reputation for masculine virility in the dust, but wear your spats by all means. All you consumers of banana splits and marshmallow sundaes, you can't afford the risk of a draught on your tootsies in such unsettled weather as this.

"Here is a bargain which every lisping wrist-watch wearer, every velvet-voiced masculo-feminine compromise, every chattering man, every gossamer winged chorus man, every human steer, should be interested in.

"Dawn-gray spats in Chanute—oh sugar!"

This, of course, was in what one of White's severest critics called his "hick strain." There is no more logic in crusading against spats than in crusading against the purely ornamental cravat. But the rural subscribers liked it and he was having fun.

Mr. White occasionally wrote *Gazette* headlines in which he revealed the same prankish spirit. One ran: "A Pell of a Harty." His misplacement of the two letters reveals what he felt about the political gathering. Another of his headlines read: "A Fraidy Calf Party."

Frequently his bubbling spirits would express themselves in a pun. He wrote about a New York City murderess under the heading "Coals to Newcastle":

"A New York judge gives La Snyder a stay. To a lady who was of late on most friendly, not to say companionate terms with a corset salesman, one little stay more or less should be no novelty."

After reading an editorial colleague's recipe for "buttermilk pie," Mr. White commented:

"Someone can be found to defend anything—anarchy, bloody murder, larceny, . . . fruit salad, and Villa. But our idea of the lowest step to which a man may sink in talent is defense of buttermilk pie."

The *Gazette* once printed an inaccurate story about some Emporia club women; after ably righting the wrong, Mr. White added:

"These feeble remarks are submitted in all humility. He who writes them is no better than others. He wishes he were; but he is not. Being human, he has the ordinary human weaknesses. Yet, also being human, he is entitled to aspire for better things, to hope for better things and even, in all kindness, to point to better things."

Once when the Kansas newspapers were bandying gaysome quips on the affected spelling of girls' names—Alyce, Katheryne, Edythe, etc.—White contributed the following:

"When a girl or her mother figures up a fool way to spell a nice old name, we have noticed that one thing invariably happens, she gets married early—early and often, and generally to some youth who has no more brains than a summer squash. She fades early and becomes a stringy looking old bean pole or a shapeless sack of bran, while the more sensible girls are hanging on to the willows of spinsterhood or are married to smart boys who keep their names off the retailers' deadbeat list. The rule may not be in the books, but it is written in the stars. A fool name makes a fool woman."

Perhaps no editor ever more frankly and wholly told his readers his thoughts, opinions, and needs than Mr. White. Once he wrote that the *Gazette* desired a stenographer to replace a capable young woman who was quitting this job for a better one. He told what the duties would be, then added:

But we want no gum chewer. And no earless wonder need apply. But any girl who will admit that she is twenty-five and looks thirty and isn't afraid of forty, who wants a steady job and can work in an office with fifteen men without nonsense, who will take one last long lingering look at her hand mirror as she punches the timeclock in the morning and another as she checks out, who can spell common words and doesn't regard the dictionary as poison, who knows about apostrophe s's without having to blink and guess at it, who keeps her hair combed and her petticoat from showing without devoting too much time to herself, and who can laugh easily and then doesn't, may find a fairly good job at reasonable wages. Apply in person. Do not write or phone.

Mr. White, as a mere amateur, offered suggestions to female would-be cooks of beefsteak:

Take a frying pan and heat it as nearly red hot as possible without cracking it. Then slam on a two-inch steak, T-bone or sirloin, and let it stay on the redhot griddle while you count slowly up to about fifty. Then turn it over quickly and count fifty. Then turn down the fire and put on the lid of the frying pan, and every other minute take off the lid, drain off the grease and turn over the steak.

And as you love your man, don't for the love of Mike—if his name is Mike—put either water, butter, lard or grease of any kind in that red hot frying pan before you cook the steak, after you cook the steak or while you are cooking the steak.

Give it an absolutely dry, greaseless treatment, and serve as you please—with such sauce as you care to make after the steak is on the platter. But a steak just so is good enough for poor folks.

One time he wrote "An Obituary for Anyone" in which he pointed out that millions and millions of men and women are "born, live and die," that they store their knowledge, which passes into tradition, which creates the knowledge of how to live "wisely and well."

Yet, [he wrote] few people live wisely or well. Most people think that maxims are for the fools. Most people think they are able to beat the game of life. Most people slyly try to slip around the ropes of good conduct set down by the wisdom of the ages.

So they fail. Life failures are made by men and women who try to beat the game of life. Health, fortune, good name, happiness— the way to them is plain. It is all written down in the books, all in the common wisdom of the people. Yet these things are attained by few people. Millions and millions and millions of them are born and live and die—over and over and over as the generations pass— not flies or birds, but men and women who are as blind and foolish and miserable and seem to be as incapable of learning the truth of life as though there were no human speech, no tradition, no books.

Under the title "Not by Meat Alone" he wrote that the music

festival in Emporia was as important as a new hotel or a hard-surfaced road to Kansas City, and added:

"It is not a question of how many people live in a community, but what kind of people live in a community that makes it great or small. A man is not great by reason of his net weight, but by reason of what he has in his head and his heart. The Music Festival will develop the soul of the town; it will make Emporia a better town—if not a bigger one, and it will help to make it bigger. . . . We should keep right on making it that kind of town—a town which appeals to something more than the material side of life."

And applying the same principle to politics, he wrote:

"Those who think there is any heaven-born solution of good government are the worst deluded people in the world. The government only reflects good people. Government of a city, a state or a nation is the direct reaction of the unselfish intelligence of the people, put into public affairs."

The *Gazette* editorials quoted here illustrate only a few of the hundreds he wrote on a variety of subjects, all dealing in the same spirit with small-town life and common things—the little crises in the community's history, the homely tasks, the petty disappointments, the triumphs, the change of seasons, the profound human experiences which make all men kin, or the interpretation of truths older than man and as young as a baby.

If Will White had never written "What's the Matter with Kansas?", if he had created not a single line of fiction or verse, if his opinions as expressed in his editorials had continued to be cast in the mold of the Republican platforms at the turn of the century, it is still likely that some historian of the twenty-fifth century would have dug his editorials from the files of the old *Gazette,* if these had somehow been preserved, and used them as a basis of a study interpreting life in the Middle West during the early twentieth century. Understandingly pieced together, they would with clarity and brilliance tell the story of a vital era in American folk life.

2. EXPANDING POLITICAL INFLUENCE

In spite of modern improvements in the art of propaganda, no presidential campaign before or afterward ever made such effective use of the printed word as that of 1896. Bryan's "Cross of Gold" speech swept the convention, his party, and a substantial part of the voting population off their feet. It projected emotional thinking into the campaign. It made "free silver" the leading issue, almost the sole issue. It nominated as candidate for president the orator, a man who had entered the convention an invisible horse rather than a dark one.

In this day the radio would have carried the speech to thirty million listeners or more instead of to the few thousand in the convention hall. But the Democratic National Committee did a good job of distribution, sending the text in batches of 10,000 to every corner of the country. Before they had done that, however, a pamphlet now nearly forgotten, "Coin's Financial School" by "Coin" Harvey, had been drawing the insurgents, especially in the West, into the ranks that marched under the standard of the silver dollar. They scattered "Coin" like hail.

The Republicans had an effective campaign slogan, "The Full Dinner Pail," but otherwise no literature worthy of special mention until Will White wrote "What's the Matter with Kansas?" True, this powerful editorial did not mention in so many words the main issue—"the free and unlimited coinage of silver at a ratio of 16 to 1 without the aid and consent of any other nation"—but it did picture the opposition as the Republican leaders wanted it pictured: a collection of crackpots who had ruined one state and were now out to ruin all the others. Before the campaign of 1896 was over, every Republican newspaper had published it and, as before stated, Chairman Mark Hanna had distributed more than one million copies of it in leaflet form.

Naturally the appeal of White's argument, the interest in his presentation and his interpretation of the opposition, made him a bright and unexpected asset to the party. Equally naturally, his party's political leaders expected that when their candidate won, White would go to Washington and collect his reward.

Important officials of the Republican party dropped off in Emporia on their way East or West to look him over. The fact that he made no references to office probably puzzled them. What was his game? Had he got it in the bag? He continued to laugh in his sleeve. Colonel Nelson, to whose training he owed so much, maintained that when a newspaperman accepted any office, volunteer or paid, private or public, he gave up part of his best asset, the right to criticize. With his uncanny ability to see and understand truths hidden from most men, Will White knew this to be so. His training under Colonel Nelson helped to make the principle a governing one in his own life, because he saw the strength Colonel Nelson gained by declining such positions.

A few years later he expressed his attitude on this point in the following words: "An editor should take no office, elective or appointive. Entering the newspaper business every young man should take monastic vows against office holding."

White was vitally interested in politics then, just as was the typical newspaperman of his and any other day. But by the same token, your newspaperman scorns politicians and political office. Kansas editors, who so frequently used journalism as the first step in the ladder leading to high public office, were not typical American newspapermen. In the American scheme of journalism, the reporter and the editorial writer are supposed to be above the struggle, interested first in getting at the truth about events, then in interpreting them, finally in commending, criticizing, or explaining the men who make the events—and all with complete intellectual honesty. That they have not all lived up to this ideal is aside from the point; it remains the ideal nevertheless. Most newspapermen hate nothing so much as bunk—even when they are writing it—but they know that an infusion of bunk is a necessary element in every political success. The moment a man runs for office he makes concessions to untruths, and when he accepts an appointment from a political party he is muzzled, he is no longer free to criticize it. If he does, all members of the party that gave him the appointment consider him worse than the bird who fouls his own nest.

Foreigners used to note as a curious fact the rarity of journalists in the field of American statesmanship as contrasted with the position they hold in Europe and especially on the Continent. Journalism there stands almost equal to the law as a ladder for a man with political ambition. Only a very few American journalists as compared with lawyers, have ever occupied high public office or even sought it.

In the national field Horace Greeley was an exception in the generation following the war between the states, and in more recent years so was Harding. Greeley was a failure as a candidate, and most contemporary newspapermen felt that it served him right. Except financially, Harding was no more of a success as a newspaper publisher than he was as a president. The attitude of most competent journalists is that they wouldn't accept the office of president for a deed to the whole United States.

Just how much of this aversion to holding public office was born of White's own wisdom, how much came from his desire for independence, and how much he absorbed from Colonel Nelson, is not material. He had no intention of accepting a reward for his political services, but the pixie in him made him keep his own counsel and get all the amusement he could from the guessing of his party and his fellow Emporians.

He ended this speculation when, in 1897, Mark Hanna invited him to visit Ohio and make a speech at a Lincoln's Birthday banquet given for the purpose of celebrating McKinley's victory over Bryan. White accepted and made a speech which from the first word to the last was a torrent of old-fashioned, stand-pat Republicanism. Every newspaperman understands why he accepted. Acquaintance is an asset in his business. Here was a chance for White to meet and to assess the powers behind the new administration.

He met Mark Hanna, of course, had a personal interview with him. As Mr. White summed him up in "Masks in a Pageant," Hanna was not the bloated plutocrat clad in loud checks and laughing at the impudence of the common people to whom Davenport, the cartoonist, gave invidious immortality. He was, however, a boss, powerful and of great individuality. White had known miniatures of him at Topeka—expansive, shrewd, dowered with a sense of humor. During the interview Hanna edged toward the question of political rewards and White, seeing that it was time to quit fooling, announced flatly that he would not take office even if it were offered to him and, what was more, he had no henchmen of his own to reward. Delighted by this original attitude, Hanna insisted that White visit the "boss" and passed him along to Canton with a note of introduction to President-elect McKinley. At White's insistence, Hanna added a line reading, "He wants no office."

McKinley was struggling at Canton with the distribution of thousands of appointments among tens of thousands of greedy applicants. Ill and worn out, he failed to be sweetened even by the unusual line in Hanna's letter of introduction. To White's boyish amusement the president-elect received him coldly, got rid of him as soon as possible.

Perhaps this unsatisfying reception didn't come solely from McKinley's exhaustion. Perhaps White himself was not so warm toward the new president. At the St. Louis convention the year before, he had whooped it up for Thomas B. Reed for the Republican presidential nomination. White never became a great admirer of McKinley's. McKinley may have felt this and reciprocated in kind.

Nevertheless, through nearly all of McKinley's full term and the half-year of his second, White supported his policies earnestly, almost blindly. In April, 1900, in an editorial, "Wobblers and Things," he stated that the *Gazette* was "for every man nominated on the Republican ticket from road overseer to President. It is for the Republican party without equivocation." While he admitted that the party was not perfect, he added, "But take it by and large, broad and long, first and last and all the time, the Republican party comes nearer being right seven days in the week than any other party organization in the world."

In his maturity he discarded these partisan blinders. Later he invariably weighed all human affairs for himself, taking nothing for granted except his own faith in the goodness of men and their motives. He already was doing that in his comments on town affairs, on men and women, habits, good and bad literature, morals, all aspects of life except politics. That room of his mind still seemed locked.

Still there had been earlier indications that he was troubled by Republican practices and procedures. Perhaps the first of these straws in the wind rose in 1893, when he joined a group of young Republicans in Kansas to climb up through the wreck which the Farmers' Alliance and Populists had made of the Republican party by creating the Kansas Day Club, which White wanted to name "The Ancient and Honorable Order of Hell Raisers." The avowed purpose of this organization was to hold each year on January 29 (the anniversary of the admission of Kansas to the Union) a Republican banquet in Topeka, to which distinguished national leaders of the party should be invited as speakers. The end they sought was to inject new spirit into the party, to substitute intelligent discussion of new ideas for the unyielding stand-patism of the stalwarts who controlled its machinery. That club still lives and serves through the years as the annual rallying place of Kansas Republicans.

During his first half-dozen years or so with the *Gazette,* Mr. White seemed to have believed that good government could be secured and justice dispensed if able, honest men filled public offices and the power of evil political bosses was restricted. And his thinking on economic subjects was largely related to their political application—like many other young men, he thought in stencils. "Socialist," for example, was a vague, invidious epithet like s.o.b., applying to people who questioned the eternal rightness of things as they were and presumably always would be.

But after his travels had given him personal contact with the vast, complicated national life, new outlook gained from personal observation made him skeptical of his earlier beliefs. Those things which he had held fundamental to good government were important and necessary, but he now began to see that they alone would not be able to make the democratic process work with necessary effectiveness. Business, according to his new conception, "must grow a conscience, be regulated." White's growth in things political was further revealed by his new discovery that the democratic process was something much more than any set of political institutions, public officials, or regulatory measures, because it "writes constitutions and amends them, it does not depend on them. The democratic process operates in many ways outside of government." He later believed it to be "that fluidity of ideals, that dissemination of intelligence backed by purpose, that establishment of custom and folk ways which seeks out and secures justice before laws come to guarantee justice. All these things constitute the democratic process in the life of the people. Government is their servant, not their master." The man who held a broader and more fundamental conception of what it takes to make a democracy function most effectively in the public interest had gone a long way from the one who once believed passionately that only the Republican party "had the know-how" to operate our government successfully. Even with a genius truth is coy.

In time Mr. White grew to believe also that these free forces which "instinctively guide a social order and establish a political government" are slow and clumsy and operate with vast waste; that they "sacrifice the tyranny of efficiency for the slower pace of common consent of common sense in promoting change in morals, in business and finally in government."

Now he began to strike his great stride, as he went on to say that although the democratic process was "awkward, sluggish, often wasteful and occasionally corrupt, despite our ideals," it nevertheless had a transcendent value which came from the fact that it left men free. This, then, was the end and goal of democratic procedure: to keep men free. And since a man cannot be both free and blindly partisan, we find Will White inevitably straying farther and farther from the ark of the covenant of his youth, the Republican party.

3. NEW POLITICAL HORIZONS

Many of Will White's Kansas friends and all his biographers have puzzled over that change in his political and social philosophy which began to be expressed about the turn of the century, and which within the next few years made him the wise, all-comprehending, and balanced liberal that he remained for the rest of his life. One of them, taking his text from the Acts of the Apostles, calls it "The Damascus Road." The figure of speech does not quite walk on all four legs, because White had no sudden conversion, caught no spiritual flash as did St. Paul. True and lasting conversions either religious or political seldom happen in this way. In his *Varieties of Religious Experience,* William James concludes that even when the sinner suddenly "sees the light," as at a revival, the effect of instantaneous change is illusory—it is instead the conscious manifestation of forces that have long been working in his subconscious mind. Such forces had been at work in Will White's mind and heart from his earliest years. He had kept them submerged, however, until—perhaps—the time he went to Chicago in the fall of 1896 to gather the first fruits of his fame.

That trip to Chicago established his habit of getting out of Emporia, of mingling in the great life beyond Kansas, at least once every year. Coming in touch with this great, interesting, fascinating world beyond and gathering impressions from it, he began to see that the small-town editor who really serves his people best must bring and interpret the outside world to them. He probably also realized more clearly than ever before that a newspaper in the provinces does not necessarily have to be provincial.

His trip to Columbus, Ohio, in 1897 further brought him in touch with men and affairs whose interests were more broad than were those of his Kansas friends. Then within a year of his first success he visited New York.

On these first trips Will traveled with his eyes open. He had never before found an opportunity to examine a manufacturing community—Kansas City during his days on the *Star* was primarily a farming, wholesale, and stockyards center. In all his early life he probably had never been inside of any factory other than a flour mill. Now he was to visit Pittsburgh with its forest of stacks, its eruptions of slag and molten steel against the night sky, and to see, growing up on the shores of the Great Lakes, industrial empires where millions of workers put in a six-day week—many of them even a seven-day week—and a twelve-hour day. Heretofore he had written again and again that the weak must go down in the struggle for existence, the strong rise to the top as it did in the frontier towns. This was the law of nature as manifested by both man and beast. To his way of thinking, to deny that principle was to "set class against class." "The same selfishness that has made the world go spinning around the grooves of progress for the last million years, is still the dominant force of human nature," he wrote in 1897. Therefore, let the rich get richer if they could; the overflow of their prosperity will drip onto the masses. This was the creed of the classic economists of that day.

Now, he began to realize that those millions working in the industrial centers might all be men with brains and characters as good as the best, but regardless of how hard and intelligently they worked there was little room for them at the top of the heap. The overwhelming majority must stay at their lathes and levers for life—their place in society had scarcely changed since the beginning of the industrial revolution. Even twenty years later many laborers of the United States Steel Corporation were working ten or twelve hours a day.

When White wrote of affairs in Emporia or Kansas he took no other man's ideas for a guide. He thought things out to their end and in relation to the whole of life in these communities. But when he followed this trail through, something—was it perhaps his mother's fundamental teachings, or was it the abiding sense of justice in his heart?—stopped him dead. More than thirty years later he wrote as he looked over some of his early stand-pat editorials, "What a curious profession is journalism! It is the only profession whose dead are never buried. The editor carries in his files the embalmed copies of yesterday's blindness. Men know him for the fool he was." He was not writing in clichés, nor with even a trace of insincerity. No man ever wrote fewer insincere lines. He meant all he said—at the time.

The impressions which changed his social and political outlook and a thousand more like them gathered in his travels were gestating in his heart and mind, waiting for the catalyst that would bring the subconscious and the conscious into combination. It did not work in a flash, however; it was a slow process and all the sounder because it was slow. And the catalyst, he himself always seemed to believe, was Theodore Roosevelt.

At any rate, some powerful agent was working effectively, more on Will White's mind than his heart, for his heart always was warm and responsive. As early as the end of 1898 the change began faintly to appear in a slight softening, a modification of what had heretofore been juvenile cocksureness, especially when he wrote on partisan matters. When he wrote for his subscribers on the failings and triumphs of their town or on their current customs and manners, he became more mellow, more tolerantly humorous. But this new color of his spirit was so little noticeable to Kansas politicians that when McKinley was still in the White House the Republicans began talking of him as anti-Populist candidate for United States senator. He viewed the proposal "with alarm." He discouraged further discussion of the subject by slandering and guying himself in the thinly veiled anonymity of an editorial.

The proof of the change in him lies not so much in a gradual acceptance of "Populist" measures as in a fugitive editorial entitled "Don't Scare 'Em," which appeared just after Theodore Roosevelt had become president by a vote of the people. White threw the throttle wide open and steamed ahead with T.R.'s program of reform. During his conservative period White had used the epithet "socialistic" as his big gun to blast radical opposition. In 1897 he had written of this "hideous doctrine":

"The socialistic colony which depends for its success upon the unselfishness of men, has failed as it always has failed and always will fail until nature changes human hearts. The cunningest man wins the battle. It is a fact of nature; laws can't change it. The man who depends upon his muscle will be the servant of the man who depends upon his brain."

But now he wrote that while ten years earlier the word "socialism" would have knocked any scheme into a cocked hat, it no longer frightened people; that the adoption of Chicago's proposal to buy the street railways had not made anyone jump. He added:

"No one doubts but that municipal ownership of street railroads, gas, water, lights and power will be as prevalent in America twenty years from now as any political custom. The people are learning more and forgetting more than their fathers learned and forgot. There is little Bourbonism in the country."

Even so, his expanding outlook on life, his clear realization that truth is revealed to men gradually, made it impossible for him, even in his later years, wholly to accept the socialist point of view. He was to write in 1920:

Socialism is a vast stupidity. It sees the gross injustices of organized society and it is driven mad by them. The solution of the obvious ills of the world is evolutionary. The solution is found by putting the best heart and mind of the world to work on today's problem; the progress of the world must come one step at a time. But Socialism is a plan for an entirely new order dreamed out by men who have faith only in material solutions for ills that are deep in human nature. Many Socialist panaceas are adopted by the world and work well. But the whole phantasmagoria of Socialism, its elaborate Utopianism, is impossible.

4. T.R. AND WILLIAM ALLEN WHITE

IN EDITORIALS, magazine articles, speeches, and personal comments, Will White gave the major credit for the change that came over his spirit and his attitude toward politics and economics to Theodore Roosevelt. (How I love to record this, for T.R. to me also "was, is, and always will be my big chief.") McKinley left him cold; Taft held his support for but a moment; Wilson's intellect and great vision commanded his respect; Harding hardly touched him; Coolidge primarily aroused his curiosity. Hoover's spiritual qualities made him mightily attractive to White, but Franklin Roosevelt was to him the "Old Smiler." Wendell Willkie's great promise gave him a place just below T.R. in White's pantheon. But after all, it was only promise; Willkie died before he was ever tested in the fires of supreme political responsibility. To White, T.R. alone had everything.

The relationship between the two men had in it an element of paradox. One was the aristocrat, the other the son of pioneers, one city bred, the other town bred. The city boy became a passionate sportsman, and the rougher the sport the better. He boxed, wrestled, fenced, tramped endlessly in jungles and mountains, rode English hunters, temperamental stallions and half-broken broncos, shot big game, served in war as a dashing soldier. The boy from a frontier village cared for no sport, either parlor or outdoor, never even walked when he could avoid it, had traffic with no horse except sleepy Old Tom who powered the family surrey, refused to kill any living thing. Playing the piano was his only accomplishment, and music his only diversion except intelligent conversation.

Yet they were intellectual brothers, spiritual affinities, meeting as equals on those high plateaus of the mind and soul which are the exclusive domain of great human beings.

It is true that Will White had long been edging toward the light. He had written that "The best partisan was the man who exposed the rogues who tried to capture his party," that "the best duty of a good Republican is to call attention to what seems a wrong position." He had begun dimly to perceive facts to which he had been blind in his cocksure days: that our unprecedented material progress had been due largely to that extension of our frontiers which had drained the unsuccessful from our more settled communities and given them another chance, that there were few frontiers left, and that when they were gone only a very few even of the more enterprising could attain a standard of living beyond the bare necessities of life— unless we reoriented ourselves.

But it was not until 1900, when the influence of T.R. plus his broader acquaintance with America and Americans began to be effective, that he began to cut loose from his moorings and express doubt of the eternal rightness of the Grand Old Party. Even then, he did it with many ifs, ands, and buts. He continued to swallow nearly all the party doctrines, and to accept its nominees, though sometimes with a wry face.

Gazette editorials for the next four or five years continued to expound the saving grace of Republican party principles, to castigate the Democrats. Then after T.R. had become president the editor's writings began to indicate that he no longer believed the Republican party to be always right.

The *Gazette* in late December, 1901, carried an editorial on "The Influence of Roosevelt":

"There is no doubt that the country has not had in a generation such a moral uplift as it is having under the administration of President Roosevelt. And all because of one simple rule he has made in appointing men to office. That they must be morally clean before the recommendation of any senator or congressman can secure their appointments."

Mr. White added that the appointments of morally irresponsible men to public office had bred corruption in politics by making it profitable. "The crooked man in politics," he said, "is there for one reason and one reason only; politics pays him. When it ceases to pay him he will get out. The turning down of crooked men by the President even in Kansas has done wonders to brace up the moral tone of the state. It makes clean politics everywhere. There is no doubt that in the purchase of good

influence President Roosevelt's new rule has been an admirable
investment."

In 1902, writing on "Roosevelt's Strength" Mr. White expressed his belief that:

Roosevelt is a great influence in America. He stands as a man
who cares more for his own self respect than for the applause of the
multitude. Roosevelt may not secure the passage of the trust law
but he will influence the people to think wholesomely on the subject and to act fairly and in honor with both sides when a national
law is made. The value to the nation and to the world of such a
man is inestimable. He is the ideal of thousands of young men. He
is a storage battery of honesty and he is making manhood in America with intelligent, fearless, simple, marvelous rapidity. His life is
a big unmistakable lesson that it is better to be square and brave
and wise than it is to attain greatness. He is a character maker for
the country.

T.R.'s influence on White's partisan thinking is further revealed in a *Gazette* editorial printed in August, 1904, "Men—
Not Measures":

Roosevelt in American politics has been an independent Republican for twenty years—wearing no party shackles, voting for men
and not measures when the question of character determined the
issue of good government. Roosevelt was called a mugwump less
than twenty years ago because he believed in civil service. Roosevelt's character and career is that of an independent and his influence more than that of any other man now living has been toward
independent action in politics. Above party when party was wrong,
and with party when party was right. . . .

And also in this same year:
". . . The old-fashioned idea that a man should be drawn
and quartered who did not vote the entire ticket—Democratic
or Republican—of his party, yellow dogs and all, has departed."
White adds that the *Gazette* will praise it when it does a worthy
thing, but that if it "sneaks and sells out to boodlers" the
Gazette will not be "mealy-mouthed" about saying what it
thinks. "For" he wrote, "he is the best partisan who exposes
the rogues who try to capture his party, and he is the worst
patriot who allows his party's interests to weigh more heavily
than his country's. . . ."

Presently he was advocating the election of the Democratic party candidate, Joseph W. Folk, for governor of Missouri:

. . . The man who votes against Folk, therefore, whether he casts that vote as a Republican, a Populist or a Prohibitionist, casts it in favor of the return of the boodlers. . . . the *Gazette* has been a straight Republican paper for a dozen years. Under its present management it has upheld the hands of every Republican state administration that has been elected since the paper was started. It believes in Republican principles and the greatness and efficient goodness of the Republican party. But there are sometimes considerations in politics greater than party—considerations of honest government. Honest government is the first thing required in this nation. Honest men in office honestly earning their salaries and giving the people full value received for their taxes—these considerations are more important than Republican victory or Democratic victory. For until honest men are in office no principles can be efficiently established by any government or upheld by any party. . . .

The closing paragraph of an editorial which appeared in the *Gazette* in January, 1923, on the fourth anniversary of T.R.'s death read:

"There is a fine Lincolnian thing about the Colonel; he was so many different kinds of a daisy that he blooms on every hill where men are fighting for any great cause. His rod and his staff they comfort us."

In his introduction to the Theodore Roosevelt Cyclopedia, published by the Roosevelt Memorial Association in 1940, Mr. White wrote that T.R. understood his time, and added:

". . . It was a complex time that could be understood in all its aspects and contradictions only by a man who could see around the corner—into the past through knowledge, into the future through imagination." Here was one key to their affinity of spirit and mind. They both clung tenaciously to the best in the past, sought to preserve and relate it to a better future.

He defined T.R.'s imagination as one that "clarified issues which to others remained obscure," and added "we are beginning now to see him in perspective. He was the first American statesman of major proportions who saw and dramatized a new phase of the truth about freedom, its economic implications."

Here Mr. White revealed again one of the two basic tenets on which rested his philosophy of life as expressed in deeds and words—the other one to which he also always gave undeviating and uncompromising testimony was the individual's worth and self respect—that of *freedom* "and its economic implications."

This latter clause furnishes a key to the change in outlook which marked the difference between the William Allen White of the period before 1900 or thereabout and the William Allen White of his middle and later periods. He too had imagination and statesmanship, could see a slum once "and make it the cradle of a social philosophy."

With his new outlook he realized that in this machine age and its vast economic surplus, "Political liberty will no longer protect men against the old tyrannies which broke the spirit of man in other days and times. All this" he adds, "Theodore Roosevelt saw and saw clearly. He lived for, fought for, and yearned passionately for this new vision of economic democracy . . . [he] did not solve the problem, but he, of all the long line of major statesmen in the millennial fight for freedom, stood at the turn of the course, pointed to the present battleground . . . [he was] a moral leader and a prophet above everything else, expounding the will of God and imploring his countrymen to obey it."

Just how much T.R. meant in his life has never been more completely or intimately revealed than in Mr. White's formal and informal remarks at the dinner of the Roosevelt Memorial Association in 1939, when he received its gold medal award.

These annual awards are nearly always made at a dinner in a small auditorium on the top floor of the house at 28 East 20th Street, New York City, in which T.R. was born. There, a group of one hundred or so of T.R.'s close friends and associates, in an intimate setting, hold one of the most distinguished and delightful gatherings it ever has been my experience to attend. They are joyous occasions, when the exuberant, colorful spirit of T.R., with all his gusto for life and for warm fellowship, seems to hover over the company.

Aside from a brief period for citations, the recipients of the medal for that year are the only speakers. It was on this occasion that Will White, more fully and unreservedly than ever before or since, told the story of T.R.'s influence on his life. Because both his formal and informal remarks should be available to the public I present them here at great length.

In his formal speech Mr. White said:

. . . I have tried to make my life a tribute to Theodore Roosevelt. This house, this good company, this empire state, in many of its attributes and noble achievements, all pay constant tribute to him. The yearnings of the American people in these times for social and industrial justice are living tributes to him. . . . He was a prophet, a sower who went forward to sow the seeds of aspiration for justice in the heart of American people . . . the sturdy, ever-hoping heart, and the faith-giving love he bore his fellow men will bloom and fruit in another resurrection.

. . . The first time I saw him we were young,—I in my late twenties, he in his late thirties. We met in Washington. I had written a little book of Kansas stories. He had sent me his "American Ideals," autographed. A mutual friend, later to be vice president of the United States, Charles Curtis, introduced us. I have held through a generation my first flash of Theodore Roosevelt—a tallish, yet stockily built man, physically hard and rugged, obviously fighting down the young man crescent of his vest; quick speaking, forthright, a dynamo of energy, given to gestures and grimaces, letting his voice run its full gamut from bass to falsetto. He seemed spiritually to be dancing in the exuberance of a deep physical joy of life. We fell to jabbering like a pair of jays. All the many things that engage the walrus and the carpenter we talked of that day. We walked from the Navy Department under the shade of the young trees that lined the streets that summer day to the Army and Navy Club, had lunch, talked and talked, and still kept talking. . . . I was a young, arrogant protagonist of the divine rule of plutocracy. I think I called it "brains." He shattered the foundations of my political ideals. As they crumbled then and there, politically, I put his heel on my neck and I became his man. In the handclasp that followed and the gesture of good-bye he became my life long liege and I a yeoman in his service.

Four years later, another picture. It was September 1901. We were in an eight room house in a side street in Washington. I had come there on appointment. The appointment originally had been made for Oyster Bay . . . Between the time when I left home and the time when we met in Washington, President McKinley had been assassinated. Colonel Roosevelt was President of the United States.

It was his first night in Washington as President. He had not yet gone to the White House. He had invited me to dine at the home of his sister, Mrs. Cowles. Admiral Cowles presided at the board. Another young man came also. A young school man from upstate New York, who was beginning to get his nose above water politically, none other than Nicholas Murray Butler. We five dined, three youths and two elders, sat around that dinner table and marveled at the irony of a fate which should bring Theodore Roosevelt so unexpectedly to that place of great power. I remember that the Admiral had little to say. The two Roosevelts, the Colonel and his sister, made the talk. I was shy, overawed, and tremendously impressed. Professor Butler was keenly observant, appreciative of the scene. After dinner we adjourned to the little front room; we three youngsters and the Admiral. I remember I sat on the edge of my chair, pop-eyed with wonder, as the young President plunged into the discussion of his plans, of his hopes, of his fears, with a kind of dynamic, burning candor that amazed me, even though I had seen him several times in action during the four years of our friendship. But now he was President, and it seemed that he should be different. But he was absolutely unchanged. The Admiral sat in a deep chair by the unlit grate in the little parlor, watching us wordlessly, occasionally grunting approval, or sniffing his doubt. We two gaping, young guests of the new President were like some inaudible, spiritual Greek chorus to his cataract solo of talk. The old Admiral sank deeper into the cushions of his chair. He had seen his brother-in-law before. The Admiral was not impressed. His eyes began to blink. The young President began to project his imagination into the years. "But," he cried, "my great difficulty, my serious problem, will meet me when I leave the White House. Supposing I stay there seven years. Supposing even a second term, I shall still be young in my early fifties, on the shelf, retired, out of it. I know that I can make a fairly good fist of it as President, given a certain amount of luck. But imagine me as an ex-President, dedicating buildings and making commencement speeches, occasionally perhaps the chairman of some convention!" We two youngsters began to protest. There we could say something. A clatter of young voices arose. It was a great night, a memorable occasion. I happened to turn to look at the Admiral. He had folded his hands across his abdomen, his eyes were closed, his rhythmic breathing told the story. What was this young brother-in-law to him? Not a President, but a pest. Brothers-in-law are always brothers-in-law. Young brothers-in-law are just obstreperous young brothers-in-law when an Admiral is in his sixties and sailing through calm water.

The next picture is over toward the end of the book. It is December 1918, twenty-one years after that first walk down "F" Street. The young elms are in their shady middle age. The Roosevelt presidency has passed. The fight for the Roosevelt policies at Armageddon in 1912 is a memory. The tragedy and heart-break of the war are over. We were planning for 1920 as we were planning twenty-one years ago for 1904. Penrose is beginning to forgive and forget. Even Barnes is softening. Among Republicans, there seems to be "one clear call" for Roosevelt. By appointment on my way back to France on a business trip, I had called at the Roosevelt hospital in the morning to see the Colonel—a man in his sixties. At the hospital desk they told me that he had a bad night and probably could not see me. I protested an appointment on the hour. I am pushed on down corridors and a young interne shakes his head seriously. A responsible doctor indicates that an appointment is no open sesame to the sick room. A valued family friend is consulted. The consultation ends hopelessly. I had little on my mind save a program of new issues for the new time and the names of some new friends who would work with us, who five years before had been enemies. I went away sad, sorry but understanding. My business occupied me several hours. When I returned to my club I had tied up the day with engagements, but two phone calls from the Roosevelt hospital were there. Another phone call came just as I stepped in the door of the club. Colonel Roosevelt wished to see me. The voice of the nurse at the other end rather insistently asked me to return to the hospital. I promised to try to break my engagements. Again, in twenty minutes, another call came—this time from the interne. I went out into the city for an hour and when I returned to the club, the doctor was calling. It was urgent; half an hour later the valued family friend was on the phone. One could feel the mounting pressure of emotion under that hospital roof. It was teetering ready to blow off. At five o'clock in the December dusk I appeared at the front door of the hospital. The interne with nervous lines in his face stood on the front steps waiting for me. He hastened me to the doctor who grasped my hand and took me to the room where the family friend was waiting, only calmed by Mrs. Roosevelt's gentle greeting. They literally hustled me down the hall. What turmoil he must have made, lying there in his bed. What a well of energy he had even there on his deathbed to keep his word to a friend. The fire still glowing in his heart! The old fire that had set a world aflame with a new hope for righteousness, was still a burning passion in his soul. I was to stay fifteen minutes. Literally, by main force, he held me an hour.

We talked of all sorts of schemes, devices, platform plans, plans not for political advancement, but for social betterment. I remember old age pension, child labor, a non-partisan tariff commission with powers, the theory and philosophy of the new tariff policy, the universal eight hour day—a thousand chimera visions, utopian wish-structures for industrial and economic justice. We sat blowing iridescent bubbles into our cosmos. Sometimes he broke my bubbles, sometimes I blew up his. It was an hour of glorious phantom fighting, shadow boxing, a gladiatorial pipe dreaming wrestling match, catch-as-catch-can, no holds barred—a gorgeous hour. My son and his son were in and out of the room. We were proud fathers. Each son had worn his country's uniform. His sons had won distinction, mine had been in a training camp. At times we purred as fathers will in low pride.

Finally, standing at the bed, we clasped both hands and said goodbye. I am glad to have that last fine memory of him. That hour of turmoil in the room and the recollection of the tumultuous uproar that he must have caused that day to bring me to his bedside. Not that it was for me. But because I shall always know he went clear to the end of his day and time like Kipling's fuzzy-wuzzy, "A first-class fighting man." There was no twilight and evening star for him. He plunged headlong, snorting, into the breakers of the tide that swept him to another bourne, full armed breasting the waves, a strong swimmer undaunted.

And so I close the album with a smile.

Later in the evening, after that year's other recipients of the medal had spoken, James R. Garfield, the toastmaster, asked Mr. White if he cared to say anything more about T.R. He responded with these informal remarks:

. . . listening to these delightful reminiscences of Colonel Roosevelt's boyhood friend, all the memories of the man come flooding into my heart. And I wondered, as I sat here thinking, when we who knew him and loved him, who understood him, we who had the experience of seeing him, living with him, after we are gone, what will others think of him? Can the next generation get hold, have that thing that we have, that exuberant personality, that joyous, burning flame that was Theodore Roosevelt? I think all of us will agree, who knew him, who even touched him remotely, that in him, in his body and mind, there was the greatest personality that his generation knew.

. . . I have pictures of him in my heart. Perhaps the first picture will interest you: a cold night, back, I think, in the '90's, a blustery, stormy night, and the men around the Holland House, around the fire, the hearth there in the lobby, along about eleven o'clock beginning to move around, moving over to the windows. One of the men there, a stranger, says, "What is it you are looking for?"

And they say, "Come here, come here. In a moment he will appear."

"Who?"

"Oh, this young Police Commissioner, every night at this hour he rides up the street, or walks, and we watch for him."

And there he comes, buffeting the storm, full of joy, vitality, shouldering his way up the avenue, out of the night, a flashing human torch.

And that picture closes, and then I remember the boy, the eternal kidder. I was in the White House one day, it was about 1902, perhaps; I had written a very mean piece in the *McClure's* Magazine about Tom Platt, I had got most of my material from Theodore Roosevelt, and Platt had been bombarding the White House and demanding that I should be barred. . . . The scene opened suddenly when I remember the President coming to me. He said, "Did you talk with Tom Platt?"

I said, "Yes, perhaps an hour."

He said, "He says he never saw you; just come here." And I followed him. He went into the office. Mind you, Tom Platt had been saying that White should not come to the White House. He sat down, and when I was comfortably seated, he said, "Platt will be in pretty soon. He won't know you. I won't introduce you, but I thought you would like it."

So I sat there through the interview with Platt. It did not mean anything to him, but it meant a lot to Theodore Roosevelt and to me.

I never saw Theodore Roosevelt with a gun in his hand. I never saw him on the various sides on which many other men knew him. We talked books a little; not much; mostly politics. There I think I knew him a little bit. On his family side, two or three times I have been in Oyster Bay as a guest, a number of times at the White House, but my side of this great elephant of a man is the politician; and he was more than a politician, of course, he was a statesman, but a very human person; never a grudge-bearer; a man who realized that today's enemy may have to be tomorrow's friend. So, on the whole, you want to treat your enemy squarely, fairly, so that he can be your friend.

I have seen him forget wounds, I have seen him work with men whom he had not thought he would be working with a few years before. But always he had a philosophy; he appealed to the best in a man. If the man was a scoundrel, there was something in him that was worth holding.

He had a common ground of meeting with Quay, the Pennsylvania senator, and you will be surprised to know it was Icelandic sagas. They talked for hours about the poetry of Iceland, and got on fine.

There was a time in 1912 when Theodore Roosevelt had some uncomplimentary things to say about Boies Penrose and William Barnes, we all did, and then the whirligig of time moved, and the last time I saw Theodore Roosevelt, he was in the hospital. I went over to see him, and he said, "I think they are now ready to take me." We had been talking about the presidential nomination. He said, "They realize that I can win." I said, "Yes."

He said, "Who do you think is now sending word that he would like to have me run?"

I said, "Search me."

He said, "Boies Penrose!" And if he had lived, he and Boies Penrose would have been singing "Onward, Christian Soldiers," in 1920; but he is in a different world, a better world, I am sure.

. . . I hope some genius somewhere will be able to gather from those of us who still live, something immortal to put into the pages of history, this unique and splendid, this superb spirit and personality, call it what you will, this combination of qualities that was Theodore Roosevelt. To me he seemed as nearly a perfect man as any I have known. He was not perfect, not more than eighty-five per cent, with a slight discount off for that, but most of them don't run over thirty.

. . . It seems to me, as I remember him, that he had not that unconscious arrogance of conscious class. To me, as I remember him, he is more like the democrat—the man who knows he is really as good as the one who is an aristocrat thinks he is. That is the Theodore Roosevelt I mean, true and brave and fine. . . .

If this discussion has strayed, for one chapter, a quarter-century beyond the story, it is only to give White's testimony for the belief that Theodore Roosevelt unlocked the last closed room of his mind, completed the connection between his able intellect and his warm heart.

5. WHITE BREAKS WITH THE G.O.P.

M R. WHITE supported wholeheartedly the presidential candidacy of William Howard Taft in the 1908 campaign. He accepted Taft as the logical successor of T.R., in full expectation that he would consolidate Roosevelt's pioneering gains in legislation leading to conservation of natural resources, control of great combinations of capital, the equitable distribution of wealth, and better working conditions and wages for labor.

In March, 1909, Mr. White said editorially:

The inaugural address of President Taft reads like a promissory note. It is short, definite, and satisfactory. After formally endorsing what is known as the Roosevelt policy, the new President gives first place in his address to a declaration in favor of restricting the excessive stock and bond issues of railroads. That seems to be the most important thing to the new President, as it is to the American people. It is the evil of overcapitalization that makes railroad regulation difficult.

The words of the new President on tariff revision have teeth in them. He indicates that he will fight. Congress will soon find that the big man is as determined as the big stick.

The whole address is a pledge to continue the work begun by President Roosevelt. There will be no turning back—no compromise.

Taft will clean off the desk and finish the work which has been piling up for eight years. Persons who are looking for the clock to go back to the good old days of Hanna, may as well sigh and take up their burdens. Taft means business.

The first rift in the lute became evident in an editorial in September, 1909, entitled "Never":

The President has had his say . . . he has rebuked the insurgents; he has lined up with the standpatters; he has endorsed the Payne-Aldrich bill as the best tariff bill ever enacted—and, considering the administration features, and the new tariff commission, the President probably is right—and he has shown himself clearly to be out of sympathy with what the dominant wing of the Republican party stands for in the states of the prairie West.

But the net result of the whole presidential program is that the President has lost his strength, now that the ideas he has combatted and the men he has refused are stronger than ever. There is not in the West a free newspaper that has even flickered for a minute. Hundreds of papers that have been unswerving in their admiration and loyalty to the President, are sad over his fearful mistake; but they are even more earnest in the advocacy of their ideas than before. The insurgent Congressmen and Senators have not lost a supporter. The people are still behind these men. The Presidential rebuke made them more heroic in the eyes of their friends and supporters, and every one of them—the Senators except Beveridge —as well as Congressmen are nominated and elected directly by the people; they are directly responsible to the people. The primary made them, and they will answer to the primary.

Moreover, the blood of the martyrs is the seed of the church.

White's first really harsh criticism of Taft, in September, 1909, was followed by another one three months later in which he said that there were obvious lines of agreement among the Republicans opposed to the stand-pat leadership which was aligned with President Taft in control of the Republican party.

The plainest of these lines [he wrote] so far as the insurgent Republicans consider President Taft—is that of disappointment. Another absolutely certain line of the insurgent sentiment is this: there is no anger, no resentment in it. The insurgent Republicans feel that the President is sacrificing too much for party harmony. They feel that he should have the faith that more Republican votes will be secured, both in Congress, and at the general election, by rigid adherence to the good of the country, than by compliance with the demands of Aldrich and Cannon, in the interest of party harmony. The party is strong only when it serves the people, and when party solidarity would sacrifice national advantages it is more harmful than helpful to the Republican party in a practical way.

In an editorial, January 13, 1910, concerning the dismissal of Gifford Pinchot as chief forester of the United States, Mr. White wrote that Pinchot ". . . is a thoroughbred. He has brought the robbery of our public domain to a crisis. He has made it impossible for the unwilling not to see the facts. From now on the fight is in the open. The machine is with the thieves. The regulars are trying to save the organization. The people have with them only such men as Pinchot, in Congress and out, in public service and out. But the people will win in the end."

One week later Mr. White wrote of "The Republican Crisis" saying:

It doesn't matter whose fault it is, the Republican party in this nation is in serious danger of a split that will cost it the congressional election. Attempts to read the insurgent congressmen out of the party, the denial of patronage to them, the snubbing by the party whips, the dismissal of Pinchot, the presidential endorsement of . . . three of President Roosevelt's most effective and implacable enemies—all these things have disciplined, not the insurgents, but the people themselves. It is the people—the rank and file of Republicans in this nation from Maine to California—who are in revolt. And it is up to the leaders to placate the people. This can't be done by disciplining the insurgents. . . . The good of the party demands the retirement of the men who have pushed it so far toward disruption and ruin.

Many other White editorials during these trying months were in the same vein. In November, 1911, he wrote of "Our Weary President":

In all our history no sadder spectacle has been presented than that of President Taft journeying painfully to a silent, undemonstrative and rather uncongenial constituency, trying to explain to the voters the consistency and righteousness of his policies. It is evident that he is tired, tired of trying to straighten out the tangles, tired of the whole thankless unhappy job.

. . . Heavy, heavy hangs over your head, Mr. President, and it shall be fine or super-fine in relation to your own choice of future policy. If you forget your judicial training, and take up militant leadership—you may regain the lost kingdom that has disappeared since the Winona speech. If not—no one may foretell what the future will bring.

By January, 1912, he was writing: "Unless Republicans change leaders, the country will change parties. A lot of finer things enter into this situation, but they are minor things. The great big important fact is this: That this country is going Democratic as sure as November comes unless the party changes

leaders. . . . Someone must take the reins who can put cay-
enne pepper on the balky horse where it will do the most good.
"It's Roosevelt or bust."

In May, 1912, when the Roosevelt-Taft battle for delegates
to the 1912 Republican Convention was hottest, Mr. White, in
speculating on the reasons for T.R.'s gain in the states which
had already held primaries, said that the liberal movement was
fundamental. If it is revolutionary, he asked, what then? And
he expressed his belief that it was not only a big, strong movement toward more popular government but that it would be
historic in American social and political life—

"Big changes are coming. Roosevelt nomination or defeat is not
important. It will go on no matter who wins . . . The movement
is bigger than Roosevelt—bigger than the Republican party. It is
even bigger than this nation. It is part of a world movement looking
for readjustment of economic conditions—to the right of the average
man to a position of dignity in the world."

Mr. White attended the Republican convention of 1912,
wrote articles concerning its deliberations for a newspaper syndicate, and tried in every way to bring about T.R.'s nomination. He went as far as to accept high political office for the first
time—that of Republican national committeeman from Kansas.
He resigned this job a few days later and gave his reasons in a
Gazette editorial. He declared that he had not acted impulsively
nor with unnecessary haste. He had done it because the National
Committee had made rulings of invidiously far-reaching importance to the nation:

The first was that any member of the National Committee who
did not give such support to the party candidate as the Committee
deemed necessary, could be removed at once by the Committee.
That is not so important. It is the second one that carries the dynamite. The second rule says that when a man is removed from the
membership of the Committee, his successor shall be appointed by
the Committee.
    It has been the custom heretofore for the State Central Com-
mittee to fill a vacancy caused by the death or retirement of the
State's party representative on the National Committee. Now by
the arbitrary action of that body, it will be possible for the National
Committee to retain its present color indefinitely, regardless of the

opinion of the people of the state that tries to express itself through the choice of the State Central Committee.

Mr. White went on to say that he was a loyal follower of T.R., that he believed the wishes of the larger Republican states, as expressed at the primary, made him the choice of the national convention; but that the National Committee, as part of the machinery of the party and intended by the rank and file to be merely a convenient instrument to record the party's will, had assumed dangerous, menacing authority. He stated that his career as National Committeeman was necessarily brief because if Kansas was to be represented, he had to resign and his successor to be elected before the convention passed out of existence as an official body.

There was no emotion and little heat in this statement, nor can any heartbreak be read between its lines. But during those trying days at Chicago when he made the choice between principle and devoted loyalty to the Republican party, Mr. White went through great agony of spirit. The night of the great decision in Chicago he called his full partner and companion by long distance and told her in a voice breaking with emotion that he had decided to leave the party of his mother, of his boyhood and his young manhood and throw in his lot with a new party.

This decision was one of the most painful of his life, yet it completed his emancipation. From then on he no longer was politically earthbound. He had freed himself and could follow his political fancy wherever it led.

In August, 1912, in commenting editorially on "The New Party," he said:

The platform of the new party is much more important than either of the candidates at the head of the ticket. Roosevelt is an episode in this contest; he will be known as the founder of the party. But the party will continue as the radical party of the nation long after Roosevelt is gone. The party is pledged at the beginning to definite social and industrial reforms. It is not pledged to prosperity, but to justice. It is pledged so to change the environment of chronic poverty that whatever the changed environment can do to ameliorate or remove chronic poverty, will be done.

The new party is pledged to the rule of the people—to all the people—men and women alike. It is pledged to justice between men so far as it may be approximated in human affairs. . . . But always it will face forward.

In October, 1912, Mr. White wrote that the problem of the new century was the eradication of such chronic poverty as is caused by the action of environment upon humanity, that poverty is a national disease, and that its cure must come through a national remedy. The causes of chronic poverty, he said, lie in "the inequities of distribution of our great surplus wealth"; we distribute our surplus wealth poorly because commerce in America is conducted by the many for the few. As for the remedy:

The Republican party as organized today is in the hands of the bosses. They are jobbers of prosperity and believe that the big rich should be permitted to thrive because they are big, so that the little boy may get the crumbs from the feast.

The basic idea of the Republican party is prosperity. Its face is turned to the days of the plutocracy of the nineties. The Republican party believes in the full dinner pail as an incident to the full automobile.

But the fundamental idea of the new party is not prosperity; it is for the full dinner pail, but not as an incident to anything. The solution of the labor problem is not dependent upon good times or bad times, but upon justice at all times to the men who do the world's work. . . . The idea will find its way into the law books and administration in due and proper time. The victory is won no matter how the election goes.

We lost the skirmish that fall, but the heirs, successors, and other beneficiaries thereof since then have won the liberal war.

6. THE BULL MOOSE INTERLUDE

Two years or more before the Bull Moosers marched to Armageddon, there had been many proposals in national political circles about the organization of a new political party. This subject is a hardy quadrennial. The election laws of the states, however, have been so tightened up during the preceding generation as to make it difficult to organize a new party. Now, therefore, the agitation seldom gets beyond the stage of talk.

Party lines were still firm, even hard, early in this century, despite the softening process which T.R. had put them through between 1901 and 1909. Hundreds of thousands of men—even millions—halfway believed that party regularity came ahead of patriotism. Some of them even seemed afraid that if they scratched the party ticket, an avenging god would strike them dead.

Other voters, somewhat more enlightened, considered party regularity a minor virtue. Few, however, were willing to consider the formation of a new political party. Will White himself had declared editorially in 1910:

Of all the fool things under the sun, talk of a third party in this country, or in any state in this country, is the foolest thing. The Republican party is coming into a new lease of power. It is about to be baptized with a new consecration. It will be a new party, but not a third party. The old barnacles that have loaded down the ship will be scraped off. The people are about to take the helm and human rights are to become in the future—as they were in the beginning of the party's history—the chief object of the party's consideration. We are going into the new emancipation—the emancipation of men—and the Republican party in every state and in every nation is to be the new emancipator. Those who talk of a new party are not the best friends of progress.

The man who wrote that had been shoulder-deep for ten years in a fight against the stand-pat leadership of his party's stalwarts in the battle to breathe reality into the new emancipation. There can be little question but that T.R., Will White, and all other members of their wing of the Republican party went to the Republican National Convention of 1912 determined to keep the fight a family one.

Circumstances gave me a ringside seat in the Bull Moose campaign. Earlier in the year the death of my youngest sister took me back to Emporia from the East where for seven years, except for vacations, I had been in school and college. Shortly before the time when I planned my return to New York City, I met White on the street. We discussed the fight between Progressives and stand-patters for delegates to the coming National Republican Convention then just beginning in Kansas. Will was the state leader of the Roosevelt forces. I asked him if he didn't need me to "help save the country." His reply was, "You work southwest to my office and get busy with the typewriter while I cover the Fourth Ward."

We went our ways. I found plenty of work at the *Gazette* office, and from that hour until election day he and I were captain and crew of the good ship Bull Moose in Kansas. The *Gazette* was Kansas headquarters for the Progressives. White operated from his own office. I fell heir to the room of Walt Mason, the prose poet. Walt was a Republican regular—had no use for such wild cavortings as those of the Bull Moose. We had hardly started our work when he announced that he would get out of there and do his writing at home because he was certain that if he remained, he would catch blood poisoning from some Bull Moose scratch.

This was a glorious adventure, an experience which enriched my life beyond measure, for ours was wholly unlike any other political headquarters that ever functioned. Neither of us knew much about party organizations and procedures, but such knowledge would have been ineffective anyway. Routine procedures were at a discount in a campaign conducted with swing, lilt, ideas, audacity, imagination, courage, and a magic name.

It was not until a year or more later that I even suspected that the standard setup of political headquarters requires such departments as publicity, speakers' bureau, finance organization, and such divisions as first-voters, preachers, lawyers, or what have you. We had none of these—only a man and a boy who went to sea in a tub and had the time of their lives. White confined his activities largely to high strategy, copy writing, maintaining contact with the National Committee, and conducting personal correspondence. The rest was mine: a fifteen-hour-a-day, seven-day-a-week job and every minute of it interesting. When my load grew too heavy, White would hire another $15-a-week stenographer. Our first concern was to get a majority of Roosevelt-pledged men elected as delegates to the Republican National Convention. White hand-picked his candidates for delegate and ramrodded his followers into accepting them with as much forcefulness as any powerful, experienced political boss. His principal mode of attack was yelling bloody murder in such a variety of interesting ways as to make the headlines daily. He was able, by this method, to get and to keep his views before the Kansas electorate. Editors who enjoyed a scrap and admired him gave him an amazing amount of space—as also did even those editors who opposed him, for his copy was too interesting to ignore.

His publicity inspired thousands of people to write him pro and con. Those correspondents who supported his cause became our shock troops. We used the term "starred list" to describe them. A man, for example, who wrote a reasonably legible and intelligent letter would get one typewritten star after his name, the writer of the somewhat better letter, two stars, and so on up to five stars. Either White or I read each of these letters and marked it with a numeral to guide the stenographers in classifying the writer. Once a man's name was on the lists, we began to send him form letters over White's signature, enclosing campaign literature designed to keep him hot, bothered, and busy.

This activity produced a steady flow of return letters, each writer telling in detail about the dirt being done at his particular crossroads, and who the wolves in sheep's clothing were. Most of the writers outlined in detail their own plans for high strategy. Naturally, we had many letters from crackpots, since any new radical or liberal party attracts what T.R. himself called the "lunatic fringe."

We had to use careful judgment, often checking and rechecking on an item of information by correspondence or long-distance, because in a political fight where feelings are as intense and bitter as in that one, doubt and suspicion of leaders is inevitable. When apparently responsible writers reported what they considered traitorous doings by men we knew to be staunch friends, White usually attempted to satisfy them by persuasive argument, but sometimes he was peremptory. One such letter concerned a Roosevelt-pledged delegate from northern Kansas named Armstrong. Our informant warned us that Armstrong would not stand hitched. White knew Armstrong well and being sure of his man, told me to write in reply, "You are mistaken. Armstrong is all right. I know what I am talking about." No more, just that. The letter quieted that informant.

As I remember, all but four of the Kansas delegates to the Republican convention voted for Roosevelt. We lost two of these in a fair fight and the Old Guard city-slicked White out of the other two.

White returned to Emporia from the Taft-controlled convention with blood in his eye, honing for the fight ahead. Our first job after his return was to cull from scores of requests the names of those who were to be selected as delegates to the hurriedly planned convention of the new Progressive or "Bull Moose" party, and while doing that to keep great quantities of pitch hot, for the devil was to pay. We also had to work out a deal with the state and county Republican organizations by which we supported the vast majority of their candidates for state and county office. Nationally we fought the Republicans, but within Kansas, where the party was truly Progressive, we joined it in the fight for state officials against the traditional enemy, the Democrats.

White went in August as a delegate to the new party's convention and was a member, if not the all-important member, of the Resolutions Committee. He helped draft "A Covenant with the People," one of the three really great political platforms written in America since the custom was initiated in 1840. (The other two were the Republican platform of 1856 and the Democratic of 1932.)

Shortly after his return from the Bull Moose convention in Chicago, which nominated T.R. for president and Hiram Johnson for vice-president, Mr. and Mrs. White left for a month's vacation in their beloved Estes Park. We at the office made an analysis of our "starred list," and found that in many communities we had from ten to fifty workers, whereas in some others we had none. We mailed form letters over White's signature to all our workers asking them to send us the names of reliable supporters of our cause in communities where we had little or no representation. The replies came in floods, bringing us thousands of new names. We checked them against our old lists and added them to a new master-list. Thus we shortly had, not a precinct-by-precinct organization, but the nearest thing to it we could get. Moreover this new setup fitted our needs—we wanted not political workers but crusaders who would spread the gospel, for we were carrying on a fight of ideas, reason, persuasion, appeals to the consciences of men, trying to get them to realize that private morals and public morals are cut from the same piece of cloth.

When the Whites returned from Colorado in early September, we were set to go. White threw his imagination and audacity into high gear, and created ways wholly new to political campaigning for carrying on our attempt to keep the all-important issues before the electorate.

Our activities were largely confined to a direct mail, publicity, and speaking campaign with occasional fast footwork by White. He wrote most of the copy for our campaign circulars, and innumerable enclosures for all letters sent out of the office. Additional copies of any enclosures were sent without charge to anyone requesting them. Proofs of *Gazette* editorials dealing with the campaign were pulled and mailed to more than two hundred Kansas newspaper editors who were supporting Roosevelt. We had a special writer interview men and women in all walks of life, lawyers, farmers, merchants, bankers, housewives, teachers, railroad employees. Each interview of about two hundred words gave the reasons for supporting T.R.'s candidacy—closely related to the person's trade, profession, or occupation. In this manner we were able to get every important argument in favor of T.R. set forth. We pulled proofs of the interviews and sent them to the editors of our co-operating newspapers asking them to get some local man or woman in a corresponding walk of life to endorse them. Thus we presented our best arguments to the voters of a community through a fellow townsman.

We raised within the state every cent we spent—the first time this ever happened in a national campaign in Kansas. This was done by appeals to our workers, whose contributions ranged from one dollar to one hundred dollars. White served as banker, personally advancing money as needed. Once when our funds were low, I wrote, for his signature, a letter which I believed able to entice a hungry dog from a meat-wagon. White read it and added two telling sentences. One was to the effect that while we still were trusting to the ravens, our faith was growing weaker for lack of supporting evidence; the other, which ended the letter was: "We are ungodly hard up." He remarked to me, "We'll catch some driftwood with this," and with a touch of genius sent the composition to a supporter in Topeka with a note—"Show this letter most confidentially to Bill Kercher and see if he'll swallow the bait." Kercher was the Topeka correspondent of the *Kansas City Journal,* an ardent supporter of Taft and a bitter antagonist of T.R. The unsuspicious Kercher naturally took this begging letter as proof that our headquarters was only half a jump ahead of the sheriff and might be closed up at any time, so he made a feature story of it in the *Journal.* Three hundred Kansas newspaper editors, opponents and supporters of T.R. alike, saw our letter, read it, reprinted it, even hammered in the point editorially. Net result: such a flood of checks rolled into our office that within a week we had weathered the storm.

One afternoon during the campaign I told Mr. White that we should be plugging for both Capper and Stubbs since both of them were supporting T.R. (Arthur Capper was Republican nominee for governor, W. Roscoe Stubbs, then governor, Republican candidate for the United States Senate.) My point was that with little additional cost we could enclose Capper and Stubbs literature in the thousands of letters we were sending out almost daily to our workers. White asked first how much this was likely to cost. "About three thousand dollars," was my guess. He said: "We don't have as much money as that and I doubt if we can raise it." I suggested that perhaps Capper and Stubbs themselves would subscribe it. He looked up at the clock and said, "Get your hat quick, there's just time to catch Six"—that eastbound Santa Fe train which left Emporia for Topeka in midafternoon. I got my hat, he hurried out front to untie Old Tom and drive me to the station. On the way he said that he'd telephone to both Capper and Stubbs and ask them to wait for me at their offices.

Both of them agreed to the proposal, and I caught the seven o'clock train back to Emporia. The next day we were working hard for three candidates. There was no agreement covering the Capper and Stubbs subscriptions, other than their oral promises to me, but we had gone ahead and were using White's money.

The way White baited the *Kansas City Journal* into publicizing our financial needs revealed the qualities of imagination and audacity he used in the campaign; the Capper-Stubbs episode, his good faith, and down-to-earth business acumen. The morning after election, when we learned from the returns that both men had been defeated, he said to me, "You get up to Topeka quick and get those checks before Arthur and Stubbs turn sour. They'll both be feeling all right for a day or two, but after that—nobody knows. And for heaven's sake be careful. Don't get killed before you collect—if you do I'll be out three thousand dollars." I was careful, and they both paid up promptly and gladly.

That, however, is a little ahead of the story; for the big event of the campaign was T.R.'s visit to Emporia with his special train. He arrived late Saturday night and left Sunday afternoon. He attended church service and visited the *Gazette* office where, despite a curious crowd, he sat at White's desk, apparently oblivious of the staring people, and wrote a long letter to Mrs. Roosevelt. The rest of the day he spent at the White home. Except for the crowd before the *Gazette* office, he escaped all of the fatigue of public attention, largely because on Saturday afternoon (White was with him in Topeka) the *Gazette* ran an editorial by Mrs. White which tells its own story of her delicacy and understanding, of her ability to get a point over effectively:

Emporia folks are the kindest and best mannered folks in the world. Every issue of the *Gazette* records little incidents of this neighborly kindness. Because of Emporia's kindness and good manners she will shelter tonight and tomorrow the most prominent citizen in the United States. Theodore Roosevelt will spend Saturday and Sunday in Emporia, the guest of friends. He is coming here for a day of complete rest. He has had two weeks of the hardest kind of campaigning and he has six weeks of still harder work ahead of him.

There is no question about the kind of feeling Emporia has for the Colonel. Now here is a way to show that feeling:

Give the man the one thing he needs most tomorrow—a chance for a day's rest. Let Emporia, Kansas, show him that if he wants to sit on the front porch and read the paper he can do it, and attract no more attention than any other man doing the same thing on the front porch.

It is up to Emporia to show her kindness and her good manners toward this tired man who is coming here to rest.

At the end of the visit White drove the great man to his special train at the Santa Fe station. A crowd of three thousand or more Emporians were massed around the private car. T.R. boarded the train, came out onto the observation platform, and, facing a sun near to its setting, in the hush of the Sunday afternoon spoke briefly. It was more a benediction than a political speech. He told of the pleasure the quiet day in Emporia had given him, emphasizing its benefit by mentioning the long, arduous speaking schedule both behind and before him, and concluded with the thought that all of this was done, "To strengthen the opportunity for honest men and honest women, decent men and decent women everywhere in the nation to live more comfortable lives in justice, in harmony with each other." A few more sentences to the same effect and the train pulled off into the twilight of a beautiful Kansas fall evening (and Kansas is truly beautiful in the fall). Men uncovered their heads; all of them, men, women, and children, continued to wave until his train became only a speck in the east. No applause followed T.R.'s remarks—it would have been out of keeping with the deep feeling of everyone there.

The day following T.R.'s visit, and each succeeding one until election, found us busy trying to keep our thousands of volunteer workers supplied with persuasive literature, appealing for money, scheduling speakers, and taking care of the correspondence. The National Committee provided us with a limited number of speakers from outside of the state, but Kansans filled the majority of our engagements. Once, after repeated failures to find a speaker, we canvassed the situation and decided that Henry Allen—who previously had declined—should be drafted for this job. White wired Allen, "If you love me, speak at Quenemo tomorrow night." Henry replied he did and would. It was in this manner, personal, intimate, and warm, that he met and solved the multitude of problems which arose daily. Such methods would have been ineffective in stereotyped campaigns conducted from the state headquarters of a political party. Moreover, no state political headquarters ever had a leader with the imagination, audacity, or devoted following that Will White had. Ours was a moral political crusade carried on in the one state which specialized in such. Since we neither inherited nor had time to create a standard political precinct organization, we put all our eggs into one basket. We improvised, or played by ear. Whenever a bright idea occurred to me we would talk it out. Being a political novice, I was never in a position to argue that it would work; I could only insist that I "had a hunch." White then would issue a statement tentatively trying the idea out by drawing the opponents' fire. It nearly always did so, and then he would take advantage of the opening we had created, and blow the opposition out of the water with his counterblast. He came in time to trust my "hunches," and in later years frequently spoke of a "Quaker hunch" as being the surest thing in the world.

When we talked the battle over on the afternoon before election day, Mr. White said two things that stick in my memory. The first was that he had done nothing in the entire campaign to which his most bitter political enemy could properly object. This was true. Clean and open, appealing to the voter's intelligence and moral purpose, educationally persuasive but hard-hitting, it was the kind of campaign that any young man with high ideals would have found to his liking.

His second remark had to do with our chances. Deep down in our hearts we did not believe that T.R. would carry Kansas. But we could not be sure. Our Bull Moosers were a voluble lot, inclined to tell the cockeyed world where they stood politically. Straw votes taken on trains or in communities showed T.R. far in the lead. We talked of these and other signs and portents, talked ourselves into belief, until White proposed satirically that we run an advertisement on the front page of the *Gazette* proclaiming that if T.R. carried Kansas, the two of us, being "free, white, and over twenty-one, would appear publicly drunk at the corner of Sixth Avenue and Commercial Street at 6 o'clock on the afternoon following election." But we lost, as our hearts told us we would.

A precious Irish inheritance from that mother of his was his ability to meet troubles, perplexities, and irritations and laugh them off. Just before election, he sent our leading workers inaccurate instructions as to one important proceeding. I had been out of town for two days and upon my return, on the Sunday afternoon before election, he was at the railroad station waiting with Old Tom and the surrey. He told me what had happened and said that we'd have to get all these people on the telephone that afternoon and evening and straighten them out. We went directly to the office, where I began placing long-distance calls and, as they came in, correcting the mistake. He sat around fidgeting until I finished the first two or three calls; then, perfectly at ease, he said he'd go on home. Everything was all right now since, as he said, "we have started to get the cattle out of the corn." His worry lasted only until steps were taken to repair the damage; then he completely dismissed it.

On the day following the election and while I was in Topeka collecting from Capper and Stubbs, Mr. White, with characteristic thoughtfulness and without a previous hint to me, had telegraphed at great length to George W. Perkins, chairman of our party's executive committee, to say that he had a young man whom the National Committee should catch quick. White belonged to that small group of men who would go to hell for a friend. I do not know exactly how much he endangered his soul on this occasion, but I saw Mr. Perkins' laconic reply: "Send your wonderful young man right on to New York."

I did not specially fancy this job, and argued with White for days. He submitted that the finest body of young men and women in the land were marching under the Bull Moose banner and that the experience of serving in such a movement would be an inspiration all my life. No young man could afford to pass up such an opportunity. He won.

Late in 1913, I stopped off at Emporia en route from the

West Coast, where I had been doing some spade work for the Progressive National Committee, to New York. White was organizing a convention preliminary to the state campaign of 1914. He asked me to return to Kansas in January in order to help out for a fortnight with the preliminaries. I agreed willingly because he needed at the moment all the help he could get. He had not found a satisfactory candidate for either governor or United States senator. Bull Moosers in western Kansas had tried to start a boom for him as the gubernatorial candidate. In an effort to squelch them he used his old device —guying himself. This time he said:

A number of Progressives at Lakin, more kind than considerate, yesterday resoluted in favor of this man White, of Emporia, for governor. They wanted him to run as a Progressive candidate. To which *The Gazette* says no—a thousand times no. For we are on to that man White, and without wishing to speak disrespectfully of a fellow townsman, who, so far as we know, may be at least outwardly decent in the simpler relations of life—perhaps he pays his debts when it is convenient, and he may be kind to his family, though that's not to his credit, for who wouldn't be—and he may have kept out of jail, one way or another, for some time; without, as we say, desiring to speak disrespectfully of this man, we know that he's not the man either to run for governor or, if such a grotesque thing could be imagined, to serve as governor.

He can't make a speech. He has a lot of radical convictions which he sometimes comes into *The Gazette* office and exploits, and which are dangerous. He has been jawing politicians for twenty years until he is a common scold, and he has shot up his so-called ideals so high that the Angel Gabriel himself couldn't give the performance that this man White would have to advertise on the bills.

So, in the words of the poet, nix on Willyum Allen. *The Gazette's* nose is hard and cold on the proposition to make him governor. He is a four-flusher, a ring-tailed, rip-snorting hell-raiser, and a grandstander. He makes a big noise. He yips and kyoodles around a good deal, but he is everlastingly and preeminently N.G. as gubernatorial timber—full of knots, warts, woodpecker holes, and rotten spots.

. . . People in the state may be fooled by the doped gait and fancy steps of this man White, but we know him. If he is a candidate for governor or for any other office, we propose to tell the truth about him . . . if his fool friends insist on playing up this self-advertising game for him any longer, we propose to abandon twenty years of guarded innuendo and prattling subterfuge, and come out with the real facts. We shall speak plainly hereafter.

A word to the wise should gather no moss!

When I reached Kansas late in January he had found a candidate for the Senate. The late Victor Murdock had agreed to accept that nomination but White was still looking for a candidate for governor. Popular Henry Allen, the logical man to head the ticket, unyieldingly refused. White and I talked the problem out. All seemed lost unless we could get a strong candidate for governor. In the wisdom of youth I pointed out that the pendulum was swinging back from the liberal to the conservative, therefore, we should look for a businessman candidate (a wholly fallacious theory, as all realize who really know the operations of politics and government. But it sounded good then, as it still does to the uninitiated). White asked me to go to the home towns of some of our Progressive business leaders and investigate them. None filled the bill and I finally telephoned White to suggest that we might get Henry Allen to accept if we could induce the *Kansas City Star* and ex-Governor Stubbs to say they would support him. White's reply was, "You get Stubbs and I'll get the *Star*." But when we reached Topeka the morning of the convention we were both empty-handed.

Now the situation seemed desperate, and especially to emotional Bull Moosers. All seemed lost save honor, and that was badly compromised. This was still the situation when Victor Murdock went out on the stage to deliver to a hair-triggered emotional crowd of two thousand delegates a magnificent rabble-rousing speech designed to force Henry's acceptance. While Victor waited his cue, White and Raymond Robins had been walking back and forth arm in arm with tears streaming down their faces. Henry Allen, while deeply moved by all this display, continued to stand alone in a corner like a bad boy a bit disturbed but still resolute. Then Victor struck the spark which touched off the dynamite in the delegates' hearts. Before he had spoken five minutes they had begun putting their hearts and lungs into the chant, "We want Henry! We want Henry!" over and over and over again—endlessly. No man could have resisted the fervor and the earnestness of that cry. Not even

Henry. His resolution broke like a dam. He strode suddenly out onto the platform and after getting a semblance of quiet said, "My friends, I don't want the nomination but I will accept it." Later when I asked why on earth he had kept us all worried so long, he answered, "I decided that it would be easier to make the race than try to explain to all those dear folks why I didn't want to run."

It was such things, qualities of the heart and spirit, that set the Bull Moose movement aside and apart from any other of this generation. It caused Mr. White and others like him to hold it deep in their hearts as a joyous memory of a great adventure.

We had hoped to duplicate nationally the early history of the Republican party—one election, a good showing; the next, victory. We reckoned without our Europe, which few Americans of that period envisaged as having any bearing on domestic politics. As the election of 1916 approached, the burning issue was not internal reform but foreign policy. The fires of war had melted and recombined all the elements of our thinking. Also we found, as religious revivalists had found long before, that it is hard to hold men at such a high emotional pitch for long periods. And the fleshpots lured many of our politicians back to the Republican fold. Nevertheless, the party kept intact a paper organization until the conventions of 1916. To the end, White was an active toiler in the vineyard, serving as national committeeman from Kansas, turning out copy, raising some of the money he needed for his own work.

Following the nomination of Justice Charles Evans Hughes by the Republican National Convention in 1916, White and most of the other Bull Moosers folded up their banners and went back to the Republican fold, perhaps wiser but certainly not sadder men. Their party had elected only a thimbleful of men to important office and a handful to unimportant office. But they had frightened politicians of all parties into action for reforms long overdue. Because of the Bull Moose rebellion the federal statute books and those of most of the states now included laws more advanced toward goals of social and industrial justice than responsible citizens had dreamed possible a decade before.

In a *Gazette* editorial, published November 4, 1912, on election evening, White wrote:

". . . The result of the election is an incident. The progressive principles, control of trusts, a scientific protective tariff, conservation of American resources for all the people, old age pensions, short hours for workers, a minimum wage for women, the right of labor to organize, workingmen's compensation—these measures have come before the American people; they are in the hearts of the people, and soon they will be upon American statute books. That is the chief thing. It is not important whether Roosevelt is elected or defeated. . . ."

The battle to create a new political party had been lost, but in losing it the war to create a finer social conscience in America had been won.

7. THE GROWING PHILOSOPHER

Although Mr. White made such gestures of appeasement toward the Socialists as I have revealed by excerpts from his editorials, he never accepted their doctrine as a whole—nor did he ever accept any other ready-made theory of government. A great many writers who began with him as muckrakers in the period of our great national awakening had gone the whole route and become disciples of Karl Marx. Some of them, conspicuously Upton Sinclair and Jack London, tried to entice White into their camp and expressed much irritation when he remained "bourgeois."

Expressed in academic terms, Mr. White had no fundamental philosophy except pragmatism. Neither perhaps has any other typical American—it is virtually an American creation. It has no other foundation than the firm one of adherence to goodness. Otherwise, in its lower lights it is merely the philosophy of getting things done, and in its higher ones the denial of the belief that there is any such thing as absolute truth. The universe grows and truth grows with it. What is truth in one generation, time, or set of circumstances may not be in another. Goodness and its practical attainment—that is the measure. Probably White never formulated all this—he and many other Americans think and act on such terms instinctively, not by the slow process of meditation.

He did, however, in this period form a working philosophy of life, government, and society upon which he acted all the rest of his life, and which ran through his editorials to the end. Let me follow that golden thread for a few pages.

As early as 1902, Mr. White expressed his belief that there seemed to be in the Christian world a wrong idea prevalent about the punishment for evil and the reward for good.

The truth is [he said] that there is no reward for goodness outside of goodness, and meanness operates its own contemporary hell. Heaven is the very act of doing right, hell is the evil itself.

Peace and happiness are as inseparable from kindness, thoughtfulness and truthfulness and simple courage as light and heat. Lying and malice and cowardice and selfishness are inseparable from woe, misery and remorse. . . . There is only one way to get to Heaven and that's to live it. Children should be taught that the important thing in life is character and not attainment. The way to attain is to be. Too often teachers put the cart before the horse and tell you that the way to be somebody or something is to attain, to get there. The fact is that it isn't at all in getting there—it's what you take there. It is not how far you go oward success that makes your happiness, but whether you go bravely or like a thief; whether you carry others or steal your way; whether you go with clean hands or smutty hands. That's what counts. The only thing in this world is character. And whatever there is in the next world can be nothing but character. Heaven and hell, here and hereafter, are in men's souls.

It is true that if you dance you must pay the fiddler. But it is also true that if you don't dance and sit and burn your heart out with unhealthy desires to dance, you will also pay the fiddler. Well, fiddlers are accurate accountants.

In 1903 he wrote an editorial, "Think It Over," in which he made a plea for fairness in all human relations, and especially for even-tempered kindness. He said:

. . . Decency breeds decency, meanness breeds meanness. Every man has his good side, his ideals, his human hopes and aspirations. Cultivate the best in your neighbors.

A kind word is about the only evidence of immortality there is in this world. . . . More grief is caused by things that are said than things that are done. Anger is a flame that burns quickly and kills . . . flares up and does fatal injury . . . the good people are divided in this world and the evil triumphs because of hatred caused by foolish tongues in anger.

Again he wrote:

"It is for the good one does in the world that he should be proud. Or for what he gives his fellows, not for what he gets from them . . ."

By instinct and at heart a reformer, even in his early days of party regularity, throughout his life he clung tenaciously to the eternal verities. About the only things he did not seek to improve were the Ten Commandments, the Golden Rule, Christ's Sermon on the Mount, Magna Charta, and the Bill of Rights in the American Constitution. These were the lodestars of his life. His Irish combativeness, his intelligent discontent, his ever undimmed idealism, drove him to talk and live reform all his useful life. And he knew the reform business from A to Izzard; understood the reformer's strengths and weaknesses.

. . . Reforms depend on no man; they are not a personal asset. They must come as a result of popular education, and unless the people are behind a reform, no matter how just it is, no matter how badly it may be needed, it will not come. A lot of reforms are frosted by reason of having got out too early in the spring.

Reformers get in a hurry too. The everlasting justice of the things they are after seem so plain to them that they cannot see why the people are cautious—and properly so. When the people get ready they will act, and although the reformers may sputter and fuss they won't hurry the people. The glacier can't beat the housefly to a given point, but the glacier stays. . . .

A great many good things are too good; and you can't impose justice on a people not ready for it any more easily than injustice can be imposed on them when they are tired of it. The government of this country will move along, about as the people wish it to move. The thing for reformers to do is not to get angry at the politicians and officers and lackeys in the service of the people, but to go to the people, arouse them, educate them, appeal to them in the name of justice and then wait—let your appeal soak in; if you're right, your seed will spring up.

There is a deadline over which reformers too often cross and become common scolds. A scold gets little done. The thing for reformers to do is to scold as little as possible; be as patient as possible and know that in the end right will prevail, and if the Lord can stand the injustice of this world you should not worry about it—just keep plugging away . . .

In a Memorial Day sermonette Mr. White wrote of the debt his generation owed the Union soldiers:

. . . We should cherish the liberty they died for; we should honor the government they saved, we should be proud of the civilization that sprang up as the soldiers fell.

And our gratitude, our pride, our honor, may be shown only by giving to those about us—our neighbors, in the simplest first-hand relations of life, the service that the hourly need requires, the kindness that smooths the roughest way. Duty is usefulness. And usefulness is happiness, and that is all there is in life. We may celebrate this day, and every man may celebrate every day best, by doing for others, what he would like to have them do for him. It is exceedingly simple, the problem of life, when one strips it of its flub dubs. It all resolves itself into the duty of the moment and the persistency of unfaltering kindness.

There is no larger good that justifies meanness and cruelty. The purpose of the meaning of life, does not require any great sacrifice to one's conscience. Life requires nothing but duty, and there is no duty save that it has in faith and kindness.

That is the lesson of the day, the day of ghosts, the day of old memories, the only sad holiday in our country's calendar.

In an editorial written about 1909, Mr. White discussed "The Success of Service" and expressed the belief that America was developing a new faith, "the religion of serviceable men":

"The reward the American people give to such success is remarkable in its impressiveness . . . man cannot help undergoing infinite processes of enlargement of his sympathies and mind and from the contact he has with people of high education and standing."

Again:

"What the world needs is a gospel of kindness and fellowship. . . . Men need faith in one another; classes need faith in each other. Nations need faith in the essential goodness of man. Lacking that faith, individuals riot and kill, classes exploit and hate, nations trespass and ravage . . ."

Once he wrote:

"The trouble with fighting the devil with fire, is that he not only has the most fire, but that he is fireproof. Moreover, he who touches pitch shall be defiled."

And:

"Liberalism is no outworn and inelastic creed, but an attitude toward life that can and must evaluate and absorb the good in every serious proposal for social advance."

Despite Mr. White's unquestioned faith in the people and his idealistic outlook on life he was realist enough to recognize the limitations of man in the mass. When an editorial colleague asked why the people will not learn some of the simple facts of life, Mr. White replied:

Chiefly, kind sir, because they can't. If people could learn, this
world would hit the millennium like Zazelle shot out of a cannon.
But they are impervious to ideas, immune to advice, and hardboiled on every front. They assimilate information, but not wisdom.
They get the facts, but shy from the truth. The wisdom of one generation is only partially preserved for the next . . .

So people don't learn. They can't learn. If people could only
learn we should be running interurbans to Heaven and back in ten
years.

This pessimistic comment, quite foreign to his customary expressions on the popular intelligence, suggests that in his realistic mind he appreciated the fact that you have to tell truths
over and over and over again before the people understand
them. You must interpret continuously, in a variety of ways, the
simple truths of ways of living and doing, preach kindliness and
neighborliness, honesty, fair dealing, and generosity, over and
over and over again, hoping bit by bit to fire the human intelligence and sharpen human vision. Such continuous interpretations and preachings would in time make an impression upon
the minds of men.

Writing about the need for and place of leadership in a
democracy, Mr. White said: "Until an idea commands the respect of high-class, stable, conscientious, unselfish men, it gets
nowhere." He held that in a democracy all kinds of men lead
the people—heroes, cowards, trimmers, wise men, stupid men,
men with charm and men with hearts, and even harsh, repellent
men. But each of them has some quality that makes for faith
from his followers. Bryan, he said, had it in oratory. That plus
courage and great personal charm made him a real leader in
American life. "With intellectual equipment, what a leader he
would have been!"

"Roosevelt had intelligence, courage, but he was not the
great emotional artist that Bryan is. Roosevelt had an engaging
personality—the gift of charm. Wilson had courage and wisdom,
but a repellent personality and his gift of expression through
the written word was unusual. Harding had more than anything else a charming personality, and so it goes.

"Leadership in a democracy has many roots to the heart of
the people."

In an editorial "Athens or Babylon," Mr. White quoted a correspondent who, traveling through Emporia, was impressed by the beauty of the town—its elm-bordered streets, flower-garlanded parks, paved streets, neat homes, well-lighted thoroughfares—and read what Emporia stood for:

"You seem to be trying to make a place where people can get the most out of life. You are not trying to assemble a vast number of people in one place to live wretchedly in what is called a hive of industry. You seem to be one of the few towns in the United States that is not striving to be a city at all. You seem to be trying to make a place where people may live in comfort and happiness. Your idea is beauty—beauty of life. . . . Your ideal is Athens, not Babylon."

Mr. White commented:

"That's about the size of it. Every town must choose between these ideals—the ideals of spiritual growth and prosperity, or the ideals of material growth and prosperity. Emporia is lined up with Athens."

In one of his lay sermons he wrote:

"The doctrine of the Golden Rule is saving humanity. Nothing can stop the terrific power of that dynamic creed from making over humanity. Organized religion is necessary to spread and to hold that creed in the heart of man. Hence the church is the cement of civilization. Any dogma is worse than no dogma. The passing of dogmas of the church which change with the centuries, are of no great importance. A deep essential faith in Jesus, the brotherhood of man and the fatherhood of God is a changeless creed that will redeem a lost world."

In the same vein, he wrote that many centuries ago a golden precept was given to the world, which received it not:

This precept obeyed would have brought a peace and prosperity to a world of order and a millennium to all mankind, but sin and selfishness flouted the precepts and brought instead, sorrow and suffering. Ceaseless wars have marked the centuries, and within our own day even, millions of men, some loved ones, have been sacrificed to war and billions of dollars worth of property has been destroyed and burdensome taxes levied, all because men forgot and trampled on the golden precept, "whatsoever ye would that others should do unto you, do ye even so unto them."

In his perceptive and discriminating editorials on morals he could at times be startling, as in one entitled "Right and Wrong":

"Murder seems wrong. It is the one inexcusable thing in the civilized world. Yet to impose that sixth of the Ten Commandments all over the earth would create, indeed in certain parts of the world has created, a very serious question."

He explained that in some savage regions, murder in the guise of head hunting had been arbitrarily prohibited. But this only brought on a social crisis because a young man contemplating marriage had to bring in the head of some human being. Thus, when he could no longer do so, he lived without marriage and flitted from lady to lady, creating a most serious problem in the tribe. In discussing marriage he admitted that in nine cases out of ten, it was the only relation between the sexes which makes for the stability of society, yet he pointed out that "the mother of Alexander Hamilton, America's greatest statesman, took up with Mr. Hamilton, the statesman's father, and lived with him without the benefit of clergy." This young woman, he explained, was married to an old man who abused her and who, under the laws of the island where she lived, could put her away without giving her a divorce. So when she fell in love with Hamilton she went to live with her lover and bore him a family of children. White concluded:

"America's most stable institutions have come to her through the genius of the child of that lawless marriage.

"So don't be too sure that you know the right from the wrong. 'Judge not that ye be not judged,' is a fairly wise precept."

Of "The Strength of the Humble," he said:

"The meek inherit the earth; not because they are meek but because being meek they are fair, and being fair and inspiring confidence, they bring home the bacon; which is a low way to estimate success, but a counter that fools can read, even if the wise sometimes have to raise other standards.

"Which is to say, it pays to be decent, and what is more it's a lot of fun."

In a similar spirit:

"There is nothing so grotesquely false in all the stupid doctrines that infest this planet as the theory that men are goaded to their highest endeavors by the money there is in it. The cheapest service the race knows is paid for in money."

Eventually, this philosophy of his tinged all his thinking; this for an extreme example in 1930:

The world cannot exist much longer half slave and half free, any more than America could a hundred years ago. We are too closely interrelated. Whether the freedom of the oppressed, underprivileged masses of the Far East shall come through the advance of Christianity or whether it shall come through economic pressure, no one knows and it is of little moment. The important thing is that this century will probably see the rise of the oppressed and downtrodden in the jungles and swamps and wildernesses of the East and the appearance of a middle class there. The stars in their courses are all set against the old pagan order.

This, he said, was "a hard nut to crack"—to determine whether economic salvation of the world will come through organized Christianity or whether organized Christianity inevitably "will penetrate the world that is rising out of slavery into self-respect."

Then came the declining years when good men soften. More and more he thought of human society on universal lines, less and less in terms of partisan politics—or any politics at all. Yet on certain occasions or in certain moods he could touch on politicians with his old vigor, his old geniality flavored with a dash of vitriol—but how much more broadly! As:

Politics is supposed to be a dull and dirty game, a scramble for place and power. So it is if one views it only from day to day and from month to month. But considered from decade to decade, from generation to generation, the dull and dirty game begins to assume a large form. It appears as a current in human affairs. Upon the waves movements ride and ideas translate themselves significantly. Tides are visible. Cross-currents bite into the flood and then slowly turn the tide to a new direction. It seems curiously mad—the whole rush, crash and twisting torrent. . . . Yet it is translatable into fairly simple terms. Politics seen in the large is the turmoil between ideas so great that men in the mass may not state them simply; so large that men wrestle only over the surface outcroppings . . . that move in the underconsciousness of mankind.

For thirty years—possibly for fifty—the politics of the world has been moved by a theory of biologists, who held that environment was more important than heredity in determining the life of the living creature. So all over the world political parties have been organized to affect the environment of humanity. The Liberal in England, the Continental Socialists, the American Progressives, the whole kit and kaboodle of uplifters, reformers, corn dancers and idealists, have been bent on redistributing the gross income of mankind so that the average man can live in better houses than ever before, eat more white bread and meat, wear better clothes, read more books, work shorter hours, ride in grander carriages, both public and private, and generally kick up more dust as he passes through this world in pilgrimage than the average man ever had produced in the world before. Parties rose and fell. Politicians lied like Ananias. Demagogues appeared, promised the voters the moon with plum jam on it and sold out or faded out or really chipped off here and there a chunk of the moon. And all because pale, cloistered scientists fifty or seventy-five years ago decided that environment was important in the human equation.

Now, the theory of environment is giving way to the theory that heredity is the governing cause in man's welfare and happiness. . . . Books are cascading out of the presses upholding the theory of heredity. Soon the controversy will have its political statesmen and then, bang, will go the old parties of the world and new issues will come. New liars will appear. Fresh spasms of yearning for the unattainable will rock our public institutions and we shall compromise on the attainable and be happy. And all because a group of biologists examining a multitude of microscopic exhibits, tucked safely under covers of the little glass, have agreed that life cells transmit characteristics immutably and that our fates are in our blood. The people won't know this. The politicians won't even dream of it. But the angels who watch our destiny and keep the sluices open in the irrigation ditches of life that we call the moving side of long events—these angels will know the truth and get their compensatory smiles from the knowledge.

And finally, almost like a valedictory:

"In a democracy the best statesmanship is patience; it is willing to take licking after licking, not caring for majorities, but caring chiefly for convincing the people, trusting the people when [they become] convinced to use such weapons as the movement provides to achieve their desire. We must learn to labor and to wait . . ."

WILLIAM ALLEN WHITE
1868–1944

MARY HATTON WHITE

DR. ALLEN WHITE

WILL WHITE AT KANSAS UNIVERSITY

SALLIE WHITE ABOUT 1900

WILL WHITE ABOUT 1900

WILL WHITE'S "EMPORIA STREET FAIR," 1898

WILL AND SALLIE WHITE, 1912

WILL, YOUNG BILL, AND MARY WHITE, 1914

THE GAZETTE OFFICE IN 1903

THE GAZETTE OFFICE AS IT LOOKS TODAY

WILL WHITE ON THE SIDEWALKS OF EMPORIA ABOUT 1880

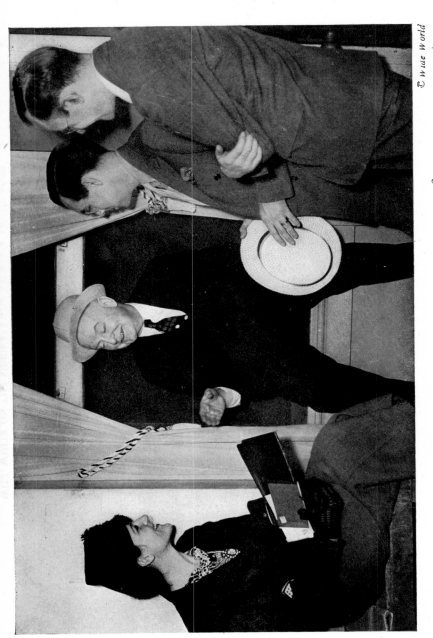

THE GREAT JOURNALIST BEING INTERVIEWED, 1936

© Wide World

©Wide World

WILL, SALLIE, AND YOUNG BILL UPON THE LATTER'S RETURN HOME AS A WAR
CORRESPONDENT, 1939

Courtesy LIFE

WILL WHITE AT HIS CLUTTERED DESK NEARLY READY TO SAY TO
HIS SECRETARY, "COME IN, MINNIE; WIPE MY NOSE AND WASH MY
FACE"

© Wide World

"I WILL LIFT UP MINE EYES UNTO THE HILLS, FROM WHENCE COMETH MY HELP."

WILL WHITE AT ESTES PARK

WILL AND SALLIE WHITE, ESTES PARK, SUMMER OF 1943

Courtesy LIFE

VETERAN MEMBERS OF THE STAFF ON THE GAZETTE OFFICE
STEPS WHO, GENTLY AND SORROWFULLY, CARRIED THEIR BELOVED
"BOSS" TO HIS LAST REST

8. MOSTLY THE *GAZETTE*

Let us go back now to those years when Theodore Roosevelt was president and when William Allen White's change of attitude was manifesting itself in a long burst of creative writing. This was his busiest and most fruitful period. He continued to maintain his interest in fiction and in that literary trade which has been called magazine reporting. He dropped his old connection with *McClure's* in the spring of 1906. That was at the time when John S. Phillips (McClure's able partner), Ida Tarbell, Lincoln Steffens, and Ray Stannard Baker departed in a bunch and transferred themselves to the *American*. For the next few years that magazine along with the *Outlook*, the *Independent*, the *North American Review*, and occasionally *Collier's*, all of which were following liberal policies, were his chief outlets for his more serious articles and character sketches.

He also contributed articles to the *Saturday Evening Post*, which moved Senator Albert J. Beveridge to propose him as the next Republican candidate for Senator from Kansas—the old nuisance again. As for fiction, he wrote for various magazines a set of short stories whose collective title when published in book form—*In Our Town*—describes them. Like almost any other ambitious American journalist with creative ability, he had in mind "the great American novel" and was building it in his mind, making notes for it.

The *Gazette*, in the meantime, was growing toward its perfected form. By 1904 he was beginning to delegate some of his functions. He made Walter E. Hughes—whom on his death Will was to eulogize as "my best friend"—business manager. Laura French became managing editor.

Even before the change in Mr. White's social, economic, and partisan outlook began to be indicated in his writings, he was cleaning up the advertising copy which he ran in the *Gazette*. He refused to take advertisements which were plainly fraudulent, such as those of the venereal disease quacks—this probably more from a sense of decency than from concern over

what they did to their victims. At that time even the most intelligent Americans were singularly ignorant of practical medicine. Through that very ignorance he continued for a while to
accept patent medicine advertisements. Then, being a thorough
businessman, he read the fine print that was buried deep down
in their contracts and found, in obscure clauses, provisions
which would have bound the *Gazette* to oppose any legislative
measures contrary to the interests of the party of the first part.
He recognized this for what it was—plain bribery. This happened before Mark Sullivan in the *Ladies' Home Journal* and
Samuel Hopkins Adams in *Collier's* had begun their attacks on
what Adams called "The Great American Fraud." Through
Mr. White's decision the *Gazette* lost thousands of dollars an-
nually, but it and he gained materially in the end.

However, he was not ahead of the procession on the question
of railroad passes for newspapermen. In the days when he broke
into the newspaper business, no Western editor, star reporter,
or business manager ever thought of paying for his railroad
transportation; neither, if he had any prominence at all, did his
family. Mr. White himself did all of his earlier traveling on
passes; and after 1896 he traveled farther and more often than
did most editors of that region.

Early in 1904, I had a severe bout with pneumonia with tu-
berculosis as a threatened aftermath. Mr. White, solicitous of
my health, told me that I should spend some months in a dry
climate and volunteered to get me a round trip railroad pass
good for a year or more to any place in Colorado, New Mexico,
or Arizona.

Two years later Mr. White commended Judge Thomas J.
Flannelly for returning passes which a railroad had given. He
said, "Flannelly regards passes for which he can give no honest
value received, as bribes. There is no question but that he is
right, a judge who takes a pass takes a bribe. The sooner this is
recognized the better it will be for the people."

By now, he himself was engaged in a hot fight against railroad rebates, which involved, paradoxically, an attempt to stop
the promiscuous issuance of passes in return for favors—not only
to public officials but to newspapermen—fighting, once more,
against his obvious personal interests. A "prep" school student,

I learned of this quite incidentally in the course of an episode which I shall always treasure in memory. In 1906, I was attending a boarding school near Philadelphia. I intended to visit Washington during the spring vacation, and wrote to White asking with juvenile innocence the favor of a note of introduction to President Theodore Roosevelt. He sent it, accompanied with a personal note in which he expressed the hope that I would "like the President. He is a good, brave, honest man." The first thing T.R. said to me was, "I have been wondering why you hadn't showed up because old Bill wrote me some time ago you were coming." He then went on to say something like this: "I wrote Bill asking him to stir things up with the Kansas delegation and get them back of me in the railroad rebate fight, and he broke the rake handle." That last puzzled me. He was referring to the fact that White had pressed so vigorously his Congressman, Charles S. Curtis, to back T.R.'s program, that Curtis had responded with a vicious attack on White in the newspapers, and in the personal feud the main issue was lost sight of completely. T.R.'s reference meant the handle of a "muck-rake." This became clear the next morning when I read the famous speech he delivered at the laying of the cornerstone of the House Office Building, a few hours after our visit, in which he put that word into the American language.

The acceptance and use of passes by newspapermen was a subsidy from corporations, nothing less, but when Congress and the legislatures began to criticize this practice, White, instead of fighting for its continuance as did many other editors, heartily supported its abolition by law.

White at this time also was devoting thought and effort to helping his regular advertisers plan their programs, even to help them write their copy. Sometimes against his own immediate interest he would advise merchants to cut down the amount of advertising space they were using. On merchants of the other sort he used unique devices to prove that advertising paid. For example, he displayed prominently an attractive picture of the more than ordinarily fine home of the leading merchant, who used a generous amount of bought space in the *Gazette*. The caption: "This is George Newman's home. He advertises in the *Gazette*." And then below it a line, "Go thou and do likewise."

He put in a great deal of work on the standards and practices of the merchants, his advertisers. For example, he initiated a campaign which he carried on for years, to prevent Emporia from becoming what he called a "cheap town"; as witness excerpts from an editorial:

. . . Having said which *The Gazette* now desires to talk to the buyers and the merchants of this town about another entirely different tendency, the tendency to go cheap, to sell, not seasonally once or twice a year, but day in and day out cheap stuff at cheap prices, promoting transactions which do neither side of the bargain any great good.

The Gazette has a larger interest in this community than that which goes with the immediate dollar. It is easy to grab off the immediate dollar, the quick, more or less dirty dollar in advertising, but *The Gazette* expects to be running here on something like the same management for the next quarter of a century. Hence we feel licensed to talk to advertisers and buyers alike and advise them to begin considering quality.

. . . Quality costs but it lasts, and in the end quality is cheaper than shoddy . . . Emporia cannot afford to go cheap. Somewhat it is the business of the merchants to see that it doesn't; but largely this is the business of the buyer. For every penny you save on cheap stuff your town sinks that much lower and your property is cut down that much. Cheap merchandising soon is reflected in vacant buildings. Vacant buildings bring lower rent. Lower rent brings lower real estate values. Up come the cloth signs and down goes the town.

ON THE EDITORIAL SIDE

He was to the end of his days a fighter and a formidable one, but with the "change" in 1901 or thereabout, particularly after he had whipped his financial problem, his methods of fighting changed, too. In his early days he fought with a bludgeon—the old-fashioned, vigorous, western style—picturesque denunciation, often far too personal. Now he began to abandon the bludgeon for the rapier, used his fund of ready humor to make an adversary ridiculous. He had infinite resource and like a good general the art of striking the enemy at an unexpected point. The time came eventually when there were few souls in Kansas hardy enough to invite controversy with him.

Fighter though he was and a self-appointed defender of fairness and justice, he occasionally ignored injustice and unfairness. For example, he paid no attention at first to the "black lists" which the Daughters of the American Revolution were distributing. Through these lists they were accusing nearly everyone in the country who held liberal views of being partners in a gigantic conspiracy to weaken our army and navy so that we would be a set-up for a Communist revolution. White held his peace until they put him on the list; then he carved them to bits.

More and more as time went on Mr. White ceased to bring personalities into his controversies. When he did, he seldom printed any name regardless of how much he disliked its owner's views or acts. A contrast in his treatment of men and their character is his valedictory on two unsuccessful competitors. This in 1900:

Editor Phillips, late editor, owner and publisher of the *Emporia Daily and Weekly Democrat,* has left for parts unknown, probably to the horror and consternation of the parts, and certainly for the general betterment of this community . . . homely truth demands that it be said of Phillips that he was, is and will be while he lives on this easy old earth, the most picturesque, unique, original, shameless, deliberate, conscienceless, malicious and indefatigable dead beat that ever pressed the sidewalk of Commercial street with his velvety feline feet. . . . He had the soft, self-deprecatory, insinuating voice of a cooing dove; and he glided into his machinations with the gentle, noiseless, hypnotic sinuosity of a rubber-tired rattlesnake. He was as bland as a sunrise and as deadly as a pestilence.
. . . Earth was a wilderness of suckers for him. He put the marks of his easy touch all over the town and when advertisers were coy he cut their advertisements from other papers, charged up the account, waited till the store keeper was out and traded out the amount of his account and twice as much besides.
. . . Poor old Phillips, he has left us. We may never look upon his like again—thank Heaven—until the sulphurous blazes of perdition illuminate the job lot in the deepest part of the seventh pit.

This in 1909:

There is something sad in the announcement of the *Emporia Daily Journal* that it has printed its "last copy." Because, on the whole, Emporia has never had a more sincere, conscientious attempt to establish an independent, uncontrolled daily newspaper than this. . . . He has fought a manly fight, and in so far as one wins who maintains his integrity, he has won. . . . He was talked into a foolish venture by men with axes to grind. They found an honest man, and they left him to find out their perfidy. But what an old story this all is in this profession. No American town, north, south, east, or west, is too large—or unfortunately too small—to have this very tragedy enacted. Every newspaper, in the nature of things, makes enemies. To tell the truth it must make enemies. But its enemies are often the best things about a newspaper. They are its assets. They are its chief source of strength in a town.

. . . in printing his valedictory, Editor Mickey, of the *Emporia Daily Journal*, quits with the satisfaction that he is no one's tool; that no one has controlled him; that he has been a man from the beginning to the end.

He will continue to run a weekly—a clean, decent, reliable weekly —and he should have the town's support.

One member of the *Gazette* force during these years who deserves special mention was Walt Mason, whose "prose poems" —rhymes run without division of lines and stanzas—became a delight to millions of Americans. Mason, an able journalist and prolific writer, had unsuccessfully fought the demon rum for years. Then when he was down for the last count and almost out, he attached himself to the *Gazette* force. With the help of its patient, tolerant, kindly, and helpful editor he won his fight. He wrote news items, editorials galore, heads, read copy and proof, did editorial chores.

At that time the paper ran daily, in bold-faced type and bordered with asterisks, a brief but important local news story, and in the same style at the head of another column a similar Associated Press story. There was no sufficiently important local news story one Saturday in 1907, so Mr. Mason as a substitute wrote a short "prose poem" which exhorted the readers to attend church the next day. Miss Laura French, city editor, recognized the copy as poetry and defying a long-standing official rule that the *Gazette* never was to publish any homemade verse, ran it.

Mr. White had made this rule, one of the few absolute orders he ever gave, in order to close the floodgates against that obituary verse with which rural bards used to deluge country news-papers in those days. When Emporians liked this effort and said so in large numbers, the boss forgave Miss French and made an exception of Walt Mason, who turned out more and more verse of this genre. It was clipped so profusely by *Gazette* exchanges that presently, and with White's generous consent, a newspaper syndicate took the feature over—to the author's great financial advantage.

By the time T.R. had entered into the swing of his second term Mr. White's notoriety of eight years before had become real fame—with the nuisances and temptations that surround it. More and more trips to Washington, more and more ap-peals from societies to improve the condition of the world, ask-ing him to serve as an officer, committeeman, adviser. Most of these he refused. But even the refusals took time. His support of T.R. and T.R.'s policies kept White running to Washington. Even known intimacy with the President brought its special obligations.

After T.R. left the White House in March, 1909, he got out from under the weight of these burdens for a few months by taking his family, wife, mother, and two children to Europe on that first trip abroad, mentioned before. The proof that he had trained and welded together as a working unit an excellent staff is an editorial which he wrote in September, 1909, upon the family's return. After remarking that before he got down to work again it would be necessary for him to clean up three cubic feet of accumulated mail, he went on:

But it is only just to the men and women who have been run-ning the *Gazette* for the past five months to say that they have been running it without strings—just as they would have run it if they had owned it. They were left no instructions, no general orders—no limitations. And they have conducted the paper as nearly in the line of absolute honesty as it is possible to conduct any human business. They have made a most interesting paper—and it represented their idea of what a newspaper should be . . . on the whole it was a more entertaining and enjoyable paper than it would have been if the owner had been here. Local stories of a most delicate nature were handled with the most admirable taste. The dead were hon-orably mentioned. The brides were sent on their way rejoicing;

politics was left hanging on the clothesline to bleach in the wind, and subscriptions are better and the advertising patronage stronger than it was last fall. If ever men and women were faithful to a trust it is these men and women who have been running the *Gazette* the spring past and the summer passing; and the trust they were loyal to was their own conscience, and their own judgment. They were true to themselves—and to everyone else.

Going back a few months we find that the year 1909, in which Taft was inaugurated, marked another turning point in his intellectual and spiritual history. During the years when Theodore Roosevelt was trust-busting and cudgeling "malefactors of great wealth," White had almost abandoned the short story as a literary form and was devoting his spare time to his first full-length novel, *A Certain Rich Man*. He delivered the final manuscript just before he sailed for Europe.

This book is still in print even though, with the forms and idioms of fiction so changed, it has now a faintly antique air. But again Will White broke ground. American fiction had already discovered the small town, but no one before him had explored what the academic would call its sociology, and showed its seamy side. That was probably his intention when he conceived his novel—that and the desire to show how one of Theodore Roosevelt's "malefactors of great wealth" got that way. Possibly, also, his unconscious mind was saying all the time, "But for the grace of God there goes William Allen White."

Novelists tend to put a bit of themselves into characters which interest them. In spots his villain-hero—John Barclay—seems to be a conscious replica of the author, as in his delight in music, his trait of drawing thought and creation from it.

The bond between Barclay and his mother may have been conscious or unconscious self-delineation. The resemblance between young John Barclay, before greed became his ruling passion, and what the young Will White must have been undoubtedly was wholly unconscious. The author's personality flashes into this character again and again—most notably in the subtlety of some of John Barclay's mental processes.

It is easy, a third of a century later, to criticize this novel. As is common with men whose fiction is the by-product of an active life concerned with practical affairs—Disraeli for example—he

editorializes much of the thought which a full-time novelist
would have digested and recreated into a significant episode or
a brief, revealing saying in the mouth of some character. The
transformation of John Barclay as the result of a tragedy for
which his greed stood responsible is too abrupt to be entirely
credible. Admit all that, and the book is still a vital work.

If, with his first successes in fiction, White had dropped journalism, gone into himself, spent his bored leisure in smelting
his impressions of life until they came out of the retort pure
gold, no one can even guess how far he might have gone as a
fictionist. But as events worked out, this, except for *In the Heart
of a Fool* published nine years later, was his last important piece
of fiction.

The election of Taft and his gradual abandonment of Roosevelt's policies threw White again into the whirlpool of politics.
He who had taken "monastic vows" against holding public office found himself forced by conscience and circumstance to go
to national conventions, to help mold and write national platforms, to participate in a fight for a new party. Liberal causes,
real and living personalities, engaged his attention more and
more.

It was for the best. He was to become "The Sage of Emporia." His journalistic writings were to grow with his interests
until the best of them crossed the thin line between journalism and permanent literature. We have had many fine novelists,
but we have had no journalist who so caught the best spirit of
his times and turned it into lasting literature as did Will White.

Part Three

THE FRUITION
1916—1944

1. THE FRUITION

THE CAREER of William Allen White up to the period when we entered the First World War might have been planned by a master architect. Now, in his early forties, he owned a highly successful newspaper in the town of his birth, which he loved above any other, and a comfortable, attractive home, presided over by a most gracious, intelligent, and charming woman. In this setting, into which he fitted perfectly, he lived a life that was symbolic of the best and strongest in Americanism, a man who knew the great world but was profoundly content with creating a rich life in a small community.

The home which the Whites had bought out of his first literary earnings was a formidable mid-Victorian mansion built by a pioneer cattle king, of red stone from the same formation as that tourist's heaven, the Garden of the Gods. A Kansas City architect helped them to redesign this mournful anachronism into a setting harmonious with their cultivation, good taste, and wide interests. Success never robbed them of their human quality of neighborliness. As though symbolically, they never fenced their yard, and the latchstring of the house was an easy one. By now he was the most eminent citizen of Kansas and this house a place of pilgrimage for some of the most distinguished people of the United States. But the poor and humble visited it on the same terms. The Whites knew no such thing as looking up to people or looking down on them.

The Whites' two children, Bill and Mary, who were in their teens, were attending public schools in Emporia and during the summers running wild in Estes Park. Their young friends, their ponies, dogs, and cats were all over the White home. White's mother's home stood next door to his. His physical and mental vigor were at their topmost point; life was an inspiration to him. He was enjoying to the fullest "the royal American privilege of living and dying in a country-town, running a newspaper, saying what we please, when we please, how we please and to whom we please."

His unassuming democracy, his engaging personality, his fairness, helpfulness, and generosity, had endeared him to the townspeople, and his national fame impressed them. But still they could not wholly understand how Will White, who breathed the same air, bought the same groceries and patronized the same tailor as they did, and merely recorded their comings and goings, their ideas, and sometimes his own far-fetched or half-baked ones, had gained such recognition. They still referred to him half pridefully, half deprecatingly; but they did love to show him off. Emporians who entertained out-of-town friends or relatives took them to the *Gazette* office to meet him. After the introductions he might say, "Now after you have seen Wild Tom [a famous champion Hereford bull] at Sunny Slope, you will have seen Emporia's two prize exhibits." Although he was on friendly terms with everyone in the county and boasted that when he spoke to them he could address by their first names over half of Emporia's population, nearly all of his fellow citizens addressed him as "Mr. White" or referred to him by the name by which the nation knew him, William Allen White. Only a few men whose innards were lined with brass sought to give an impression of intimacy and called him Old Bill White or just Bill. His few really close friends called him Will. In the early period of the *Gazette,* most members of the staff referred to him affectionately as Father White. But to the later generation he was simply "Boss." Both terms fitted the man, for there was in him the touch of the patriarch—sound in judgment, wise in counsel, patient in trouble, understandingly kind—and no one who worked in that shop doubted who was running it. Conversely he had a tendency to be paternalistic, but the majority of his employees who were most critical of this tendency of his were those who were the recipients of his especial benevolence.

During the period now under consideration—the eve of the First World War and of the great transformation in American outlook—White was molding the *Gazette* into its final form. He was still to make some changes, demanded by modern conditions, both in the product and in the organization that turned it out. For example, after years of struggle between personal taste and public demand he yielded to the pleadings of his staff and admitted comic strips. Not that he had any snobbish aversion to that diversion of the young and intellectually immature. It was only that he could use the space, he felt, to better advantage. But the spirit and working methods of the newspaper did not change essentially during the last quarter-century of its owner's life. In short, when the shot at Sarajevo called him, as it called so many others, to wider fields of thought and action, he had learned his trade of country editor and publisher.

One who worked for him or with him in those days thinks of him first not as a power in the land but as the friendly manager of a happy little sheet in a country town. His patience with the staff of the *Gazette* is a tradition in Kansas journalism. He had no need for demanding loyalty from them; he earned it. They stood by him because he stood by them. Whenever they got the paper into trouble, he backed them up. If the mistake was sheer carelessness, he called attention to it without any upbraiding. If it was ignorance, he enlightened the culprit—and bore the brunt of kicks and insulting letters. Once a canoe powered by a professor of the State Teachers College was swept over the dam at Soden's Mills on the Cottonwood River. The *Gazette* printed the story; the professor came back with a letter impugning its accuracy. Mr. White printed the letter and answered it in a footnote. The reporter, he said, had a good record for accuracy, and the information came from a reliable eyewitness whose version the *Gazette* preferred to that of a professor "who didn't have sense enough to keep out of a canoe when the river was up."

As the best American university in the nineteenth century was "a log hut, with only a simple bench, Mark Hopkins on one end" and a student at the other, the best American school of journalism in the twentieth was William Allen White and a cub reporter sitting side by side at a pine table. He taught his student how to see "the story"—the essential fact—in any event, small or large, how to develop it, in case it was important, by perceiving and recording day by day new phases and features, how to search out its larger meaning. He coached him in writing clearly and concisely, in avoiding stock phrases, and, still more, stock attitudes of mind. Above all, he tried to blow up to a flame any spark of humor or imagination he had discovered in his cub's mind.

The *Gazette Style Book* warned the staff that "Reporters may be fired for faking news stories. Never guess—verify! Make every story answer who? what? when? where? why? and how?" Even with such standards and practices, false tips received through the mail or lies deliberately fed to reporters sometimes deceived the *Gazette* as they do all newspapers. Touching on this subject in print, Mr. White mentioned a newspaper in a near-by town which had in good faith published the notice of a wedding which never took place. His attention having been called to the error—probably most forcibly—the editor apologized to the alleged bride and bridegroom and offered a cash reward for information as to the identity of his deceiver.

"When an editor gets stung like this (and we all get stung once in a while)," he commented, "he crawls on his tum-tum until the buttons pop off his vest like the report of a machine gun. What a curious business this is—selling rumors and capitalizing hypotheses, and betting on the truth with the odds against us. It's a wonder that we have even the rudimentary respect of a civilized world—we editors—and maybe we don't. Maybe it's all fear and contempt camouflaged by politeness!"

The *Gazette Style Book,* revised from time to time to cover new horrors which his latest generation of cub reporters had uncovered, was the office Bible. No flaw in the *Gazette* pained him more than violation of its precepts.

Under "Don'ts" it told the staff:

. . . Don't split infinitives. If you don't know an infinitive when you see it, look up the definition.

Don't use these words:

Very. (If you must use this word, the Boss says to make it read "damn." Then the copy reader will be sure to spot it and kill it.)

Quite, rather, somewhat, some, a number of (meaning several, few or many).

. . . Do not write:

"At the present time," for now.

"In the near future," for soon.

"Reports" or "states" for finds or says.

And never, never "family have" or "crowd have" or "sorority have" or "committee have," for has.

"Make their home" for live.

. . . "Passed away" for died.

"At death's door" or "very low" for seriously sick or critically ill.

"On account of" or "due to" or "owing to" for because.

. . . Cut out "proceeded in a body" and "marched in a body"— they went.

. . . Do not say "local" when referring to an Emporia person or institution, at least not more than once a year. Use the word "thus" with the same discretion.

Do not use the word "professor" except in referring to a corn doctor, a stage character, magician, etc.

Never use "Hon." or "city dads" or "city fathers"; or "canine" for a dog.

. . . The word "lady" does not go in the Gazette except when you refer to a woman in police court and such like stories. Same applies to "gent."

. . . Don't say "proceeded to the dining room" or "repaired to the spot"—they went.

. . . Don't say "accepted a position"; say "has a position" or better still, "a job."

. . . "Occur" and "take place": Events occur by accident, and take place by design. Weddings, parties, sports events take place, automobile accidents occur.

Do not say one autoist drove his car into another. Say the two cars collided, or ran together. It is not the purpose of the news story to place blame.

. . . Complex spelling; make it simple, spell it program, cigaret, quartet, sextet, duet, etc.

Be sparing, on general principles, in the use of adverbs and adjectives.

Avoid superfluous words; say "Ten men were present" instead of "There were 10 men present." . . .

One year when a group of Emporia schoolboys left to take gainful jobs in Colorado during the summer, the Gazette ran the story and their names. One proud mother telephoned next day to the Gazette to say that her precious offspring was merely going for a vacation. The Gazette published a mild retraction, but above it giggled a headline that Mr. White wrote. It read: "He Will Not Work."

Rolla Clymer, the *Gazette's* star reporter for several years from 1910 on and now publisher of the *El Dorado Times,* wrote when Mr. White died:

[He] possessed such marvelous power of personality that even the smallest of his daily acts was not commonplace. His relationships were so vast and of such compelling interest, the body of his contacts have been inextricably woven into the state's legend.

In the days of his active editorship, he was accustomed to "running around through the office in his shirtsleeves." This meant that he had a hand everywhere, suggestions for timely news stories, interpolation of copy here and there with some twist of his own that raised ordinary reporting to a high level, apt headlines that spoke volumes. During the years that he and Walt Mason were actively associated together, the Emporia *Gazette* was the best-edited, most interesting paper day after day that this deponent ever saw—large or small. Both White and Mason occasionally wrote display heads in rhyme, main lines and sub-decks making full sense with a jingle. We have never seen this done in any other newspaper office before or since.

While he was kind and helpful to his employees—just a big buddy on the staff—he had the knack of inflicting a rebuke which one never forgot. One time, this deponent was "holding copy" for a white-sale advertisement and ignorantly mispronounced the word, "chemise." Mr. White heard him, looked up quickly and said, *"Chemise, chemise.* You are a strong young man. Butt your head into that wall."

One of my old friends, Calvin Lambert, of Emporia, who served as reporter or city editor of the *Gazette* for seventeen years, in sending me some sidelights on Mr. White wrote that he hoped they would help develop the "human side of the best boss I ever knew."

In his notes, Mr. Lambert said that for many years Mr. White prohibited smoking in the office but later canceled the rule by overlooking it.

He often said he hated whiskey because it had killed several of his best friends. I don't believe he ever smoked and I never saw liquor in his home. He didn't fish nor hunt and would not drive an auto. He seemed very fond of young people and often after the paper was out, he would come into the newsroom, gather up the entire force and take us over to a drug store for "cokes." He didn't care for athletics. I never saw him at a ball game, but he permitted us to have a sports page, even on days when the *Gazette* ran only six pages.

If there was anything wrong in his relationship with the staff it was that he trusted us almost too far, seldom read our copy before it went to the printer and asked for proofs only when he was interested in the story. Sometimes, though, he exploded. We always took him the first paper off the press and he glanced at the headlines. Once in a while, he would see a glaring mistake or read a story in which he didn't like the angle we had taken. Then he would storm into the news office and in a voice that made us quake, yell "Stop the press!" We'd stop it, make the corrections and bring the paper to him. Usually, he would take us over for "cokes" to soothe our feelings.

It always seemed to the staff that Mr. White's fear of committing libel in the *Gazette* verged on the morbid. He had reason, however. In termtime, droves of undergraduates from the College of Emporia and State Teachers College tramped through the office, looking for part-time jobs. Perhaps because he remembered his own beginnings he found it difficult to say no to them. What with these and the promising young cubs he was training, the *Gazette* had a surplus of human material which didn't always know intellectual pabulum from journalistic dynamite. In later years, he carried libel insurance. But he kept that fact secret from the news staff for fear that the reporters would get careless if they knew that the paper was protected. Even the insurance did not quite ease his mind; and so the police reporters overworked the word "alleged."

But libel, like lightning, always strikes in an unexpected place. It was one of his experienced reporters who gave him his greatest scare. To a story of a bank robbery in Illinois committed by a gang in a green car, he carelessly hooked up the tag end of a story about a man who often visited Emporia in a green car. The result was an odd but plain hint that this upright citizen had committed the crime. Promptly the innocent victim came into the shop announcing to all and sundry that he had hired a lawyer and was going to bankrupt the filthy sheet with a libel suit for big damages. White, pale around the gills, managed to force a smile as he asked the visitor into his private office and gave him a fatherly talk. It had happened, he said, and he regretted it as much as anyone. He would do anything he could by way of retraction. But as for court action—think! And he threw all his eloquence into a description of the ghastly ordeal which a plaintiff in a libel suit must face when he came into court. Fifteen minutes later the city room, waiting with bated breath beside silent typewriters, saw the two men emerge smiling, saw them shake hands at the door, and sighed with relief. White came back to the city room trembling. "Gosh, that was a narrow squeak!" he gasped. "He'd have had us dead to rights if he'd sued. Where's ——?" he added in a steely tone, naming the reporter who wrote the story. Every brave man has his Achilles' heel. White's was libel suits.

Relatively indifferent to his own personal appearance, he seemed to take pride in having a spruce staff. Perhaps memories of the old Bohemian days in journalism, when the city editor, sending a reporter to interview a magnate or a social leader, had to search the city room for a man with a clean collar, inspired him in that. A sloppily dressed reporter was a poor advertisement for the paper. He never admonished the staff in this regard, but when one of them appeared with a new dress, suit, hat, or tie, he was likely to notice it and to remark on it pleasantly. By the same token, when he instructed a green cub about to report a lecture or public meeting, he always added, "Notice his clothes, especially if there's anything unusual about them. And get that into your story."

He was, of course, the *Gazette's* own best reporter, as Mrs. White was its best tipster for events in Emporia. But in his heart, then and always, he was an editorial writer, concerned less with fact than with interpretation. So he encouraged all members of the staff to write editorials for his page. He never butchered their copy—"The worst form of commercialized vice is mental prostitution," he said once. But he would often throw in one or two filling phrases or add an effective snapper at the end. When other newspapers reprinted any such editorial, he took the clipping to the writer and stood by enjoying his satisfied expression. He always found a way to reward good work— sometimes cash, sometimes a shy word of approval which meant more than a whole oration from any other man.

In this period, he was still pounding out his own copy on his old, blind, rickety typewriter. Then writer's cramp began to trouble him and he took perforce to dictation. He would talk off his editorial at white heat, slash it all to pieces in the typewritten transcript, butcher it again in the galley proof. In the case for his glasses he always carried a little card on which he jotted down in short phrases or even single words his ideas for editorials as they sprang into his mind.

The *Gazette* had few sacred cows. There was one conspicuous example, however: the position which Arthur Capper, White's lifelong friend, might take on any political question. White believed without reservation in Capper's integrity and high sense of public service, and admired his independence. Hence members of the staff learned to approach the subject of Capper with care and discretion.

In keeping with his preachments on keeping one's temper, White seldom lost his. Once it happened when he heard a reporter swear at a woman, a fellow member of the staff, and once again when a county official whom the *Gazette* had been taking to task came into the office and began to abuse the editor. Suddenly White's jaw set. The visitor was about as big as Jess Willard. But when the little plump editor jumped up, took him by the ear, and marched him to the outer door, he was so surprised, and probably so awed by the fiery courage of the man, that he walked along like a dog on a chain. As long as he held office, he never entered the *Gazette* again.

Even before he worked out a fair, enlightened policy toward the occasional conflicts between the advertisers and his readers, he was publishing the kind of newspaper that is described by the motto which now decorates the masthead of the *New York Times:* "All the news that's fit to print." What news is fit to print and what unfit? There must be a line somewhere between suppressing news which should be printed if the reader is to know the flaws in his community and his nation, and the promiscuous publication of news which will make the reader's eyes pop out but which also will break hearts and ruin lives. Censors of books and motion pictures have begun to learn that discriminating between decency and indecency is a matter of art, not of set rules. Our courts are more and more recognizing that principle.

So it is with news that's fit to print. If White had written or read in proof every line that appeared in the *Gazette,* the question could have been left to his own subtle good taste in human conduct. But for an editor who so often roamed abroad, that was manifestly impossible. He must have certain broad rules for the staff.

He worked these out over the years. He never collated and printed them, as he did the rules in the stylebook, but simply imparted them to his executives and the cub reporters whom he was training, until they became part of the office tradition.

Perhaps the first of these had to do with juvenile delinquents. Except in most serious cases—which did not occur once in a decade in Emporia—the name of a child offender, even the offense itself, did not appear in the *Gazette.* That would not seem a very advanced policy today. But this was years before sociologists, criminologists, and enlightened chiefs of police began looking into the relationship between juvenile delinquency and criminal careers, and educating the decent newspapers. In the period when he established his own policy, journals which still considered themselves models of taste and propriety were printing the name and offenses of little boys along with those of hardened adult criminals. In going against this policy, White was almost a pioneer.

Divorces—this was a special problem in a state with liberal divorce laws. The press might print the testimony in even the most scandalous case. And of course the more highly flavored this testimony, the better news it seemed to most editors. With his novelist's divination, the happily married Will White perceived the agonies of heart and soul which precede any divorce, and felt that publishing the details served no useful public purpose. When a suit was filed, the *Gazette* ignored it, because a reconciliation was always possible. If the divorce was granted, there appeared an item as brief as a birth notice. This cleared him of the accusation of suppressing the news. Further, suppression of any mention of a divorce might encourage such frauds as deliberate bigamy; and finally, any sensible couple would want the bare fact known, if only to avoid social embarrassment. It goes without saying that the *Gazette* never ran gossipy hints about impending scandal.

White early in his *Gazette* career made another rule which, as so often happened, cut slightly into his revenues. He announced that the *Gazette* would no longer accept "any more advertising of the fellow who gives public notice of his refusal to pay his wife's bills. We have been nursing a grudge on him for several years . . . the court rather than the newspaper is the place to air such differences. We don't want the money of the poor devil with the fool wife and we don't want the money of a tightwad husband with a good wife so nix after today on the item from the husband who refuses to pay his wife's bills."

As early as 1903, he jarred some of his conservative-minded readers by giving notice that the newspaper would print no more resolutions of respect evoked by the death of more or less prominent citizens. And also "No more cards of thanks will be printed in this paper at any price. They are in wretched bad taste . . . Don't advertise your gratitude and sorrow. Only cheap things are advertised."

When physicians drafted to sit on insanity cases decided that the subject of inquiry should be sent to an asylum, his relatives and friends tended to boycott them. The doctors laid their grievance before Mr. White. He saw the point, knew from experience the danger of leaving a "harmless lunatic" loose in the community, and agreed to suppress their names in all such stories. Later, in the period of the great depression, the number of insanity hearings increased alarmingly. Thereupon the *Gazette* stopped publishing the fact that the patient had been committed to an asylum, and merely named the town to which he had been taken.

There were always odd special instances which fitted no rules, and on which White himself had to decide. One of them, which has its humorous aspect, happened late in his career. In 1936 and 1937, a false business revival followed the long depression. People began to buy automobiles again. In a town of Emporia's size, the fact that Bill Smith had bought a new car constituted news. Suddenly the dealers, who under normal conditions encouraged the publication of such news items, descended upon Mr. White with the complaint that the stories were ruining their sales. Their publication brought a flood of dunning letters from merchant creditors of the new car purchasers and frightened off similar prospects of the car dealers. White took their complaint under advisement and, acting contrary to his own immediate interests as usual, ordered stories of this kind out of the paper.

In a town as small as Emporia, and in a prohibition state, a conviction in police court on a drunk and disorderly charge was news. After he established his own code of journalistic ethics, White never published news of a first conviction on this or any other petty charge. He allowed any man or woman one slip. But, as he looked at it, the man who filled up with whisky and then made a fool of himself was on the way to becoming a public charge and "publicity is the only way to keep him straight."

"On his second offense, no matter how high or low he is, his name goes in . . . when the drunks come around asking us to think of their wives and children, or their sick mothers or poor fathers, we always tell them to remember they had fair warning and if their fathers and mothers and wives and children are nothing to them before taking, they are nothing to us after taking."

All these years, as he thought out in bursts the ideal country-town newspaper, he took the readers of the *Gazette* into his confidence. Gathered into a volume—as someday they may be—these wise observations would make a useful book for any school of journalism. Because he was essentially a moralist, they are often wisest when they deal with the ethics of the craft. Here are a few selections:

Concerning the duty of a newspaper to its community:

It is like the chief end of man—to serve its subscribers and enjoy them forever. . . . A newspaper is [a matter of public concern] as much as the street car, the telephone and the gas plant, and all the other municipal utilities.

An editor is really a trustee, entitled to his profits if they are clean and decent . . . but not entitled to take his profit at the community's loss. Unless he can give the public some valuable things —information, guidance or entertainment—he has no right to his profits. The newspaper is certainly a public utility.

The editorial policy of a successful newspaper should combine three things—intelligence, courage and kindness. If I were making a one-sentence formula for a newspaper it would be like this: Think straight, act bravely and remember the other fellow has his side.

He had heard some fantastic and invidious rumors about his own personality and doings when he wrote good-naturedly:

An editor with any philosophy in him will grin and let it go at that . . . it all comes out in the wash . . . generally the bad stories about a man have their foundations in the hearts of those who hate him. Only the good things are the true things. And the temptation to tell good lies is not powerful. . . . So in considering the kind of man your neighbor is, gather the good stories, discount the bad ones ninety per cent and take fifty off, and you will have him sized up about right.

Generally speaking, a newspaper, if it be worthy of the name, reflects a man. One man may write but a small part of it, but . . . when you know the editor of a paper, how it "sounds like him!" You can hear his voice, see his smile, chuckle with him or listen to the blast of his bazook. The newspaper that doesn't in some way reflect a man's personality, isn't much of a paper, and if it isn't much of a paper, it does its town no good.

A newspaper . . . should be judged as a man should be judged; largely and on the whole. No man lives a perfect life; no editor prints a perfect paper . . . A newspaper is bound to make mistakes; in getting news it must necessarily take hearsay. But if, in the long run and in the main . . . a paper stands for decency, for honest thinking and clean living, if it speaks fair for those who are trying to do good, and condemns sneaks and cheats and low persons, that is a good paper.

Politics, White once wrote, interests nine out of ten readers only in campaign time. But politicians have egged editors on to overplay political copy—

Politicians fancy that newspapers make public sentiment. They do not make public sentiment at all—even locally. They merely voice sentiment already made; sometimes newspapers organize it, give [it] leadership . . . but that is all. They create no sentiment. When a politician thinks that by starting a newspaper he will help himself in politics, that politician is pounding sand in a rat hole . . . A newspaper generally hurts a politician; for if he controls it the people know it, and the mistakes of the newspaper—which are just ordinary human mistakes—are charged to the politician.

That habit of thinking on paper, of recording the stages through which he argued himself pro and con until he reached a sound and permanent conclusion, has given William Allen White an undeserved reputation for inconsistency. Still, he was half Irish and as such a creature of moods. Here are two contrasting moods inspired by reflections on journalism. The first is notable as one of the few instances of White's boasting—even, as here, by inference:

The *Gazette* [is] printed in a community where there are 13,000 people, without a pauper, with every man at work; without a millionaire; with as many telephones as there are homes, with as many automobiles as there are families; as many schools as the children need, as many books in the library as the public will read; with a municipal band, a bathtub in nearly every house; and the people in our jails came into town to get there, and we haven't an able-bodied person in the poorhouse.
That's the kind of town a paper should strive for.

But when he sat down to write "Our Annual Grouch," the title described his mood that day toward Emporia, the newspaper business, and his own corner in it:

The *Gazette* is no better than most newspapers and not so good as some, but—the business, the newspaper business—what an everlasting joke it is! . . .
Some day when the time comes we propose to get out a special edition, and for once in a long and useless career . . . to tell how many dollars the various busted fair associations owe us for advertising which was never paid; how many men the *Gazette* has supported for office who went around declaring that the *Gazette* did them more harm than good; how many times we have got behind the town . . . wasted our time and space in good black ink and white paper and in the end had a lot of ivory-handled chumps hold a lodge of sorrow over a typographical error and moan about the fact that the *Gazette* never does get anything right.
Some day, some blessed day before the mists are cleared away, we hope to be able to print a paper that will tell the truth about quack preachers and all the gorgeous hypocrisy of the infernal, mechanical, clap-trap done in the name of the Lord. Heaven knows the Gazette

is ashamed of its various piano contests, and we hope we will have the moral courage to turn down the alluring temptation the next time it comes around. But we do hate to see a piano contest run in the name of religion, and sometime we are going to take a day off and say so. And while we are saying it we are going to print the truth about at least one phase of the woman question. People are getting tired of the use of the phrase "white slave" as applied to some shameless old hen who gets caught in a commercial liaison with a man, who has been sending a lot of men to jail, and establishing a kind of double standard in favor of the woman . . . the "weemin" in some of the white slave cases that have come up recently should go to jail also—that is, if anyone should go to jail, which is a debatable question. The *Gazette* is nearly ready to cut out the use of the words "white slave" altogether.

That is about all; it is at least enough. Otherwise this is a pretty decent universe. Men pay their debts, love their wives, are fair with their neighbors and serve the Lord in a reasonably acceptable fashion. Most institutions are as good as the people that live under them.

So with these few remarks, and hoping this will find you the same, we remain yours truly until death do us part and by way of postscript will say this, that having it out of our system we feel a lot better.

Appropriately, a **William Allen White School of Journalism and Public Information** has been created by his Alma Mater, the University of Kansas. The university has assigned a building for this purpose and will provide the faculty for the school. The William Allen White Foundation is enlisting the co-operation of journalists and leaders in the radio, television, motion picture and book publishing fields for the purpose of providing instruction in all these arts of communication. The White School will place emphasis upon the broad and basic fundamentals of the truly educated man and woman. In this the university only follows its most distinguished alumnus when he wrote:

Newspapermen don't know enough. They jump into the game half ready.

The best preparation for a newspaperman would be a college education—as highly cultural as possible; classical insofar as his four years' time will allow, with a lot of energy devoted to science and great emphasis put on English, sociology and economics. A man can't get enough college education to spoil him in the newspaper business if he has any sense, and if he hasn't any sense, he doesn't belong in the business . . .

With the shrewd business instinct which some Emporians denied him, White, in 1899, had bought for the site of his permanent *Gazette* building a set of lots adjoining the corner where the federal government proposed to put a new post office. When it was completed and occupied in 1903, light from the post office lawn poured into its great windows. This and free entry to the breezes vital for tempering the hot Kansas summers made working quarters in the *Gazette* exceptionally pleasant. The newspaper plant's proximity to the post office also provided inexpensive and convenient mailing facilities.

By the time of the great change in American life, the *Gazette* had fully found itself. Adequately and comfortably housed, fully equipped for its purposes, ably staffed, a modest but permanent money-maker, it had other claims than the eminence and popularity of its editor to high credit rating. For while at times he did not seem so, White was essentially a good businessman. As previously stated, he had no yearning for wealth as such. Once he remarked, "The Lord shows how little He thinks of money by the kind of people He gives it to." Security with comfort and as much modest luxury as was good for his soul was all the material reward he wanted out of life. It is notable that when he had paid for his plant and building he continued to invest in the home town the surplus which he earned from books, magazines, and syndicated articles. He never owned a share of stock or a bond, other than government bonds. When he died he left three business buildings, three residences, and one apartment house—all in Emporia. His tenants said that he was inclined to drive close bargains but that he also was just and fair. If one of them got into business difficulties, and many of them did over the years, and asked for a reduction in rent in order to meet the crisis, White would grant it with the provision that when business improved the rent would be increased. Sometimes he would haggle over what he considered an unnecessary expenditure of a few dollars—and in the next hour give a thousand dollars to some public cause or institution.

No one knows—and no one ever heard that he tried to com-
pute it himself—how much money he gave away. A friend in a
position to speak of his financial affairs has estimated that
White's contributions to institutions and individuals in Emporia alone were well in excess of $100,000—they easily might have
been double that figure. Even this is guesswork. His contributions usually were listed "anonymous" or "a friend." He once
told me that he had contributed at one time or another to the
construction or repair fund of every church in Emporia, and in
some instances heavily. This does not include cases where he let
not his right hand know what his left hand did. Once thirty-
five years ago an Emporia woman asked him to contribute to
some cause. He stopped her appeal short, put his hand in his
pocket, pulled out a bill, and dropped it into her palm. "I want
to help. Take this. I don't know how much it is," he said, and
turned to his work as she went away dazed with a twenty-dollar
bill. That was big money in Emporia in that day.

What the total of his contributions both in and out of Emporia may be is pure speculation, but it is virtually certain that
he gave away more money while living than the value of the
estate he left—something less than $200,000.

On the other hand—or was it?—his attitude toward the pay-
roll was that of an honest businessman getting the most for his
money, and no more. If, as happened at times, one of his employees got into a jam, White helped him out just as between
man and man—and absolutely in secret. This seeming contradiction probably was one manifestation—as his philanthropy
was another—of the Yankee blood in him. It probably also resulted from the fact that he had come up the hard way and had
learned the value of a business dollar.

But he looked after the staff in other ways and not always
cheap ones. Long before health or accident insurance became
a common policy of enlightened employers, he made them a
part of the *Gazette's* operating policy, which he continued until
federal insurance of employees became law. By the same token,
until quite recently the older employees shared in the *Gazette's*
profits. "Why not?" said White years ago. "If a businessman
provides amortization for machinery, why shouldn't he do as
much for men?"

Most of his employees were getting more than wages out of him, at that. The younger members of the editorial staff, and to a certain extent the business staff, were taking a free post-graduate course in their departments. The proof of this pudding is the avidity with which the world ate it when cooked—the number of *Gazette*-trained men who passed on to high places in national journalism. And he was always trying to help them on and upward. One of his graduates remembers that he asked the boss for a raise from his fifteen-dollar-a-week salary and got a flat refusal. A little later, he saw an opportunity for a business of his own, but he had no capital. He told White his need. The result: White endorsed his note for $5,000, a sheer moral risk. When White found that a man simply would not fit in, he looked round and found a job for him that was better suited to his talents. In his whole career, he fired only one employee outright.

The reputation of the *Gazette* as a shop where a master craftsman paid a young journalist a living wage while training him spread through Kansas and beyond. From his applicants he could have recruited a staff large enough for the *New York Times*. Over the years, many other ambitious boys and girls, too young as yet to expect a job, wrote him for advice. To all these letters he replied courteously; to those whose writers gave evidence of real ability he gave special consideration. One reply of this kind he reprinted in the *Gazette:*

Stop, look, and listen, boy. If you expect to make much money in life, don't go into the newspaper business. If you expect to have an easy time in life, avoid it. Avoid journalism unless you are looking for "hard marches and long bivouacs." Unless you are looking for a chance to take leadership without material rewards, unless you "dare to be a Daniel," unless you "want to be an angel and with the angels stand" with nothing much but your harp and your crown at the end of the journey, stay out of this profession.

But if you really desire to make your own private sentiment public opinion, if you are a sower who wants to go forth and sow even though others may reap your planting, if you are content to be self-respecting and if you think you have enough sense to be really honest and enough courage to be kind in trying circumstances when it takes good brains to maintain an understanding heart, all right, go in.

He took the same benevolent and helpful interest in the personnel of the business office. They were part of the paper; if they got into trouble, he stood by them, backed them up even when they were a bit wrong. Sometimes an advertising solicitor made a mistake in calculating a rate and sold space at a price which meant loss of money to the *Gazette*. When this happened, White honored the contract. On the other hand, when an advertiser charged bad faith on the part of one of the paper's solicitors—as once did the Emporia manager for a chain-store system—he backed the employee and laid the advertiser out cold.

White had sensitive perception of office intrigues and of those personal clashes which tend to lower the morale of an organization, and dealt with them in his own way—sometimes a fatherly lecture, sometimes an investigation into the personal causes behind the trouble. Once when he noticed a great deal of behind-the-hand whispering going on about the office he asked what was up. On being told that a *Gazette* employee was rooming at a place where homosexual practices had been discovered, Mr. White blew the gossip out of water by saying, "Hell, I never did care a damn what a man's religion was."

The *Gazette* shop was coeducational; White never believed there was any sex distinction in brains. And, as might be expected, the office was also something of a matrimonial agency. Many courtships began within those walls. Sometimes he volunteered advice on employees' love affairs. One young woman made a flippant remark to him about a fellow worker who was paying her attentions. White answered in a flash, "He's a clean-minded, pure-hearted boy—and they're blamed scarce nowadays, they're blamed scarce!"

These working methods and human relations in the *Gazette* office during William Allen White's middle period did not change with time. Neither did the increasing fame which was to come with the years after World War I abate his loyalty and affection for Emporia one jot or tittle. His roots were deep in this town of his birth, of his first college experience, of the beginnings of his journalistic career, and of his lifelong friendships. He found fame and power over men's minds there. His dreams came true in Emporia.

The town was the perfect environment for the part he was to play on the broad stage of American life. He always was in character when he wrote or spoke as a citizen of Emporia, Kansas. Some local critics said that he overdid the act, and jealous persons in the metropolis spoke of his "hick pose." It was not an act or a pose; it was the man himself.

In only one respect was the William Allen White whose imagined picture so many Americans have graven on their hearts a conscious creation. He had quite evidently determined, early in life, to be himself. If he has those natural good manners which spring from fine perception of human feelings, an educated heart, and inborn good will, plus a likable personality, a man gets on in any company with which he happens to find himself. All these, and genius, White had. If he had tried to ape metropolitan manners, to soften his open-mouthed Western accent, to adopt London dress or New York sophistication— that would have been a pose. As it was, all his days, he met on equal terms the loafers in a village store and the diplomats of European chancelleries, and they all liked him.

So he never lost the Emporia touch nor relaxed his interest in the town of his life and love. Perhaps he did overidealize Emporia, and perhaps, to one of his keen insight, he did not.

The real significance of his middle years to Emporia—and especially to the generation growing up in it—was the constant run of editorials on the affairs of his parish, on homely things, on everyday problems in morals, manners and comely living. These editorials counted more to them than those on politics which then ran from newspaper to newspaper in the United States, or those thoughts on things in general which people afterward gathered into books as models of literary journalism.

He had pulled some of the wild Western weeds from the style in which he wrote for Emporia, filed some of the rough edges from his ideas. But he still spoke to his own people in their colloquial language, still used slang or ruralisms without shame or apology—like the town philosopher talking in the drugstore of nights.

For a homely, intimate example, this from his answer to the young man who, as "Star Boarder," complained that his landlady never varied the monotony of round steak and pork, both fried hard:

For less money than fried round steak costs she could give you broiled round steak, slightly underdone. It goes further, and makes more blood and strength. For less money than round steak costs she could give you stewed shoulder or brisket of veal with dumplings. For much less than hard fried round steak costs she could give you shoulder or brisket of mutton with rice and curry. For half what fried pork and round steak costs she could give you hamburger steak —with lots of meal and pimientoes and onions mixed in it, served with gravy from the steak. For a third less than fried round steak or pork costs she could give you short ribs of beef, pot roasted with onions, carrots and potatoes with oodles of brown gravy. For what round steak costs she could buy a shoulder of mutton, cover it with flour, rub garlic on it, and roast it, serving it slightly underdone, and make it go further than round steak, with lots of mutton gravy. And for less than round steak she could give you pig hocks boiled with cabbage and turnips and potatoes.

There is a list of edible food as long as the moral law, that costs less and tastes better—for a change—than round steak fried hard or fried pork. The trouble with the boarding house keeper is that she won't take the trouble to get out of the beaten track. It's easy to think up round steak fried hard or pork, and cooking is always a work of imagination and mental effort.

Now and then he brought his readers upstanding with an opinion in advance of its times such as this, printed in 1913 and headed "Motherhood":

She was a young girl; she was happy. Life filled her, she loved. It was too much for her; life overcame her, and one day she knew that the great mystery of motherhood was coming upon her.

She faced it—faced the shame that society put upon her. The baby came—a nameless baby, and society, which makes such a to-do about motherhood, shamed the nameless, helpless child, the nameless child she loved as only a mother loves. . . .

Great miracles of iron and steam and electricity have changed the face of the earth in one hundred years. But chiefly these material miracles have opened human eyes, and are opening human hearts. In another hundred years miracles of love may change the world, and make it more wonderful in justice and mercy than iron and steam and electricity have done. . . .

In speculating on news and the newspapers' duty toward it, he said once that when an editor began to favor his friends and family, he was gone. Following this policy, he kept the doings of the White family out of the *Gazette*. When he or Mrs. White traveled, he printed a single line: "W. A. White left for a trip of two weeks to the East." "Mrs. W. A. White returned Friday from a visit at Kansas City." Occasionally editorial essays based on trivial events or circumstances in the White menage were pardonable exceptions, as were such ventures in whimsy as this, headed "Public Notice":

Mrs. W. A. White has gone to New York, called there by the illness of her sister.

Mr. W. A. White is in Emporia.

How about Sunday dinner?

This is not only an opportunity, but a duty, as we have said before in many cases of public need.

Don't all speak at once, but phone 28 after six o'clock.

The Whites had lost their dog. And this unpaid advertisement appeared in the *Gazette:*

LOST. A dog—a little white fox terrier with liver-colored ears and dark, intelligent eyes; an oldish dog as dogs go, being past twelve, and slow moving, a bit deaf and maybe not so clear-sighted as he was once when two little children used to tumble him over the grass at his home ten years ago. He has always been a good, moral dog, and if he had his love affairs and romantic adventures, he was always in by nine o'clock. But now he has been gone two days. Possibly he has been crippled in an accident; it is also possible that he is sick, and it is barely possible that he may have gone to a home where there are children, though such perfidy seems unlikely. But at any rate, anyone who knows of such a dog who left home Sunday morning will please call up phone 28 and tell the news, be it good or bad, to an anxious family to whom the little dog is a living link to a happy and beautiful past.

Later the *Gazette* noted:

The little dog's name was Teddy. A few weeks after we found him, he died. He went away to die, down under the mock orange bushes in the garden. He was probably going away to die when we brought him back. Sometimes dogs seem to have a sense of their

approaching doom and seek to pass out of life alone; something
like men and women mortally stricken, who turn their faces to the
wall to start on the long journey.

During the long, serene life of the family driving horse, Old
Tom, to which White stuck for years after other prosperous
men in Emporia had automobiles, White often mentioned
him favorably in his editorials. Other Kansas editors took up
the topic and poked fun at Tom. White came back editorially:

Old Tom, of course, is no Maud S nor Joe Patchen—for several
reasons. But he has the same number of legs attached and his heart
is true. He makes no claim to speed, but his carburetor always
works, and while he has but two cylinders, he brings his guests back
in one piece and leaves them at home, rather than down town at the
undertaker's to be assembled by total strangers into their aliquot
parts.
What if he isn't speedy; what if his best record is a mile in fifteen
minutes? So far as that is concerned, the pyramids have been four
thousand years making a distance that Tom can do in a few desul-
tory minutes, and no one sneers at them. There are too many smart
alecks running newspapers who jeer at useful things merely to raise
a laugh. Old Tom may not have a windshield or speedometer. But
what would he do with them? He is fully equipped with a few kind
words and a whalebone whip. Tom, like Spartacus the gladiator,
has "faced every form of man or beast the broad empire" could
produce. . . .

Now and then, he burst into unadulterated praise, shameless
local pride, in his state and his town.
This concerning the allure of Kansas:

. . . It may not be defined. It escapes analysis. It is in the air.
There is a little sluggish creek in Kansas whose water has a flavor
and a sparkle dearer than any wine. There are scenes in Kansas—
all over Kansas, more thralling than the rugged grandeur of the
mountains. The restless, sighing winds of Kansas tell a thousand
tales that are undreamed of by the winds that blow in other skies.
There is a certain wholesome manhood in the character of the Kansas man that is very comforting to know. His talk, his point of view,
his something of sprightly picturesqueness of speech is good to
know. Not everyone can talk the Kansas language. It is an accomplishment. There is no dialect in it—especially—it is a form of imagi-

native poetic hyperbole. It is full of short cuts to meanings. Single words speak paragraphs.

These things—the air, the water, the scenery and we who fill these scenes—hold many and many a man to Kansas when money would tempt him away. . . .

Here are the still waters, here are the green pastures. Here, the fairest of the world's habitations.

One winter morning he saw and heard a redbird, that vivid characteristic splash on the Kansas landscape, flitting and singing among the bushes round his house. He went to the office and wrote an editorial which told of the thoughts and images this glimpse of beauty had stirred in him:

. . . vibrant, exultant, triumphant. He is the very king of optimists among birds, with his gorgeous color, his swift movements, his joyous song. He was man's companion in the ancient woods. Before the dog came to the fire, or the cat to the warm hearthstone, before the cow or horse pastured with man, this red bird was singing for untamed man, thrilling him with a vague, wordless happiness.

The red bird has sung man through calamities unnumbered, through catastrophic convulsions in nature, through the oppression of wicked dynasties, through the weaknesses and frailties of humanity that make more sorrow and suffering than cruelty itself. The red bird has seen revolutions come to cast down the haughty, famines sweep over the earth decimating mankind in agony. The red bird has seen fires and floods. He has sung on blithely as external change has reflected man's inner visions and ideals while man went groaning up the stony, tortuous road of progress.

And through it all, in sickness and in health, for better or for worse, the red bird has thrust that quivering shaft of song—his buoyant paean of faith; the song of hope, of love. Modern man will have no more sturdy friend in the calamity that is now hovering like a cloud over the world. For the red bird knows no halting in his cheery song. When it is done and over, when the cataclysmic change has come which shall remake our civilization in the next half a century, and so release man from many fetters that have bound him through the past millennia, the red bird will still sing; sing on even then of another, happier day than that which is now dawning, sing of a still better world.

The red bird is the flickering, quenchless fire of the kindly gods made audible in song, forever heralding the promise of the larger life that man finds unfolding from his own mysterious heart.

Lay sermons were a specialty of Mr. White's. On Good Friday in 1912 he wrote:

Today commemorates the saddest day in human history. Nineteen hundred years ago in Jerusalem a young man from the little community of Nazareth in Judea—a young man in his early thirties, full of youth and hope and enthusiasm—was cruelly tortured to death by the Roman soldiers. The young man was a carpenter—the son of a carpenter. He had grown up amid the oppressions of Rome and the decay of his own nation; he had seen robbery and rapine and pillage and heartbreaking injustice practiced by the conquering nation upon the peace-loving Jews, and his heart was full of a plan to throw off the yoke of the oppressor. He was a man of great spiritual power. . . . He burned to make his people free—even as Moses before him had burned. So he went about agitating, preaching, exhorting, showing the people their wrongs, denouncing the powers that were plundering the people, and instilling into the hearts of the poor and the common people a brotherhood that should make them rise together and resume their former national and spiritual dominion in the world. He saw that his people were degraded, so he preached self-respect and love, which is the soul of self-respect. . . . He was preaching love in a loveless age. He was preaching justice in a time when the people were being ravaged. He was preaching repentance to the rich, and—what is much more dynamic—self-respect to the poor. . . .

In his editorials to his own people, he tried constantly to bring Emporia to flower spiritually. He instructed his reporters to watch for stories of homely heroism or unassertive civic service. And he himself wrote now and then in praise of humble people, unknown to fame but high of soul. One of these praised Robert Smith, a workman who plodded faithfully on during the hot weather, shirking nothing, grumbling at nothing, in spite of the fact that a shriveled leg made every step he took painful.

That is the *Gazette's* idea of a hero. He wears no uniform; no drums stir him up to his heroism; no battle cry urges him on. But quietly in pain and suffering, doing a day's rough work for those he loves, he is going through life a real man. How many millions like him, unknown and unhonored, are doing their work in the world, making it better, making life easier for others; doing their full duty in the humble walk and way? That is the kind of hero stuff that keeps the level of human kindness rising slowly in the world. It is the home-made heroes that are really conquering the world—conquering selfishness, conquering greed, conquering carelessness, laziness, lying and lust. It is the great army of these plain-clad heroes—men and women—who are fighting the real battles of humanity. It is the grand army that will rescue the world in the fulness of time.

A strain of nostalgia ran through many of his editorials of merely local interest—longing for the "dear, dead days beyond recall." Each fall was almost certain to produce a lyric editorial singing, the merits of the pawpaw, that wild Middle Western banana-shaped fruit with enormous seeds, the taste for which definitely has to be acquired. One of his best pawpaw editorials appeared in 1912, when he mentioned that the first of them, following a light frost, had reached town, but unfortunately, he noted:

. . . not many; for with the narrowing fringe of timber about the Kansas streams the pawpaw is becoming rarer and rarer. The Indian, the coyote, the mover's wagon, the saloon, the hoopsnake and the gambler have left Kansas, and the pawpaw, which is a fruit of the wilderness, is only standing on the order of its going. In another decade, the pawpaw will join the "innumerable caravan." The pawpaw links the civilized man of Kansas to his neolithic forebear. Men ate pawpaws before they built fires, before they polished their weapons of war and defense. Therefore the pawpaw takes us back into the days that were.

Smell a pawpaw—hold it to your nose and take a long deep breath. You inhale the woods and the deep tangles and soft earth of the deep ravine; there comes back the picture of still, green water, and cool, sunny days, of the turtle on the log, of the watersnake curls of the tree over the slough; smell the pawpaw and you feel your youth come whisking out of the past; youth and play and the secret places in the woods. What a world of memories comes out of the pawpaw as you hold it to your face—memories of fighting bass, and shining drumheads, memories of silent oars dipping into quiet waters, memories of wild grapes and festoons of overhanging vines, and walnuts falling away through the woods, and a glow of foliage touched with autumn splendors! . . . What a magic talisman it is!

In spite of his openly expressed opinion that the average citizen was interested in politics only in campaign time, White could not keep off the subject for long. Again and again, he announced "no more politics for awhile"—and then slipped back into the old habit. But in this period, his political essays for Emporia widened constantly in scope, dealt more and more with eternal principles and large tendencies, less and less with temporary situations or perishable men in power. He preached a tolerant but not muddy liberalism, a sense of civic responsibility, a faith in democracy, in spite of its faults, as the ultimate salvation, a pride in the dignity of man, a burning conviction that a better society began with and rested upon better individuals.

On the seemingly material side, he was a town booster. Every editor of a small-town newspaper has to be. But it was boosting of a different, a unique kind. His aims for Emporia were perhaps best expressed in one of his pieces for the *Gazette* which, as often happened, grew out of a trivial incident and blended with a long editorial. According to him, a woman who had lately moved to Emporia from Wichita came into his office for the sole purpose of popping off. She was fed up with Emporia. "Whenever the *Gazette* harped on the string of this good, kind, wise, decent, neighborly town, she just wanted to go out into the back yard and throw up—at least that's what she said." And, as White reported her, she went on:

"You pie-faced people here in Emporia make me tired. You think you've got such a fine town. Well, your streets are so dirty that they would stink a pig out of a hog pen. You can shoot a machine gun down Commercial Street any week day afternoon except Saturday and it wouldn't wound even a cur dog, they're so empty. I haven't seen a man carrying a tin bucket since I came to this mangy town. You've got three or four little piddling industries—a packing house, a cheese factory, something that takes care of the surplus cow's milk in these parts, and something that scrapes up the country's soybeans. . . . You are so complacent and self-satisfied that you think this Indian village is goddle-mighty's heaven. Well it's not!

"Look, you're just a little bitty, teenie, measly country town. And when you get so bored with yourself that you can't stand it any other way you begin to brag about your culture! Culchaw, I call it

culchaw! What does culture buy you? Two little motheaten colleges and not a man in the whole outfit drawing down as much salary as a good Santa Fe engineer or conductor. When I go into a
crowd and see these stoop-shouldered, goggly-eyed, wobbly-jawed
professors and their anemic wives who never had a square slice of
joy in their lives, I take the number of this town to be 23—which
means out, nits, nuts, nix!"

The visitor, according to Mr. White, went on to talk about
the dialogues given by the college students which they called
plays, and the big public hall which people packed within an
inch of their lives to hear the philharmonic orchestra, and of
the community-chest rackets, and then broke out:

"In the name of all popeyed tin gods why don't you get out and
get you a great big bustling industry, something like oil, something
like a milling industry, something that will produce dinner pails?
You go around bragging that a big industry would blow your little
culchaw off the map . . . of this little sophisticated, worm-eaten
burg, lousy with a lot of college professors and merchants that get
their goods in cardboard boxes only three days in advance of a sale!"

Mr. White added:

Well that's her story. That's the Wichita perspective. What do
you think of it? We shall be glad to print any comments in the
Wailing Place [That department of the *Gazette* where White let his
readers express themselves] from anyone who has any ideas about
this matter. It certainly is a point of view. It is worth considering. . . .

She had the Wichita idea—get the money and get it quick; don't
sentimentalize, don't moon; keep your hands on your pocketbooks
and distrust anyone who says he is trying to make this a better town;
search him for the goods and see what he wants.

Some of the hyperbole and figures of speech which cut into this
tirade were inevitably out of the vocabulary of the *Gazette's* editorial department. But the fires of her tirade and the venom in her
heart were real.

Emporia took her pen in hand; for days letters, pro and con,
filled the Wailing Place. White won. Most Emporians liked the
town not perhaps as it was, but as it was trying to be and as he
was trying to make it—a better, brighter Emporia, but not necessarily a bigger one.

But an influential minority, whose members did not habitually write letters to the editor, agreed with the lady from Wichita. Happy homes, healthy, well-fed children, an empty jail much of the time, spiritual and intellectual growth—the preachers could take care of that. Practical men knew what else Emporia needed—industries, oil development, bigness! Oil exploratory work in the town's trade territory brought the White conception for Emporia and that of the practical men into sharp focus. White's slant was that, while oil brought wealth to a community, it also brought a lot of other things, most of which were undesirable.

Much later—early in World War II—this element cornered White and forced on him the civic task of going to Washington and laying their case before the authorities. With all those war industries being handed out, they wanted a slice for Emporia. When Emporia's most eminent citizen returned empty-handed, one of his close friends asked, "Will, did you really try to bring home the bacon?" White's only reply was a faint nictation of one eye. Almost without exception as the war wore on and they saw the problems which war-industry towns face, Emporians agreed that in the long view White's business judgment was far wiser than theirs.

Whether or not his dream for Emporia was wise, this is sure: most of what the town has of civic finish derives from William Allen White. Back in 1911 he started an agitation for a real town hall—which he finally got. Year after year, he pleaded for a building where Emporia could hold livestock and poultry shows, county sales-day auctions, merchants' winter fairs, a farmers' institute.

"And when the portable seats are in the hall," he wrote, "we could have band concerts all winter, a spring music festival, union religious meetings, big spectacles like 'Ben Hur' or grand opera, revivals, political meetings, town mass meetings, state conventions."

Year after year, he proclaimed the need for this building, but the dream did not come true until 1940 when Emporia, with the help of a WPA grant, built a civic auditorium at a cost of $600,000. His was the spirit behind those philharmonic concerts which so bored the lady from Wichita; no American town of its size has better ones.

When an editor in near-by Alma wrote of Emporia as a friendly town, White, in acknowledging the compliment on behalf of this town, enlarged on the theme:

"Emporia has grown in wealth and standing chiefly because it is as the Alma editor says, a friendly town. We have essentially a kindly attitude toward life here in Emporia. We are not quick and accurate grabbers for trade, but we appreciate the society of our times, the fellowship of our friends. We are willing to bet on the Golden Rule as a workable principle in life."

The essence of Emporia's spirit, he added, explained why in a town of fifteen thousand there were three libraries, two branch libraries, more than one hundred acres of parks, two colleges and a business college, four swimming pools, two good band organizations, three small orchestras of more than thirty pieces each, and as many choruses.

We have well established, well financed permanently organized activities to look after: Unemployment, undernourished children, crippled children, scantily clad children, sick children from any cause needing hospital care, the tubercular, children's eyes and teeth. And where other towns boast of their oil, their mills, their factories, we are proud of our two big modern hospitals, our Welfare Building, our Y.M. and Y.W. buildings, our efficient city and county commissioners, our low taxes coupled with high service, our municipal water plant, our Chamber of Commerce, our organized credit bureau association, our Farm Bureau, Farmers Union and the Grange. . . .

We have quit struggling to get all the money in the world or all the population wandering loose over the planet. We want to live equitably, happily and well. That's the kind of town we are, and why they find us a friendly community.

He might have said with truth that most of the civic improvements and benefits that he listed had their inception in his own active mind, owed their fruition to his faculty for getting things done.

The hard core of White's conception of the small town's importance in American life can be observed frequently in his edi-

torials over the years. It appeared in many guises. It seemed to
be about this: The American small town can successfully support only one major industry, that of producing with the aid of
good schools and the proper community environment the boys
and girls who tomorrow, because of their character, integrity,
and civic ideals, will become the leaders of the nation. No industrial center nor any great city, regardless of its other advantages, he held, ever can compete successfully with the small
town in turning out this product, indispensable, even above
price, to the nation—perhaps to civilization. If a small community performs that mission well, he seemed to say, all other
things will be added unto it.

To most if not all these civic institutions he or Sallie White
or both had given money, gladly and generously, nearly always
secretly. The last gift was all their own—Peter Pan Park, a
playground and a fairy ground for the children of Emporia.

Some time after their daughter Mary died, they began buying
land between the southwest city limits of Emporia and the Cottonwood River. When they had assembled fifty acres, they land-
scaped it most attractively and gave it to their friends and
neighbors as a memorial to Mary with the stipulation that no
plaque or marker of any kind stating their purpose or carrying
the White name should be placed there.

Its trees and gullies, artificial lake, camp and supper sites,
walks and benches, tennis courts, its natural amphitheater ac-
commodating thousands of people for outdoor plays, its flow-
ering shrubs and decorative trees, make this the most beautiful
spot of its kind in the Middle West. In late May, 1945, on a
beautiful Kansas spring evening, Sallie White took me for a
walk over the entire park and told in touching detail how she
and Will had carried out all their plans, using helpful nature
to the utmost in creating for their friends in Emporia an outdoor place of beauty. In the closing hours of the day of our visit
it took on the spiritual atmosphere of a great cathedral.

2. CONVERSATIONALIST AND CORRESPONDENT

As a CONVERSATIONALIST, Mr. White had no equal and few runners-up. He had no interest in "society" in Emporia or elsewhere, but he did have a great deal of interest in many people who passed as socialites, primarily because they were interesting. What he liked most was to visit satisfyingly with old friends, for his recreation ever continued to be good talk. Actually he was more of a listener than a talker, but whatever he had to say was wise and usually witty. Sparkling epigrams, quips, wise observations or interpretations bubbled from him as easily, naturally, and endlessly as clear water from a strong spring.

Once when an aviator was flying low over a crowd he remarked, "That's just some damn fool exercising his ego." At a pancake party given to promote *Gazette* circulation, White said that it probably would have gone over better "if I had promised free cigarettes to mothers with nursing babies." And how he hated cigarettes, editorialized about the evil things they were! So far as I know, he never lectured anyone for smoking them in his presence; at least he never criticized me for it.

How he could tickle one's fancy with his quick flashes of wit! Once in 1912 he and I made an overnight trip from Emporia to Chicago. A mother and her six- or seven-year-old daughter had berths in the same car. I told stories to the sweet, charming child in the evening. The next morning, as we were getting our coats preparatory to leaving the train, the little girl came to my seat, climbed up on it, and kissed me good-by. It was a natural, spontaneous act. White looked on, shook his head, and remarked gravely, "It's agin the law, son. You have to throw 'em back unless they're six inches long."

A few years ago, a day or two after he had spoken at an important labor and management meeting in Washington, I asked him how his speech got over. The question was prompted by the fact that he had been pretty rough on both capital and labor. He replied that the going was tough during the first half or two-thirds of the speech, but that later on the audience had thawed out satisfactorily. "You see," he said, "I used an old T.R. formula, spanked them and then petted it." Parents who have spanked their children in love instead of anger know how effective this is.

Once when he was in Kansas City in 1928, he was discovered in the lobby by some Democrat friends who were on their way to a banquet in the same hotel, the guest of honor being an unsavory politician. Members of the dinner committee, they literally dragged him to the banquet. When, just after the diners were seated, the toastmaster asked Mr. White if he wouldn't give the invocation, he hesitated for a second and replied, "I better not. I don't want God to know I'm here."

Early in 1914 Walter F. Brown, later postmaster general, and I met in Des Moines on a political mission. During the day Walter received from Mr. White a long, critical telegram based upon an inaccurate newspaper story of an Ohio Bull Moose–Republican party reconciliation. Walter, after reading it, remarked with a dry smile, "Poor Kansas is still bleeding." Handing it to me, he said, "You speak the Kansas language and know the facts. Won't you answer this in my name?" White's reply to the answer was: "It is every man's privilege to make a jackass out of himself once each year. This is my annual exhibition."

Judged by his letters to me, covering a thirty-nine-year period, Mr. White sparked as well as a correspondent as he did as a conversationalist. In his letters, even more frank than his outspoken, personal *Gazette* editorials, he told exactly what he thought about men and movements.

Once he wrote a friend who had sent him a book, "You cannot know how you have broadened my mind by adding a desire for homicide and arson to my natural catholic taste for pleasure." In reply to a request of mine that he undertake to get a Democratic administration to give one of our mutual friends an important job, he said, "I have no hesitancy about walking into the Democratic buzz-saw and coming out twins on the other side but it would not help our friend which was what I wanted to do. Perhaps in Washington, if I could have been there and had a senatorial token, by winning ways and loving kindness I could have seduced enough Democrats to join his cause and do him some good, but I am unable to do it with the equipment I have."

In another letter written at the end of the Hoover administration, he expressed regret that it had not made a greater effort to keep on friendly terms with the northwest Progressive group: "A little social attention, a little political consideration, a little walk and talk in their direction would have saved the situation. It takes so little to win them, it costs so much to lose them." He added plaintively: "And David, I do wish before this Administration leaves the White House, some one in it would have a realization of sin."

Writing a few years later of a trip he and Mrs. White had taken to Mexico, he said:

We really had a swell time in Mexico. We were gone five weeks and never enjoyed ourselves more nor got a more complete rest. It is a Mediterranean culture; in the towns very much like Italy. In the country like Eastern Europe, Greece or Bulgaria. But certainly not what we are wont to call Anglo Saxon culture. They've got an easy-going butter-fingered socialist revolution going on there but you'd never know it if it wasn't called to your attention. Running a communist totalitarian state in a country where economic surplus is utterly unnecessary by reason of climatic conditions is a tough job. For the average peon and average industrial worker doesn't just naturally give a tinker's dam about the lofty ideals of his political overlords and yearners.

Once he and I were trying to bring about the appointment of two different men to high office. I queried him as to which of these appointments we should tackle first. He replied that, as he viewed the situation, we couldn't move in Jones's case until Smith's appointment was settled and added:

"Gosh! This sounds like patronage broking, but it really isn't. Yet I suppose every habitual thief thinks he is merely promoting distributive justice and every booze lapping, cocktail heister feels that he is corroding his intestines in the interests of 'freedom's holy light.'"

Toward the end of his life he discussed in a letter various topics of mutual interest and said in one paragraph that it might interest me to know that Blank, a public official in Kansas, was scheduled for a licking in the coming election, "for which he is to blame more than anyone else."

Not that he is dishonest—for he is as straight as a string—not that he is dumb—for he is intelligent; not that he is a demagog—for he believes tremendously that he is right, and I expect that is one of his faults. To him the world seems all black and all white—those who support his causes, and those who do not. He has found it so easy to make enemies out of his adversaries—he has lived by the sword, an arrogant, unbending Isaiah of a man, with more morals than manners, and in the two years that he has held office, he has glutted himself with the blood of his enemies politically. So he will die by the sword. He has made a good public official in a bad way, being content with bull strength where charm and tact were necessary.

Mr. White was uninterested in political patronage as such, but if he learned that a bad appointment might be made, he actively backed a good man for the job. He invariably refused to ask for the appointment of a personal friend to office on the grounds of friendship. The few men he backed for either appointive or elective office had to be honest, able, and well qualified for the job in question.

Occasionally he spoke out of turn, to the consternation of his fellow partisans, for the purpose of clarifying a situation or curing a fault. In the mid-nineteen-thirties he "nominated" Mayor La Guardia of New York for president. Immediately throughout the nation editorial and political pots boiled over. The pros and cons of his proposal were weighed seriously and critically. Hardly anyone recognized that Mr. White was dramatizing elements in a situation rather than advancing an individual's political interest. When the comment was at its height he wrote:

As I wrote you I had no illusions of his being a presidential candidate but I wished to swing a red light of danger in front of the plug-hat section of the Republican party to let them know that there was a large body of available votes in the LaGuardia following in the lower urban middle class which they must have if they win and which they cannot get if they pick a plug-hat nonentity . . . and try to run him for President in 1940.

In another letter on the same subject, he said:

Personally, I greatly admire LaGuardia for his courage, his honesty and his executive competence. . . . He is a young man yet and by the time he gets through . . . the political map of this country is going to be greatly changed. Probably one little spot on the map, infinitesimal but dear and important to me by that time, will be my grave. But if I have helped him and helped the people to understand him so that in the new line-up he can go farther . . . I think the country will be richer.

Mr. White always was keenly interested in policies, which constitute the high strategy of political action. And he was at his best in interpreting situations. In a letter written in November, 1930, he discussed the political unrest in the country and the troubled Republican party situation. His judgment was that:

In a crisis like this an executive in a private concern can make ground by waiting, but America is more than a going concern in industry and if a President makes three mistakes in five they will forgive him if his two moves are good. But if he makes only two moves out of a possible five they will damn him for lethargy or indifference. And the people thought that Hoover did not care and was indolent, when he was merely careful when he took the executive habit into the leadership of a democracy.

Once in an exchange of letters on the subject of organizations that sought to influence public sentiment, Mr. White explained to me why he had become affiliated with many liberal movements:

It is so easy for men of some standing and some property to line up on the right. Lining there they convince those who do not have standing and property that society in its privileged strata is aligned against them. It inclined to make class feeling. So, as you know, I have always lent my name to organizations that went a little farther to the left than I would be willing to go if I had any executive responsibility in government or any administrative organization. I have done this deliberately, willing to sacrifice my name to an extent that I might persuade what for the want of a better word, we will call the under-privileged that some of their well-to-do neighbors have a sense that there is a real problem of adjustment to be worked out under the democratic process now, and in the next decade and generation and in this century. It seems to me the emphasis of our politics in this century will be largely upon that readjustment of income and perhaps to an extent incidental thereto, a readjustment of title in property—not all property, but certain property affected by public use. This readjustment will come slowly. Where revolution tries to hasten the process, the friction of compulsory confiscation and the probable bloodshed thereunto appertaining will slow down the march of progress and I feel dead sure that the underprivileged, (again using the word for the want of a better word), will come more nearly under the democratic process if they feel they are not alone than they will otherwise. So I have stepped across the border of division many times as you know. If I ever expected to hold office, my words and my position would rise to mock and damn and defeat me. But I do not want to hold office. I do want to be an influence for the stabilization of the social conflict, which I feel it will take nearly a century to achieve.

3. A VARIETY OF ACTIVITIES, INCLUDING
BOOK-OF-THE-MONTH CLUB

How Will White ever found time to accomplish all he did is an unfathomable mystery to ordinary men who are forced to work so continuously for much smaller results. He had first of all a full-time job as editor and publisher of a successful newspaper. This activity seemed only to stimulate his work, for writing was both vocation and avocation to him. In all he published twenty-three books, several of them of great significance, and more than two hundred magazine and newspaper syndicate articles.

Aside from his duties as author and journalist, he also was a leader in every local civic betterment undertaking and in many national and international movements of public interest. The local activities which he led or actively supported would alone have demanded the time and energy of most other men. He conceived and promoted county fairs, was active in the establishment of YMCA and YWCA organizations, and in raising money for their operation. The College of Emporia frequently found him its best worker and most generous contributor. Whatever the civic need, he was there to advise, to push or pull, to plead or beg as the case might be. He was not a "joiner," but he did belong to the Rotary Club, and although he repeatedly refused to serve as its president he was a willing worker and always maintained a keen interest in the organization and its activities. In 1922 he wrote John Hilton, then president, from the *Mauretania* thirty miles off Naples to say that he had just come from a Rotary lunch on shipboard and enclosed the menu, which he called "Bill of Fare," so that he "like a true Rotarian could call it by its first name." He mentioned the dessert, *omelette au rhum,* and told Hilton that "It was wonderful. If we could only get hens in Lyon county that would lay that kind of eggs we could beat the band."

By 1915 Mr. White had gained national recognition as a distinguished author, humanitarian, and philosopher. He was the friend and equal of the great of the nation. His influence and reputation had become such that few national movements for public betterment were initiated without their sponsors making an effort to enlist at least the moral support of the "Sage of Emporia." He contributed much in time and wisdom to many such organizations or movements. A partial list of those for which he served as trustee includes the Rockefeller Foundation, the Roosevelt (Theodore) Memorial Association, the Woodrow Wilson Foundation, the Walter Hines Page Foundation, the Pacific Relations Committee, the National Illiteracy Association, and the League to Enforce Peace. He was a member of the Pulitzer Award Committee, president of the American Society of Newspaper Editors, and chairman of the Committee to Defend America by Aiding the Allies.

In time the list of his honorary degrees became formidable. It included Washburn and Baker Universities in Kansas, Knox College in Illinois, Beloit College in Wisconsin, Northwestern, Brown, Columbia, and Harvard Universities. The citation by President Conant of Harvard, when conferring the degree of Doctor of Laws on him in 1935, referred to Mr. White as ". . . a citizen of this Republic who has devoted his life to democratic ideals and labored increasingly for the public good."

The first gold-medal award for distinguished service to American journalism and letters by the American Society of Newspaper Editors during the first twenty-one years of its existence was voted unanimously to Mr. White in October, 1943. He learned of this honor when he was at the Mayo Clinic. The presentation was to have been made at its annual dinner, which was not held until after his death.

Politics, often to the exclusion of his countless other activities, fascinated his Kansas heart. He served the Republican party as committeeman from his precinct for many years, as its national committeeman from Kansas for a few minutes, and as the gadfly of its conscience all of his long, busy life. He served also for four years as Bull Moose national committeeman from Kansas and he ran for governor of his state as an independent candidate. Over and above these activities, he tried continuously for nearly fifty years to get honest, qualified men nominated for and elected or appointed to office.

Few men could have filled so many jobs, and all of them well, as did Mr. White, and found spare time to travel. But he did. He accepted appointment to public office only twice, both times by presidential appointment. President Wilson gave him the first appointment at the Paris peace conference, naming him special minister to conduct negotiations with Russia's representative at Prinkipo, but this conference was never held. Several years later President Hoover named him a member of the Haitian Commission, whose duty was to formulate and recommend a Haitian policy for the United States Government. In the middle 1930's Mr. White, as an official representative of the United States Government, attended the inauguration of Quezon as president of the Philippines. None of these offices paid a salary.

All of this, however, was in the future. The present point is that by the end of this century's first decade, what with economic security and freedom from the grind of establishing a newspaper, he had leisure to use more effectively his great spiritual and intellectual powers. The first step to accomplish this was to learn for himself what was beyond his old horizons. In 1909, on his vacation in Europe, he first saw the actualities of men's finest dreams as they had been immortalized in painting, sculpture, and architecture.

It was in Europe, too, and on this first visit, that Mr. White seemingly discovered qualities and virtues of a kind wholly different from those he had known and clung to in his boyhood frontier life. He had learned from his early years to hold in high regard those spiritual Anglo-Saxon, Protestant virtues which stem from the Golden Rule and are given manifestation by free men in the form of democracy. This Protestantism did not require physical miracles, did not ask the Lord to make fields or folds fertile. If in drought years a weakening survivor of flood, grasshoppers, or windstorm did plead with Providence for rain, he afterward seemed somewhat ashamed of the fall from grace. The religion in which White's faith had been nurtured was a spiritual one whose God was apart from the material universe; one that concerned itself with "faith and morals which affect conduct, and after that concerned itself with little else."

This religious outlook had amply satisfied White's spiritual needs until he first visited Europe. What he saw there convinced him that his Middle West also sorely needed "the more distinctively Catholic qualities, a love of beauty, a sense of reverence, a capacity for faith in authority, that yearning for perfection which develops sainthood."

The discovery of this new truth helped in a significant way to broaden his sympathies, to prepare him for his later role, that of a leader in the fight for tolerance and for international good will.

Previous to his first trip abroad he was almost if not entirely unknown in London or on the Continent. He had met most of the brightest literary lights while there through the good offices of William Dean Howells, who supplied him with letters of introduction to many of them. Thus he came to know them slightly, but when in 1912 he emerged as an actor in a leading role in national politics, he began to command the attention of European intellectual leaders. His experience in the national political field, in which he was playing such a direct and important part, combined with the things he saw in Europe, along with the vast, varied interests and problems which absorbed T.R. and inevitably Mr. White, served to condition him, upon the outbreak of World War I, for sloughing off his former insularity and emerging as a champion of international co-operation.

In the Heart of a Fool, published in 1918, was virtually his last piece of fiction, but during the years from the middle '20's on, he wrote three more books. First came *A Puritan in Babylon,* an analysis and interpretation of the Coolidge era, and second, *Masks in a Pageant.* Later he delivered a series of lectures on the new West at Harvard University. These were the nucleus of the last book published during his life—*The Changing West,* written with all his old vigor and flavor of the soil, a profound contribution to the understanding of the social currents of our times. This book, published in 1939 when he was seventy-one years old, was, except for his forthcoming autobiography, his swan song in literature.

His absorbing interest in his last years was current American history in its relation to permanent and universal history. Most of his magazine articles and books in these later years were written on this subject. *Masks in a Pageant,* published in 1928, consisted of biographical and critical essays on the presidents he had known up to 1928—and he had known them all from Grover Cleveland on—together with thumbnail sketches of the men who surrounded them and influenced them. There he gave final verdicts on most of them. Other writers have only filled out the details.

Mr. White was in great demand as a speaker. Invitations to address meetings came to him from far and wide and he accepted as many of them as he could. Parenthetically, he was almost the world's worst public speaker among great men. An intelligent audience interested in content rather than artistic presentation found him thrilling and inspiring because he had a message for such people. These audiences always followed him closely, perhaps in part because they felt so sorry for him on account of his poor delivery. He once remarked to me that he preferred to speak extemporaneously even though he lost his verb and had to stand there and try to find it and get it back in place. But the emotional audience which felt rather than thought was cold to him.

Early in the Harding administration it became apparent to Mr. White and most other farseeing men that the United States' repudiation of Wilson's working League, the Versailles Treaty, the World Court, was the verdict not only of a group of "willful men" but of the American people. We were passing into a mood of isolationism as starry-eyed and romantic as ever exaggerated the idealism of the war period. This was to last twenty years.

Writers and lecturers were revealing to the public the horrors of the First World War, describing the new instruments of destruction which might make it seem like a skirmish compared to the next one, and trying charily to draw the moral that the only way to escape this calamity was to unite with other peoples and nip the foul growth in the bud. With the absorption of an audience at a horror film, the people listened to the prophecies of war as it would be and drew their own morals—the wrong ones. America must sit tight inside her borders, refusing to have anything to do with those foreign kings and Bolsheviki. As to the policy of this isolationism, the country divided into two factions which were presently to have a little war of their own. One was for disarmament, absolute pacifism, the other was for a strong navy and a conscript army, but solely for defense. For us international co-operation was a dead issue.

And in this truce between the two wars domestic issues also left Mr. White stranded. The social reforms of the Wilson administration stood, the Progressive party was dead, and the old parties were now mainly absorbed with the problems of postwar recovery. We were prosperous—yes, but what prosperity! Political liberalism was out of fashion. Even the workers, stilled with money, spoke no words of vigorous protest against things as they were.

Never, since he sprang into fame or notoriety in the last years of the nineteenth century, had he been less interested in politics than he was during the Harding and Coolidge administrations. Thinking in type in the pages of the *Gazette,* as he always did, he seemed to be feeling his way toward the final stage of his personal philosophy, obtaining his full spiritual development, forming a complete union between his liberal religion and his liberal political thinking.

Although he did not parade the fact, he was at the bottom a deeply religious man. As many of the *Gazette* editorials show and as his life demonstrates, he believed in a God with purposes higher and more benevolent than those man could conceive and would easily accept, believed in the philosophy of Christ as set forth in the Gospel.

Then, as throughout his life, Mr. White was indifferent, even contemptuous, of theological hair-splitting or sentimental religious hysteria. In the reckless young mood of a sub-editor of the *El Dorado Republican,* he had offended many of the unco righteous by an editorial on the passing of hell. Two or three times in the period when his *Gazette* was struggling for a foothold, he got himself into trouble by attacking those hysterical revivals which still held over from the mores of the frontier. He was roasting or guying them as late as 1926. In an editorial he remarked how they tear towns to pieces:

. . . In the name of religion such orgies of intolerance are launched, such torrents of bigoted abuse are released, such weird ideas of God and the universe are preached as mock religion and merely get the people excited for nothing.

That kind of a revival does more harm than good. It is merely a modern expression of the voodooism of the jungle. The tabernacle, the choir, the bawling evangelist—all set up an emotional spree in modern civilization. And it's a bad thing. Emporia has revived from the last revival sufficiently to be a normal, man-loving, God-fearing town!

Heaven preserve us from another!

He frequently lost subscribers by such forthright statements, but he always got them back again with interest, because Emporia found by experiment that it could not live without the *Gazette*. In that period he expressed the new harmony which was growing in his heart by a loathing for war as an institution, a mood verging at times on the isolationism which he repudiated in 1919, and which he was to repudiate more effectively in 1939. War to him was a denial of all that Christ taught. War was organized murder. He had seen its face and found it horrible. This mood prevailed at times all through the boom decade.

The basic tenets of his working creed, as has been stated before, were the Golden Rule and the command to the Apostles— "Preach the Gospel to all men." Democracy to him was the social manifestation of Christianity. As such it knew no distinctions of race, creed, or social condition.

During the middle '20's Mr. White found a new, vital outlet for public service which until his death claimed far more of his sustained interest than did either politics or writing. It came second only to his *Gazette* and his benevolent Emporia interests, which from the day he bought the paper had been one and the same thing. This new interest was the Book-of-the-Month Club. He became a judge for that organization in 1926 and continued to serve as one until the day he died. As he once explained in the *Gazette*, he considered the work he did for this organization to be in the nature of public service.

For a dozen years now on the award committee of the Book-of-the-Month Club, it has been my luck to have my finger in the lit-

erary pie of the United States. The Book-of-the-Month readers
have picked in advance more than ninety per cent of the best-sellers
of a dozen years' literary output. Moreover the Pulitzer awards in
biography and fiction have come from the Book-of-the-Month list
in seven cases out of ten. In addition to having kept abreast of literary currents of the time—that is in addition to keeping a dodder-
ing old frame quick and alive by reading three to ten stimulating
books a month, either in the manuscript or in the proof—it is a
certain satisfaction and delight for a small town editor to feel that
his literary prejudices are, in some measure, helping to guide the
purpose and direction of American literature. So when Emporians
drop in at 927 Exchange in the evening and find the host and the
hostess with their noses deep in books, the visitor should not be
deceived, these two old parties are not whiling away an idle hour.
They are trying to earn an honest living and govern a sovereign
people by remote control through books the people shall read and
the thoughts they should think and envision, . . .

Moreover it's a lot of fun. Nero fiddling over Rome, never got
half the kick out of it that we do! Darby and Joan in their vine-
covered cot on the lone prairie!

When Mr. White was unable to attend the regular meetings
of the Book-of-the-Month Club's judges, he telegraphed his
decisions on the books that were currently under consideration.
Harry Scherman, president of the club, courteously gave me
these telegrams, from some of which I selected the following
brief quotations:

. . . On all others I have rather emphatic nix but I am probably
wrong and will know it when you all differ with me.

. . . Nor to my notion is "——" which strikes me as most trivial
and we might be hauled up by the Aunt Netties of our list for
sending it out and Aunt Nettie is not to be sneezed at. . . .

The three biographies, Villard, Tarbell, Jane Carlyle are tops . . .
Villard's is controversial but a powerful job. Often I disagree with
him but his craftsmanship and his integrity of purpose give his book
force and compelling interest . . . Far and away the best novel is
"The Grapes of Wrath" but it would be a mistake to buy it. Thousands of our readers would be offended by its necessary but to me
quite inoffensive indecency. . . .

. . . I am hardboiled and mean in my tremendous dislike of "——"
as Book of the Month choice. It would queer us with a large crowd.
Why take a questionable book when you have half a dozen sure
shots? Now is the time to cross the Rubicon on the dirt question.
. . .

. . . "Mr. Skeffington" is rather a sweet package high in cellulose
and low in protein and hardly our dish. But might work in as dual
choice with heavier Look. . . .

. . . "Gentleman from Stratford" mere synthetic, bloodless, academic, literary strutting, a wax veneer on basswood without real
guts. But I am all burned up about Mencken's, Aikman's and
Rauschning's books. . . .

First choice "Walk like a Mortal." Second choice "Voice of Destruction." Third choice "Trouble in July" if one espisode is
deleted, otherwise, "No, a thousand times No". . . .

Seems to me an exceptionally fine list. Feel as though I had had a
post graduate college education. We could afford to take all five of
them. . . .

By all means buy Hemingway's "For Whom the Bell Tolls" . . .
As a second fiction choice after Hemingway I would say "Sergeant
Lamb's America"—beautifully done. Absorbed in narration and not
too scholarly. I should greatly like to stock up with Allan Nevin's
"Rockefeller" far and away the best biography of modern business
I have ever read. . . .

. . . Book needs editing, I mean cutting down unless we need a sea
story which God forbid now or ever. . . .

. . . a waste of time even if the last chapter is the best tale of a sea
battle I ever read. But not worth wading through two hundred
thousand words of brackish dish water. However if Chris [Morley]
likes dish water because it's briney let's take it. . . .

. . . Like William Byrd's Diary but think its academic flavor might
make it hard for most readers to take though it is peach. I am still
hoping and praying that you will not take the —— opus even for
dual choice. Have tried half dozen fairly sophisticated western

literati and they all get stalled in the second third or splash through it mystified weary and in end annoyed at its pseudo fiction.

. . . "——" which has restricted audience sort of "Gents Only" book, heavily spiced hamburger out of bull meat with Rabelaisian sauce but tasty as far as it goes. . . .

. . . I don't like "——" the adulteries become too monotonous and after first half dozen they are repetitious and one longs someway for good vigorous criminal assault and battery . . . I should say, speaking broadly, when a writer multiplies his dirty love affairs until they become mere biological case records he has lost the rabbit's foot of his art and become a mere chronicler of pathological incidents. . . .

Go ahead if you want it but it's just a dry academic research to me with a spoonful of synthetic mineral oil gravy on it. An ersatz dish to my palate.

. . . "——" is just a paper from a woman's club on Flemish art done as a cyclorama. It reads as well forward as backward and up as well as down . . .

. . . I should say third and a poor third "——." The decorative ornate writing of first half makes it pretty terrible, I mean those lugged in and pinned on metaphors, similes and tropes which are like pimento strips on a salad or paper panties on a mutton-chop. . . .

My choice above all others is "The Raft," a straightaway adventure story, real sea yarn. I am getting so weary with the books out of books . . . that again I clamor for book without style or any academic qualifications . . . Nix on "——," but in choosing it see if I care.

Seems to me by all odds the best buy is "The Year of Decision." It will stand up with "Washington Reveille" although not so interesting a period and of course with no great figure in it but still it is dignified job of which we can all be proud. The Italian book . . . is carved in basswood and the characters are pure theatre and for me, at least, the interest does not rise. "——" is the dirtiest book I ever read. Not that I was shocked by it. The fences barns and out-

house walls of childhood's Golden Hour gave me great familiarity
with general idea of book. I feel that it would outrage at least a
third of our readers. . . .

. . . "Hostages" is only bad in one spot but unless the author will
cut the bawdy house chapter I could not stand for it. It is lugged in,
has nothing to do with the plot, and no trimming or rewriting
would do it any good. . . .

. . . Whichever one of this lot you take you have my benevolent
malediction. . . .

"The Fifth Seal" is a curious book. In the first place I had and still
have trouble in connecting the title with the content and purpose
of the story. In the second place, as I read along the first quarter or
third of the book, I got the impression that I did not care for it. It
was a kind of an oblique account of life and I said "No" to it. But
after the first half, I caught myself wetting my finger to turn the
page before it was time to turn, which was a sign that I am interested in a book even though I deny it. The story gained power
under my eyes and before I realized it, I was particularly interested
in some new characters in the book. Notably an old Bolshevik Communist who was not reconciled to Stalin's kind of socialism, as a
matter of fact, the whole book is cast upon the theory of showing
how a diplomatic delegation from Moscow reacts when it comes out
in the capitalist world—a new idea in fiction. And several of the
characters beside the old Bolshevik are strangers in the fairly well
established cast of characters that walk the stage of modern fiction.
    In the end despite my own protests, I came to enjoy the book and
I can recommend it for its originality. It has a new squint at modern life. It is worth reading. And I say this despite the fact that
after I had spent three or four hours on it, I turned my thumbs
down. Probably it will affect the average reader something like that.
Most likely when he has finished it he will have, as I had, a curious
feeling that his time was well spent in reading it for he walked off
a little time in a new, strange world.

Obviously most distinguished and really best book of the lot is San-
tayana's Autobiography. . . . I personally enjoyed reading "Colonel Effingham's Raid" better than any other book but I realize that
my taste is low and I shall only obliquely suggest it curtsying and
pulling a forelock after which Merry Christmas, a transcription
from "Tiny Tim."

4. AN OBITUARY WRITER

WILLIAM ALLEN WHITE wrote for the *Gazette* the greatest
of his journalistic masterpieces—his obituary of his daughter,
Mary. As with the others, from "What's the Matter with
Kansas?" on, it swept the country without any of the preliminary advertising that precedes a book or a magazine article. The
newspapers discovered it for the general public, Christopher
Morley for the literary public. Some years later Alexander
Woollcott read it over the radio to an invisible audience that
wept with him. It is already a classic. Except for Dr. John
Brown's "Marjorie Fleming," that tender, humorous appreciation of a Scottish lass who died young, it is unique in the literature of the English language.

There is a long background to any masterpiece; a long maturing of the author's touch until the theme and the mood work
together and carry him to his heights. And in their praise of
this great essay, the critics have missed a salient point, apparent
only to one who has searched a half-century of *Gazette* files.
William Allen White was at his best, his supreme best, when,
with a sense of deprivation stirring him to his depths, he sat
down to summarize the life of a man or woman. Even when the
newly dead merited scorn or half-approval, as in the case of
Frank A. Munsey and Woodrow Wilson, a glow of feeling ap-
propriate to the supreme adventure shines through words. Almost certainly, he was the greatest obit writer that ever lived.

They are not always, they are not usually, funeral sermons
over those great of the earth whom he knew so well. The best
of them, taken as a whole, give a touch of immortality to
humble Emporians of whom the world outside would never
have heard but for his eulogies at their passing. Into them he
put all of his novelist's sense of pity, irony, and subtle perception of human values, all his own special warmth of sympathy
and understanding, and finally—for it is all too easy to slop over
when writing obituary literature—his good taste.

Here are a few typical examples:

MARY A. WHITE

. . . For nearly thirty years she had lived in this town, most of the time in her own house, and always in her own way. Any kind of fetters galled her. The Irish love of freedom ruled her soul. She was sentimental to a fault. When Grover Cleveland was first elected in 1884, her husband was dead. But she knew he would rejoice, so with grim loyalty holding back her tears of rage at the elevation of a Democrat to the Presidency, this black Republican abolitionist put a lighted candle in every window of her home when the news of Cleveland's victory came. Then she went to the back of the house where she could not be seen when the Democratic parade came around. It shamed her but she was proud of her shame. She was like that always. And so often was most unhappy, having small sense of humor. As the years came upon her she had grown more and more grim, more and more doleful at the restraints of life. She has had a long journey—nearly ninety-five years of it, yearning passionately for a freedom that she could never quite define. So it is with all of us, in our heart of hearts. And yesterday she had release—into the world of truth, into the land where our visions blurred by the earth's dull circumspection come true and satisfy the soul. I am sure, and so I am most happy that whatever survives of my mother today is young and free and happy beyond human words. For the iron that bound her heart chafes her no longer. She is the captain of her soul.

May 7, 1924

TOM WILLIAMS

Tom Williams, who died yesterday afternoon, was my friend. He was black, coal black. Probably his Ethiopian ancestry went straight back to Africa without a white cross to mark the journey. I was about to say he had never done a lick of honest work in his life. That would hardly be true. I can remember when he used to do housecleaning. But it irked him—not the work, but the regular hours of commercial employment. Occasionally he would do chores for a friend but even then he would rather have the service established on anything than a money basis; an old suit of clothes, say, or a place to sleep or best of all a cup of coffee now and then, or the right to a chat in the kitchen and a sandwich. He was almost exactly my age and I have known him for more than 40 years about as well as I have known many a white man in town. He claims to have been in the penitentiary three times. I think he was bragging.

I can only remember twice, both times for arson. Publicly he claimed to be innocent. He never told me that. The tale of his innocence was for casual acquaintances and strangers.

He was not a thief in the strict sense of the word. He wouldn't take anything that he thought anyone wanted or could use. But he picked up trifles around that were out of use and either used them or traded them off—preferring barter to sale. Other colored folks said he stole dogs. He told me the dogs just naturally followed him. I think—with certain reservations—this is true, more or less! But you could always go to Tom when you wanted a dog of any particular age or breed and give him a month or two and Tom would show up with it. He would not lie much about the breed unless he thought you were the sort of a man he had to lie to in a trade. Many white men have the same sort of virtue. They don't lie unless their fellow bargainers force them into it . . .

. . . Because I was sometimes an issue but never a candidate in city elections, it pleased Tom to abuse me roundly and wildly. Then he would shuffle around and tell me about it and assure me that he didn't mean it at all. I once had a white friend that had the same weakness. He liked to slam me and slip around and laugh about it. Looking back at the two, who are both dead, I am not quite sure which was a better friend. . . .

. . . He was a night owl and saw too much of the doings of many people to have an abiding faith in the morality of human nature. Other colored people who knew stories such as Tom knew were inclined to laugh at white folks. If we white folks knew how much colored people know about us and how we are tagged in colored circles as we shall appear before the Great White Throne, we white folks would not patronize colored people as we do. We would respect them, maybe fear them. But colored people are kind and wise in their charity. So they only laugh. But Tom did not laugh. He never snickered when he told me of the subterranean night life in Emporia. He was terribly in earnest though not offended, not stricken in faith, just interested, in knowing why men strayed and women fell and how the devil kept his fires going.

Tom was not a busy-body, not a peddler of gossip. He kept his counsel, mostly told few friends, chiefly white, to whom he could talk in self-respect as a philosopher; not as one who compensates for hardships of his own sad morality by reveling in the misdeeds of others. The records on the Lamb's book of life will probably be set down with something like Tom's philosophical detachment; the record of an inquiring mind and an understanding heart. Which

remark is not intended to be profane and smart. It explains why I
clove to Tom Williams as a friend. . . .

Thinking it all over—that 40 years and more of acquaintance
which became a sort of friendship—I suppose the basis of my affection for Tom Williams was the fact that he came to me in trouble
and always showed me his best side. One of God's major blessings
upon me, I see now in the declining years of a long life, probably
comes from the fact that men who are full of flaws and weaknesses
and who visit upon others the curse of their weaknesses turn to me
only their good side, never victimize me. Most likely this unfortunate trait which blinds my eye to faults that others see and shun,
furnishes the clue and key to my regard for Tom Williams. . . . To
the town he was just old black Tom Williams, shiftless, idle, crooked
and at times half mad—just one of the town "characters." To me
he was a man of some parts and consequence despite his failings,
and despite the complete and abject inconsequence of his life.
What more than "town characters" are most of the town's best
known citizens? Their wealth and fame have sifted away after death
as Tom Williams' dogs have gone. Some of us a little queer in one
spot, others soft in another—out of plumb a bit here and there—sag-
ging in secret moral decay or bulging with a facade of rococo recti-
tude. We are known by our neighbors as much for our odd streaks
as our good ones—famed here on earth only as "town characters,"
and "town characters" all of us stand before the Good God's throne
of grace!—in 50 years forgotten of men! The tremendous handicap
of his race, of course, weighted Tom heavily. Yet I have known so
many other men with fewer virtues and with many of Tom's defects
who have gone much further without even Tom's brains!

Reading this over in the proof I'm sure if Tom could see it he
would be so inordinately proud that he would denounce me on
Commercial street and then toddle over to the *Gazette* office to correct what he would surely call certain "inadvertent inaccuracies!"

December 1, 1936

HOLMES PASSES

Former Justice Oliver Wendell Holmes died this morning in
Washington. He had served his country seventy years, boy and man;
as soldier, servant and statesman . . .

Justice Holmes carried to his grave a Civil War bullet. Yet he
was the broadest of statesmen fifty years ago in all his attitude toward the South. In his veins coursed the blood of the Massachusetts

Brahmins. Yet he was the most liberal of our modern statesmen, standing shoulder to shoulder with men like Theodore Roosevelt, who brought him to the Supreme Court, with the elder LaFollette, whom Holmes admired greatly, and with every forward-looking man of whatever party, Republican, Socialist or Democrat who joined the American quest for social justice.

Personally, he was a sweet and kindly man, greatly beloved by three generations. His attitude in the Supreme Court has been an example to other lawyers in other courts. America is saved from a Pharisaical plutocracy largely because Oliver Wendell Holmes followed the inner voice in his heart. He escaped the warping with which fame twists many a man, and so he lived simply, naturally, beautifully to the end of a full and happy life.

March 6, 1935

DAVID TIPTON

There was buried today in Maplewood one of the best citizens of the town—David Tipton by name. He was not a white man; they say he had Indian blood in his veins, and though he was of African extraction, he was born a free man, of free parents, and all his life he looked every man squarely in the face without blinking. He was a handsome man, was Dave Tipton—tall, angular, broad-shouldered, strong as an ox, clean limbed, keen-eyed, blunt spoken, straightforward . . . one who bore the handicap of his race like a gentleman. He never whined. On the other hand, he found something he could do and he did it well—better than any one else in this part of the world. . . . His was a successful life. He had sense—lots of it. . . . The *Gazette* extends the heartfelt, fraternal sympathy of the community that is the loser for this hard-working, right-minded, kindhearted man.

January 20, 1910

REST IN TRUST

Frank Munsey, the great publisher, is dead.

Frank Munsey contributed to the journalism of his day the talent of a meat packer, the morals of a money changer and the manners of an undertaker. He and his kind have about succeeded in transforming a once-noble profession into an eight per cent security.

May he rest in trust!

December 23, 1925

WHAT IS A MAN PROFITED?

The other day in Emporia, the longest funeral procession that has formed in ten years followed the Rev. John Jones three long miles in the hot July sun out to Dry Creek Cemetery. Now, a funeral procession may mean little or much. When a rich and powerful man dies, the people play politics and attend his funeral for various reasons. But here was the body of a meek, gentle little old man—a man "without purse or scrip." It won't take twenty minutes to settle his estate in probate court. He was a preacher of the gospel—but preachers have been buried before this in Emporia without much show of sorrow.

The reason so many people lined up behind the hearse that held the kind old man's mortality was simple: they loved him. He devoted his life to helping people. In a very simple way, without money or worldly power, he gave of the gentleness of his heart to all around him. We are apt to say that money talks, but it speaks a broken, poverty-stricken language. Hearts talk better, clearer, and with a wider intelligence. This old man with the soft voice and the kindly manners knew the language of the heart and he spoke it where it would give zest to joy. He worked manfully and with a will in his section of the vineyard, and against odds and discouragements he won time and again. He was infinitely patient and brave. He held a simple, old-fashioned faith in God and His loving kindness.

When others gave money—which was of their store—he gave prayers and hard work and an inspiring courage. He helped. In his sphere he was a power. And so when he lay down to sleep hundreds of friends trudged out to bid him good-by with moist eyes and with cramped throats to wish him sweet slumber.

And then they turned back to the world to make money—to make money—what a hollow impotent thing! What is a man profited if he gain the whole world and lose his own soul?

August, 1901

WILSON

God gave him a great vision.
The devil gave him an imperious heart.
The proud heart is still.
The vision lives.

February 4, 1924

JANE THOMAS MOON

This afternoon among sorrowing friends they laid the mortal remains of Jane Thomas Moon away to mingle with the mold from which they came; to spring up again in trees and flowers and prairie grass, to thrill in bird-songs that shall be—into that physical immortality which is as sure as the never-ending procession of birth and life and decay upon this earth. There passed with the human form also into an immortality as sure as that of physical change, the memory and the sweet influence of a kindly, happy life, a very sunshine of a life that warmed and cheered and stimulated to all good things, the lives of those about her. These two immortalities none may dispute . . . when into this world of ours there comes so real a thing as a radiant human soul like the soul of this woman who has passed beyond the realm of finites, when such a soul glows into our eyes, touches our lives in love, beams in a whole existence of beauty and use, when such a soul comes into this planet, full-grown, splendid in its power to make life sweet and joyful, something has entered the earth not of the earth; something has come into life not of the things of life. It came; it has gone. It always was; it must always be. The hearts that know such a soul need no strength added to their faith. They have seen the miracle; they have known of their hearts the presence of this holy spirit, this divine spark that comes into humanity and lifts humanity to the eternal stars. . . .

A few years ago, in writing about the "Mary White" editorial, Mr. White said:

Since this was written, the Mary White editorial has been published in twenty-three different books for high school and college reading, required and supplementary reading. Christopher Morley discovered it first as book material. Since then it has gone on and on. This would be the immortality that Mary would love to live in the hearts of her own people, youth in the teen age and the twenties. Probably if her father has any sort of lasting fame beyond the decade following his death, it will come from this editorial. I shall go as far as I go, which very likely is only a little distance, along the path where Mary's hand may lead me. That also is enough fame for me.

Many of its readers have remarked the unusual qualities of a father who could write with such art, such poignant beauty on his daughter's death the day after her funeral.

Actually the Mary White editorial was not the work of one man, one mind, or one heart, but of two people, two minds, and two hearts, who were united as one in marriage, life, understanding, hopes, and purpose. Those two people were Will and Sallie White.

In May and June, 1945, I was a guest for three weeks in the White home in Emporia. One afternoon when I came in Sallie White said, with great joy: "Oh, David, I've just found the original of the Mary White editorial. It's been lost for twenty years and we have looked and looked for it but today I found it in an old box full of manuscripts."

There it was. Four typewritten pages on ordinary newspaper copy paper, fading, blue ink, double spaced, a few words x'd out, penciled interlineations—all just as it went to the printer twenty-four years ago.

And she told me the story of a story, which then revealed the completeness and significant beauty of the union between Will and Sallie White.

"Neither of us had slept any the night after we put Mary away. We had tossed all night. When morning came, we got up and ate some breakfast from habit, but neither of us wanted any. When we had finished Will said:

" 'Get your things, Sallie, we must go to the office and take care of Mary.'

"I said to him: 'I can't do it, Will, I can't do it,' and he replied:

" 'But you must, dear, you must. We always have done everything together and we must do this together. Besides, I need you. I can't do it alone.'

"So I got ready in a daze, for I was so numb I couldn't think, and we started walking to the office. About halfway there I became conscious, as I went along with my eyes looking down, for the first time in my life of people we met looking at me, and I said, 'I can't go on, Will, the way everyone is looking at me.'

"Will said to me, 'Look up, dear. They are our friends. Look into their faces. We must take care of Mary and I can't do it alone. I need you now more than I ever have before.'

"When we reached the office Will closed both doors and began to write. In a little while he handed me some copy and asked if it was all right. I read it and said: 'Yes, it's all right, but don't forget this or that, Will.' He said to me, 'That's one reason why I had to have you, Sallie.' He went on writing and showing me what he had written and I suggested other things that should be included, five or six altogether. One was about Mary's dinner for the folks at the poor farm. When Will had finished writing and had corrected the copy he called Cal [Calvin Lambert, then *Gazette* city editor]. Cal brought back the galley proofs as soon as it was set. I remember holding out my hand to Cal for something but until today when I found the copy I never could remember why I had done that—I was in a stupor then and did everything automatically. I've been hunting everywhere for it because I wanted to give it to the library. It belongs there." (She was referring to the new William Allen White library at the State Teachers College of Emporia.)

When, the next day, I told this to some of the old-timers at the *Gazette*, they recalled the staff's excitement when Mr. and Mrs. White came into the office together and closed the doors. The staff felt that something fine was going to happen, but no one had a guess of how human and how transcendently beautiful it would be.

This poignant expression concerning the most universal of deep, human experiences, the loss of a loved one is reprinted in full here as Will and Sallie White wrote it:

MARY WHITE

The Associated Press reports carrying the news of Mary White's death declared that it came as the result of a fall from a horse. How she would have hooted at that! She never fell from a horse in her life. Horses have fallen on her and with her—"I'm always trying to hold 'em in my lap," she used to say. But she was proud of few things, and one of them was that she could ride anything that had four legs and hair. Her death resulted not from a fall but from a blow on the head which fractured her skull, and the blow came from the limb of an overhanging tree on the parking.

The last hour of her life was typical of its happiness. She came home from a day's work at school, topped off by a hard grind with the copy on the High School Annual, and felt that a ride would refresh her. She climbed into her khakis, chattering to her mother about the work she was doing, and hurried to get her horse and be out on the dirt roads for the country air and the radiant green fields of the spring. As she rode through the town on an easy gallop she kept waving at passers-by. She knew everyone in town. For a decade the little figure in the long pigtail and the red hair ribbon had been familiar on the streets of Emporia, and she got in the way of speaking to those who nodded at her. She passed the Kerrs, walking the horse, in front of the Normal Library, and waved at them; passed another friend a few hundred feet farther on, and waved at her. The horse was walking, and as she turned into North Merchant Street she took off her cowboy hat, and the horse swung into a lope. She passed the Tripletts and waved her cowboy hat at them, still moving gayly north on Merchant Street. A *Gazette* carrier passed—a High School boy friend—and she waved at him, but with her bridle hand; the horse veered quickly, plunged into the parking where the low-hanging limb faced her, and, while she still looked back waving, the blow came. But she did not fall from the horse; she slipped off, dazed a bit, staggered, and fell in a faint. She never quite recovered consciousness.

But she did not fall from the horse, neither was she riding fast. A year or so ago she used to go like the wind. But that habit was broken, and she used the horse to get into the open, to get fresh, hard exercise, and to work off a certain surplus energy that welled up in her and needed a physical outlet. That need has been in her heart for years. It was back of the impulse that kept the dauntless little brown-clad figure on the streets and country roads of the community and built into a strong, muscular body what had been a frail and sickly frame during the first years of her life. But the riding gave her more than a body. It released a gay and hardy soul. She was the happiest thing in the world. And she was happy because she was enlarging her horizon. She came to know all sorts and conditions of men; Charley O'Brien, the traffic cop, was one of her best friends. W. L. Holtz, the Latin teacher, was another. Tom O'Connor, farmer-politician, and Rev. J. H. J. Rice, preacher and police judge, and Frank Beach, music master, were her special friends, and all the girls, black and white, above the track and below the track, in Pepville and Stringtown, were among her acquaintances. And she brought home riotous stories of her adventures. She loved to rollick; persiflage was her natural expression at home. Her humor was a continual bubble of joy. She seemed to think in hyperbole and metaphor. She was mischievous without malice, as full of faults as an old shoe. No angel was Mary White, but an easy girl to live with, for she never nursed a grouch five minutes in her life.

With all her eagerness for the out-of-doors, she loved books. On her table when she left her room were a book by Conrad, one by Galsworthy, *Creative Chemistry* by E. E. Slosson, and a Kipling book. She read Mark Twain, Dickens, and Kipling before she was ten—all of their writings. Wells and Arnold Bennett particularly amused and diverted her. She was entered as a student in Wellesley for 1922; was assistant editor of the High School Annual this year, and in line for election to the editorship next year. She was a member of the executive committee of the High School Y.W.C.A.

Within the last two years she had begun to be moved by an ambition to draw. She began as most children do by scribbling in her schoolbooks, funny pictures. She bought cartoon magazines and took a course—rather casually, naturally, for she was, after all, a child with no strong purposes—and this year she tasted the first fruits of success by having her pictures accepted by the High School Annual. But the thrill of delight she got when Mr. Ecord, of the Normal Annual, asked her to do the cartooning for that book this spring, was too beautiful for words. She fell to her work with all her enthusiastic heart. Her drawings were accepted, and her pride—always repressed by a lively sense of the ridiculous figure she was cutting— was a really gorgeous thing to see. No successful artist ever drank a deeper draft of satisfaction than she took from the little fame her work was getting among her schoolfellows. In her glory, she almost forgot her horse—but never her car.

For she used the car as a jitney bus. It was her social life. She never had a "party" in all her nearly seventeen years—wouldn't have one; but she never drove a block in her life that she didn't begin to fill the car with pick-ups! Everybody rode with Mary White—white and black, old and young, rich and poor, men and women. She liked nothing better than to fill the car with long-legged High School boys and an occasional girl, and parade the town. She never had a "date," nor went to a dance, except once with her brother, Bill, and the "boy proposition" didn't interest her—yet. But young people—great spring-breaking, varnish-cracking, fender-bending, door-sagging carloads of "kids"—gave her great pleasure. Her zests were keen. But the most fun she ever had in her life was acting as chairman of the committee that got up the big turkey dinner for the poor folks at the county home, scores of pies, gallons of slaw, jam, cakes, preserves, oranges, and a wilderness of turkey were loaded into the car and taken to the county home. And, being of a practical turn of mind, she risked her own Christmas dinner to see that the poor folks actually got it all. Not that she was a cynic; she just disliked to tempt folks. While there she found a blind colored uncle, very old, who could do nothing but make rag rugs, and she rustled up from her school friends rags enough to keep him busy for a season. The last engagement she tried to make was to take the guests at the county home out for a car ride. And the last endeavor of her life was to try to get a rest room for colored girls in the High School. She found one girl reading in the toilet, because there was no better place for a colored girl to loaf, and it inflamed her sense of injustice and she became a nagging harpy to those who she thought could remedy the evil. The poor she always had with her and was glad of it. She hungered and thirsted for righteousness; and was the most impious creature in the world. She joined the Church without consulting her parents, not particularly for her soul's good. She never had a thrill of piety in her life, and would have hooted at a "testimony." But even as a little child she felt the church was an agency for helping people to more of life's abundance, and she wanted to help. She never wanted help for herself. Clothes meant little to her. It was a fight to get a new rig on her; but eventually a harder fight to get it off. She never wore a jewel and had no ring but her High School class ring and never asked for anything but a wrist watch. She refused to have her hair up, though she was nearly seventeen. "Mother," she protested, "you don't know how much I get by with, in my braided pigtails, that I could not with my hair up." Above every other passion of her life was her passion not to grow up, to be a child. The tomboy in her, which was big, seemed to loath to be put away forever in skirts. She was a Peter Pan, who refused to grow up.

Her funeral yesterday at the Congregational Church was as she would have wished it; no singing, no flowers except the big bunch of red roses from her brother Bill's Harvard classmen—heavens, how proud that would have made her!—and the red roses from *The Gazette* force, in vases at her head and feet. A short prayer; Paul's beautiful essay on "Love" from the Thirteenth Chapter of First Corinthians; some remarks about her democratic spirit by her friend, John H. J. Rice, pastor and police judge, which she would have deprecated if she could; a prayer sent down for her by her friend, Carl Nau; and opening the service the slow, poignant movement from Beethoven's Moonlight Sonata, which she loved; and closing the service a cutting from the joyously melancholy first movement of Tschaikowski's Pathetic Symphony, which she liked to hear in certain moods, on the phonograph; then the Lord's Prayer by her friends in High School.

That was all.

For her pallbearers only her friends were chosen: her Latin teacher, W. L. Holtz; her High School principal, Rice Brown; her doctor, Frank Foncannon; her friend, W. W. Finney; her pal at *The Gazette* office, Walter Hughes and her brother Bill. It would have made her smile to know that her friend, Charley O'Brien, the traffic cop, had been transferred from Sixth and Commercial to the corner near the church to direct her friends who came to bid her good-by.

A rift in the clouds in a gray day threw a shaft of sunlight upon her coffin as her nervous, energetic little body sank to its last sleep. But the soul of her, the glowing, gorgeous, fervent soul of her, surely was flaming in eager joy upon some other dawn.

5. NATIONAL POLITICAL ACTIVITIES
1916–1924

As HE HIMSELF SAID after that defeat of the Progressive party which was half a victory, he "had enough of bolting." To most of the Progressive faction, Wilson was a not disagreeable alternative, especially when he began his administration by going beyond his campaign promises and instituting social and financial legislation advanced for its times. Presently, in spite of the temperamental dislike of his idolized Theodore Roosevelt for this schoolmaster in politics, White found himself going along with Wilson in the domestic policies which absorbed our political attention until August, 1914. Even in the campaign of 1912, White believed him to be "clearly the strongest man in the Democratic party," and early in 1913 he said, "Wilson is talking right." He felt that it was "refreshing to find an administration wherein money does not talk," that these were grand days for "them damn literary fellers." Wilson's was "an amazing administration," a political curiosity, because here was a "mild-mannered, rather soft-voiced man, who has a supercilious, sometimes hoity-toity way with him—an exalted schoolmaster, but with two years of political experience, moving gently down on Washington and taking the leadership of a great party—notoriously untamed and turbulent—and, by his sheer intellectual force you see him playing upon office hunger and patronage with impartial skill, making that rampant Democracy 'mild and lovely, gentle as the summer breeze.' " And, White added, "The people are with him."

Early in 1914, it seemed to Mr. White that Wilson's "advent marks an event at the end of an era in American politics—the definite downfall of a dynasty. The dynasty as it fell might be called a business dynasty, to distinguish it from the political dynasty of the first period of American life, and from the slave holding dynasty. . . . He is a leader worthy of his times; and these are great times. But only the beginning of greater ones."

In early 1916, Mr. White said that "on the whole" the country had admired the Wilson administration. "It appreciates what a miserable handicap he is working under as leader of a reactionary party, in getting progressive legislation . . . we cannot accept his doctrines, but we can respect the man."

Mr. White, after his four-year emotional jag with the Bull Moose party, found the Wilson-Hughes campaign uninteresting, with not a "rocket's red glare or a torchlight in sight . . . not a roorback . . . boomerang . . . connive. Did you ever see the like . . . or did anyone give a hoot in an oil well what happened?"

The political rally, he wrote, "resembles a compromise between a memorial service and a director's meeting . . . the candidates sobbed mournfully over the shortcomings of their rival . . . no one is accused of being a bank robber or train wrecker . . . the platforms are read in sorrow, not in anger; the whole atmosphere of the campaign is lachrymal and doleful."

Mr. White, in the 1916 campaign, held that Judge Hughes was "candid enough, and brave enough and wise enough," but that there were wide areas of his political horizon in shadow; whereas Wilson's best, by and large, "had been unsatisfactory," he had moved in the right direction, "but his direction is biased."

In May, 1917, Mr. White called Wilson "a wonderful man." He said that the great man who had come out of these times was Woodrow Wilson, and added: "If democracy—which is but another name for Christian brotherhood—makes a long forward stride in humanity out of this world crisis, more than to any one individual in the world credit should fall to Woodrow Wilson. He has risen to big opportunity in a big way."

Highly critical in 1918 of what he called President Wilson's "terrible mistake" in asking for a Democratic Congress, Mr. White said that the people, in heaving rocks at Wilson, had ignored the great service the President had rendered humanity with his leadership in the war at home and abroad. Mr. White admitted, however, that President Wilson had his deficiencies: He was human, could be petty, a partisan, and "timid in personal contacts with those who differ with him."

In October, 1920, in an editorial, "A One-Line Head," Mr.

White described a conversation between the *Gazette's* managing and telegraph editors, who were trying to decide whether or not they should run President Wilson's "appeal to his countrymen" with a deck head on the first page. Mr. White commented:

"But how the mighty have fallen. And all because in his human relations he can't get on with the common run of men. Napoleon was the most democratic of autocrats; Woodrow Wilson is the most autocratic of democrats. If he were just a little more human. . . . So—because the faith of humanity is weakened by America's wavering—he gets a one line head."

In early March, 1921, in an editorial, "His Last Day," Mr. White said that this date was the last day "in the White House for the man who entered with such high hopes eight years before, that it is no mere chance that today marked the ebbtide of his fame—a minus tide . . ."

The thing that Wilson had tried to do, White said, would bulk larger than his failure, because his failure "was due to the human weakness of him, and it will die with him. His aspiration was from the divine kinship of all men with the great source from which they came, and that will live. . . . For his failure was the most tragic thing which the modern world has seen. And it was greatly his own fault."

HARDING

In June, 1920, after the Republican convention had nominated Harding, Mr. White expressed lukewarm support of the nominee, but he said, "If Harding calls about himself wise counselors and follows them he may be led in the direction of a liberal policy."

Late July, 1920, Mr. White announced that the *"Gazette* is supporting Harding. He is a better man than Cox and his election will mean more to the Republic than will the election of Cox, dominated by Tammany. . . . Also, doubtless Senator Harding is a man of many varied qualities of mind and heart. But his fool friends are doing him more harm than good by exploiting him as a man of the McKinley type."

Two months later he expressed his belief that "every Republican in the United States should vote his ticket this fall," that there was no reason for a bolt "which sometimes accomplishes something, gets Republicans" nowhere this year. He said, "The issue is one of party and not men," that both Harding and Cox were honest men, and that it would be difficult "to vote enthusiastically" for either.

Following Harding's election, White expressed the hope that "he will face forward and forget old normal things."

After the make-up of Harding's cabinet had been announced in late February, 1921, Mr. White said that "the one joyous thing about the Cabinet is that it is not a subservient Cabinet. It will teach Harding rather more than he will teach it. It is a sign of a great man to surround himself with his superiors. Harding is certainly beginning well. Luck to him."

In summarizing the first three months of the Harding administration in June, 1921, Mr. White said:

"Harding is making few mistakes, few friends, and no enemies. He has no strong purposes and no strong prejudices. He makes a good President but little history.

"It is likely that he has no reserves of force and that the three months which the nation has seen will typify the three years and nine months before us of his first term."

Mr. White's interest in national politics for a year or more about this time, following the death of his daughter, was at an extremely low point, as indicated by the almost complete absence of *Gazette* editorials on that subject.

In March, 1924, writing under the heading "More Trash," Mr. White stated:

Day by day it becomes evident that Attorney General Daugherty is staying in the Cabinet because it is safer fighting for his life in, than out of the Attorney General's office.

He is surrounded by the dirtiest lot of trash that has gathered around a cabinet officer since Grant's administration. . . . Daugherty was a bad appointment of a weak and good-natured man, who seemed to let more fools into the administration than any other President. What a God's mercy to him it was—his death.

COOLIDGE

In 1923, Mr. White wrote:

President Coolidge is a strong man as the term is used in connection with our Presidents. He is not talkative, but he is not a silent figure either. He is mentally alert and has much more capacity for the logical processes of thought than the average American President—more than Harding had, much more than McKinley had. He is well informed, given to reading books, and is possessed of an exact knowledge about where to find the expert sources of information upon any particular subject. He thinks his way to conclusions, where most statesmen feel their way. . . .

. . . his mistakes will not come from ignorance, nor cowardice, nor base motives . . . he may fail to reach the people. But he will on the whole and in most matters, get at the truth and follow it.

When the 1924 campaign was over and the returns were in:
". . . [Coolidge is] a quiet, passionless, cautious little man, who is trying to be honest with himself and with his fellow Americans. He could not be a spellbinder. It is not in him—not in his head and certainly not in his heart. He lacks the enthusiasm. He probably lacks the conviction which makes enthusiasm. . . ."

In October, 1925, Mr. White stated that a number of the *Gazette's* liberal friends were impatient with it for not getting out and beating the tom-toms against Calvin Coolidge, the conservative leader of the Republican party. His answer was:

"Our reason is simple. We are for majority rule. We believe in democracy—which, by the way, does not mean minority rule through the accident of political manipulation. Coolidge by every test, is entitled to lead the party, to rule this land. . . ."

Mr. White's final editorial estimate of Coolidge, written in January, 1933, after the ex-president's death, follows:

How quickly careers are made in America. Here is a man who twenty years ago was unknown outside of his state, and fifteen years ago remained a local figure; yet he has risen to the highest office in the land in a decade and a half and has been in retirement for four years. . . . He quit the presidency full of honor and with the affection of his country; he quit when the quitting was good, of course—Coolidge luck. Of course there was Coolidge judgment in it.

He was a queer man. He preached parsimony when people were extravagant and urged spending when times were hard. He spoke little in public and was rather voluble in private to his intimates. He calculated every move, yet he seemed at times spontaneous in his taciturnity and his habit of caution.

Above all, he was honest. And he was also courageous but he never let his courage get the best of his judgment. When in doubt he stopped. His mistakes were of omission rather than commission. But he made a good President when the world was on the upgrade. No one knows what he would have done on the downgrade. His name is safe for a generation. What history will do with him no one can say. Millions will sincerely mourn him who knew him only as a public servant. There was something in his flinty heart that inspired affection.

6. FREEDOM OF SPEECH AND OF THE PRESS

WILL WHITE went to Emporia in 1895 with only one dollar and a quarter in his pocket and the Bill of Rights in his heart. During his forty-nine years there he gave away one modest fortune and saved another one; but of infinitely greater importance to society were the contributions he made to the clearer interpretation and definition of the principles of freedom of speech and of the press.

Immediately, at the beginning of his career, at a time when he was a zealous partisan, when he lambasted what he considered "crackpot" ideas from whatever source, he vigorously defended the right of the proposers of those ideas to present them to the public. In 1900 he was forthright in defending Professor E. A. Ross, of Stanford University, whom he called "socialist," after Mrs. Stanford had had Ross dismissed from the faculty because of his radical attitude.

To anyone who thinks in modern terms, that editorial carried one bright, shining glimmer of light, even though White plainly regarded Ross, who was a radical for those times, as an "academic fool" and a "loose talker." Even so, White endorsed the principle of academic freedom of expression. With his well-developed understanding of individual men and women, he expressed sympathy for Mrs. Stanford's predicament, because he realized that Professor Ross's opinions directly affronted her idealized memory of her husband, who had founded the university. White wrote that "the expression of her resentment, as it has been expressed, is a blow to the university; that it has all the seeming, if not the reality, of that most serious calamity in a university, the repression of the free utterance of honest opinion, cannot be realized in its fullness by Mrs. Stanford."

"*Lehrfreiheit* and *Lernfreiheit* do not mean that in a university any more than anywhere else a fool saying and doing fool things is to be forever borne with and sustained. A fool in a university has no more excuse for being than a fool outside of a university, and he should have no more privileges nor better protection. Let the fool killer gather his own."

A *Gazette* editorial in 1910 carried another excellent expression of his on the subject of free speech. In referring to a speech delivered by the Socialist leader, Eugene V. Debs, who had opened his party's campaign in Chicago by attacking, with specific or implied charges, the honesty of Samuel Gompers, Theodore Roosevelt, John Mitchell, members of the Supreme Court, and various other organizations and individuals, Mr. White granted that Mr. Debs sincerely believed these men were worthy subjects of his indignation; that Debs "is a sincere man who often sees red." His "denunciation of these men probably would be regarded by many men as wrong," he wrote, and as a result "many well-meaning people would like to see Debs put into jail and kept there. . . ."

Certainly if these well-meaning people had their way, that very thing would be done. And it is everlastingly sure that if Mr. Debs were clapped in jail, if free speech were denied the men who see things differently from the average man, even men who see things red, and who see things dead wrong, the country would suffer.

For free speech in the end harms no one. In the case of Mr. Debs the good his speech does, and the harm it does, depends entirely upon the amount of truth there is in it. The error in it ultimately poisons the whole speech. This is true of free press, as well as of free speech. It is true of the propaganda of every movement or cause, political, commercial or religious. Error poisons itself. Its triumph is short lived. . . . Free thought and free speech are the first requirements of progress.

To White, freedom of speech, with due consideration for the rights of others, for all of the people everywhere, all of the time —not some of the people some of the time—is one of the first goals of free men. It implies that men are equal, self-respecting, self-disciplined, considerate, and responsible. And, equally important, the duties it places upon men are as personal and as fundamental as the rights it confers. Being an individualist and having a due regard for the rights of others, he long strove to get this basic principle of society more clearly understood and strengthened.

In 1920, in referring to the Socialist members of the New

York legislature, who were expelled because of their political creed, he took the position that if a man had a crazy platform, that was no reason why those who agreed with him should not advocate it freely. Such people were entitled to a hearing, should have their say; "reason alone, not the force of majorities, should deny them representation."

In 1921, he condemned the refusal of the Barton County, Kansas, Defense League to permit former Senator Burton to talk for the Nonpartisan League in that county. He called it an "un-American outrage worthy of the Germans in Belgium." He had, he wrote, "the lowest possible opinion of Burton and for twenty years had held to contumely everything that Burton stood for," and it was his belief that the Nonpartisan League under A. C. Townley was a menace to good government.

But so long as J. R. Burton conducts himself within the law he is entitled to the law's protection. And so long as the Nonpartisan League is under Townley and men like Burton, it is so weak in its leadership that it carries its own poison. If it has mailing privileges under the government it should have the right of free speech in conducting its propaganda.

The outrage to free speech and the American constitution which these Barton County people commit under the "Defense League" is vastly more un-American than anything Burton can say. And Burton's career and conduct has not been such that he deserves the martyrdom which they thrust upon him. . . .

The next year White hurried to Townley's defense, saying:

The action of the American Legion men in warning A. C. Townley, of the Nonpartisan League, to leave Salina establishes a dangerous precedent. It is in effect lynching free speech. Townley himself is not a model of Americanism. But he is an American citizen. And as an American citizen he has an absolute right to free speech. Nothing that he has done in the past can in any way impair that right. If he shall attack American institutions traitorously, then the law will get him. But so long as he does not attack American institutions traitorously he is entitled to speak till the cows come home. . . .

The fact that he is a Socialist does not bar him. The doctrine of Socialism is superbly foolish and fantastically unprobable; but holding to it is not a crime and preaching it does not bar a man from the ancient right of free speech. . . .

In 1922 the railroad shopmen in Kansas went on a strike contrary to the orders of the Kansas Industrial Court. White had
been a supporter of the Kansas Industrial Court from the inception of the idea, but when it took the position that merchants
and others should remove from their show windows posters
reading "WE ARE FOR THE STRIKING RAILROAD
MEN 100 PER CENT—WE ARE FOR A LIVING WAGE
AND FAIR WORKING CONDITIONS," White promptly
displayed one of those cards in the *Gazette* window. He changed
it to read that the *Gazette* was for the strikers 49% that day.
He promised, however, if the strike lasted until the following
day, to change the per cent to 50 and move it up a little every
day. With his characteristic fairness he added that he didn't believe that anyone was 100 per cent right, not even the *Gazette,*
but he held the strikers were right somewhere between 49 and
100 per cent. This was not a question of whether the men were
right or wrong, "but a question of the right of an American
citizen to say what he pleases about the strike. Either we have
free speech and a free press in this country, or we have not. Now
is the time to find out."

The appearance of this editorial in defiance of the order of
the Kansas Industrial Court placed his lifelong intimate and
trusted friend, Governor Henry J. Allen, in a most difficult position, because Allen, as governor, sworn to carry out the laws of
the state, had no choice but to call for White's arrest for defying
the court's order. Few men in Allen's place would have acted
with such singleness of purpose. Hot words were passed as the
situation developed. Mrs. White told afterward of hearing Mr.
White a block away the day his arrest was ordered, as he came
home for lunch, clump-clumping his heels hard upon the sidewalk, the one time she ever had seen him really angry. In this
blazing anger he wrote an editorial entitled "To an Anxious
Friend," which was awarded the Pulitzer Prize for that year:

You tell me that law is above freedom of utterance. And I reply
that you can have no wise laws nor free enforcement of wise laws
unless there is free expression of the wisdom of the people—and,
alas, their folly with it. But if there is freedom, folly will die of its
own poison, and the wisdom will survive. That is the history of the
race. It is the proof of man's kinship with God. You say that free-

dom of utterance is not for time of stress, and I reply with the sad truth that only in time of stress is freedom of utterance in danger. No one questions it in calm days, because it is not needed. And the reverse is true also; only when free utterance is suppressed is it needed, and when it is needed, it is most vital to justice. Peace is good. But if you are interested in peace through force and without free discussion—that is to say, free utterance decently and in order —your interest in justice is slight. And peace without justice is tyranny, no matter how you may sugarcoat it with expediency. This state today is in more danger from suppression than from violence, because in the end, suppression leads to violence. Violence, indeed, is the child of suppression. Whoever pleads for justice helps to keep the peace; and whoever tramples upon the plea for justice temperately made in the name of peace only outrages peace and kills something fine in the heart of man which God put there when we got our manhood. When that is killed, brute meets brute on each side of the line.

So, dear friend, put fear out of your heart. This nation will survive, this state will prosper, the orderly business of life will go forward if only men can speak in whatever way given them to utter what their hearts hold—by voice, by posted card, by letter or by press. Reason never has failed men. Only force and repression have made the wrecks in the world.

Most Pulitzer Prize editorials, no matter how wise, how able, or how beautifully written, are doomed to perish with the memory of the passing events that evoked them. But this one laid hold on the eternal. It has not passed, nor will it. With John Milton's *Areopagitica,* it stands among the finest words ever written in English on the freedom of utterance.

In February, 1923, Mr. White, referring to the struggle for liberty going on in the world, expressed the opinion that an Irish anarchist in New York had violated the law by distributing circulars which demanded the overthrow of the American government and that Governor Smith, in granting him a pardon, ignored and practically annulled the law in so far as New York State was concerned.

Clearly we have turned the corner in our thinking upon the question of freedom of utterance. . . . It is clear that the American people are coming to feel that the menace of suppression is worse for stable government than the threat of revolution. . . . We are coming to the conclusion that a just government has nothing to fear from fools. This is a glorious discovery. It disarms the fools. The only danger we face in anarchy and Communism and all the well-known hell's brew of European proletarian misgovernment begins when we clap the poor fish in jail who talks a drivel that we dignify with legal disapproval. If the drivel has any merit, bars will not hold it. If it is without merit, it will not propagate in a happy land.

One of Mr. White's last editorials on the subject was written in March, 1937. He pointed out that free speech was dead in most of Germany.

We account free speech and a free press as one of the blessings of liberty. And at that, in many ways, speech is not so free here as it is in England, while the press here has more leeway. So long as our liberties are guaranteed, so long as every American has the royal right to make whatever particular kind of fool of himself his heart may desire to emulate, this country is safe. But in that sad day when we have to limit the kind of fools we are and have our wisdom channeled out by government, danger will begin to wink its red lights at us.

This seems sheer madness to the dictator. But it is the lamp of truth to Americans.

One of his last "free speech" editorials was published in 1939. In it he wrote, "the pride of our democracy is that America reaches her decisions after full debate and a free discussion. In those discussions every side, indeed any side, however odious its point of view may be, has its fair hearing."

He described a great mass meeting that had been held shortly before in New York City at which "Mayor La Guardia, half Jew, gave police protection to the crowd of Jew-baiting Nazis who recently had packed Madison Garden"; La Guardia "had done a fine thing in the American tradition." He paid his respects to the Nazis, who "in power would not have allowed La Guardia to have his say. This was no answer to the democratic demand that these bigots be heard. They had their say. What they said was terrible. But they were entitled to say it and present their case. . . . So long as that principle is active, the flag will wave and no man will be in danger."

7. TOLERANCE AND THE KU KLUX KLAN

W HEN, early in the boom era, the Ku Klux Klan burst into Kansas, Will White had no need to do any thinking on paper. From the first he ever heard of it, he knew exactly how he felt on that issue. One great quality which he kept reserved in a special place in his fine heart was sympathetic understanding for those who held views differing from his own. For the right to express dissent from his own opinions he would fight with the zeal of a Voltaire. In his earlier years he gave some evidence of being arrogant, but his warm sympathies for men, and especially for minorities who were subject to attack, early made him an opponent of the intolerant, a defender of the oppressed. To him, tolerance stood as "the first requirement for social security," even though it is one of the last qualities man develops in his social evolution. To him tolerance in America was "a deep, crying need." As early as 1900 he was writing sympathetically about the Jews, and expressing the conviction that "the Jew in American life has come to stay." This probability, he said, "speaks well for America and well for the Jews. They are thrifty; they are frugal; they are as honest as Americans will let them be. They are sober, conscientious, God-fearing, law-abiding people." He went on to point out that they "are believers in the home and the family." They stay at home of nights, pay little attention to orators or demagogues, have hard sense and a "severely practical" religion. "They don't lie and they don't steal. They keep out of police court and mind their own business." (This editorial was written long before the gangster days when so many second-generation Americans, Jews among them, went wrong—notables in this list were Lepke and Gurrah.) He concluded:

". . . In short, they are good citizens and America has been the gainer in welcoming them. They are becoming Americanized and would be less clannish if Gentile prejudices did not force them to be. Some day that prejudice will pass—as witch burning has passed, and the hatred of cripples. The Jew is a

great man. He has been a great man for ages, and in America
he is coming into his kingdom."

No expression of his shows how greatly he had grown in
sympathy and understanding since 1896, when he wrote his
"What's the Matter with Kansas?", than an editorial of 1903
on the anarchists. He began by saying that they were wrong because their theory of leveling by destruction is opposed to all
principles of building known to science. He held that "to level
permanently one must build up." Then he added:

But—

Supposing the case: Supposing you worked hard till your back
ached every night in dirty, grimy work, that made you look like the
devil. Suppose the standard of living had been increased—through
no apparent fault of yours—so that the best you could get out of a
day's work was a little house in an unpleasant part of town, and
that your children were not so warmly clad as you would like, and
your wife had to go without a girl at those times when it tore your
heart to see her bending over the washtub. Suppose that when she
was sick she had to work right along, and that death came to her
and took her from you when a few dollars at the right time would
have saved her. Suppose, then, that when you were at work some
man who you knew came to work at nine o'clock and went away at
half-past three, looked at you at your grimy work with that horrible
leer of patronizing pity that heartless, spotless men give to their
fellows in the mire; suppose that you knew his wife and children
were alive and happy by reason of their money; suppose you should
overhear a remark which that spotless chap made which indicated
that he didn't think of you as a human being, but as a unit of labor,
merely a working animal . . .

Think of the man in the muck as your brother; be decent and
square; give no charity, but give him justice. It is all right to be
smart, to be keen in business, to be forehanded. But with your surplus of brains don't grind the man under you . . .

This country needs more Christianity, more kindness of heart,
more justice between man and man, and the need is from the top
more than from the bottom. We need more business morality, more
political morality, more humanity in our dealings with each other.
We are all in the same boat, and the man in one end of the boat
who doesn't pull his weight is as bad as the lazy agitator in the other
end. Sam Parks went to the penitentiary, as he should have done.
He was a scoundrel. But the big jug-shaped rascals down in Wall

Street, who hire high-priced attorneys to let them rob and plunder inside the law—they should follow Sam Parks.

There is anarchy in high places as well as in low places. Neither justifies the other, but the rich man has less reason for his lawlessness than the poor man. Each is selfish; each is wrong; each will make the world unhappier for his living. There is no peace nor contentment nor good except in unselfish kindness one to another . . .

When in 1907 some of the University of Kansas students refused to back up their debating team because a Negro undergraduate had won a place on it, White held that:

The color of a man's skin is of no importance, if the color of his brain is good and gray. If the colored man beat the white man fairly, the white men are mighty poor sports and exceedingly cheap pikers not to get behind him, when he represents the university. Here was a black man who by hard work and honest effort had risen above his fellows. He had risen further than the white boy's defeat, because he started from the jungle only a few centuries ago, while the white boys have been thousands of years coming his distance. Why then as gentlemen should not their sporting blood rise to honor this poor slave's grandson who has come so well so far? . . . A few miserable flukes like that will make Kansas people wonder whether they are educating thoroughbreds or scrubs at their big state school.

In 1908, he wrote critically of the Jim Crow legislation Oklahoma had adopted which, he said, "classed her with Mississippi and sundry other semi-barbarous southern states. . . ." Again, concerning a Tulsa riot in which some Negroes had been killed, he wrote: "The white race will have a sad time convincing the black race of its superiority so long as the white race lets its bums and idlers and nobodies kill and burn and maim, unchecked and unpunished."

Outraged over the fact that some decent colored girls were being subjected to insult by white men as they went through one of Emporia's parks to their homes, he told the community:

. . . It's a brave thing to do! God knows that the colored girl who is trying to rise is carrying a handicap that would crush the average park loafer into a grease spot. There are men in this world so mean and low down that when they all die and are rounded up, the devil will have to establish a segregated district in hell so as not to contaminate the ordinary run of thieves and murderers and liars and house-burners entrusted to his care.

In 1921, after the Santa Fe Railroad brought to Emporia large numbers of Mexicans as maintenance-of-way workmen, Mr. White neither liked the way they were housed nor their treatment by the townsmen. Writing under the title of "Americanism," he asked:

If you lived in a boxcar along the railroad, and all your friends lived the same way;

If you were the lowest paid working man in the community, and did some of the most important work;

If your children had irregular schools, and sometimes no school at all;

If you attracted no interest in the town, except from the city marshal, the bootlegger and an occasional padre;

If you were treated like an animal, housed like an animal and given no social consideration nor economic or political position in the community—

What a lot of balderdash you would call the talk about the "flag of the free," the "home of the brave" and 100 percent Americanism! Do you ever think what the average Mexican thinks of America as he walks the streets of Emporia?

Did he ever meet our boasted Christian civilization on Commercial Street? Is it in his box car home? Is it in the merchants who sell goods? Where can he find the spirit of Jesus Christ?

And like an advance hint to the Klan, about the same time, he wrote:

"Probably more bigotry and reaction just now are hiding under the phrase, Americanism, than ever hid under one word before. If Americanism means anything, it means freedom of speech, freedom of thought, freedom of press. Every wicked, greedy force in America today is trying to strangle discussion under the guise of promoting Americanism. And as a result of the repression every mad political folly is thriving . . ."

Only a man with unshakable faith in men and their best purpose, only a man with great perspective and profound understanding of the creator's purpose could have been so sure of himself that he never feared the truth.

It was not until the Ku Klux Klan had risen to the height of its power in the early 1920's, however, that White was to be recognized throughout the nation and the world as the spearhead of the opposition to the attack on Negroes, Jews, and other immigrants. His vigorous, resourceful, and courageous fight against the Klan made him the hero of oppressed minorities in the United States.

Three public activities of Will White's stand out head and shoulders above all his others: his leadership in the Progressive party; this fight against the Ku Klux Klan; and finally, his leadership as chairman of the Committee to Defend America by Aiding the Allies. In each of these he dramatized the fight, clarified the issues, and thereby enabled all the people to see more clearly the heart of the question which was troubling them.

The Ku Klux Klan was a disagreeable social phenomenon which followed the First World War—as such follies tend to follow all wars. We had been through a debauch of stimulated hatred. Psychologists have noted that certain temperaments take an inordinate pleasure in hate. The Christian conscience bottles up a few of them, but when someone invents for such people a moral justification the cork is drawn. This group missed something out of their life—their dream hate—when Germany was beaten and humbled. Cheap demagogues, fanatics and racketeers capitalized on this mood. Intolerance, whipped up by propaganda which advertised imaginary dangers and flashy remedies, flourished as never since the bad days following the war between the states.

And so, about 1921 when the Ku Klux Klan, founded in the days of the war by a small-time preacher and promoter of fraternal orders, suddenly grew from an obscure racket into a national menace, Mr. White put on his armor for the crusade which was to absorb his best mental and spiritual energies during the next two or three years.

The Klan's ugly record needs little mention here. It was a secret immoral order, founded to establish the supremacy of "white, native-born, gentile, Protestant Americans." It had in it every one of the seeds which, falling on a more congenial soil, grew and fruited in the noxious growth of national socialism in Germany under Hitler's leadership. The Klan's founders had motives identical with those of the Nazis, a greed for power, genuine fanaticism, and the racketeer's yearning for easy money. They appealed to identical master methods of promotion, i.e., they set up a straw man and focused righteous hate on him. They used the same impulses. The obscure, the frustrated, the unsuccessful who had little cause for pride in themselves could work up a vicarious pride by the thought that they belonged to a master race. A penetratingly observant traveling salesman remarked at about this time: "You could almost spot a Klansman when you saw him. He appeared to be American of the old stock but terribly dull in the eye, low in the forehead and narrow between the ears."

The Klan flourished for a time with falsehood, lying propaganda, torture, and secret murder. Its membership increased by shoals, and political support of the Klan by conscienceless politicians became the rule. The Klan, taking a tip from that successful minority faction, the Anti-Saloon League, seldom nominated a ticket of its own, but worked by the balance-of-power method. Probably hundreds of men who since have attained high office were once members of the Klan—secretly, of course, for membership was always secret—between 1920 and the collapse which began in 1924.

Ku Klux Klan leaders, noting that Kansas had but a small foreign-born population and remembering the tendency of the state toward political crazes, marked it early as a promising field, sent their best organizers there, and soon had a large following.

Mr. White probably was the first American newspaper editor of much consequence to attack it. He began his fight when it had only 100,000 members or so, and had as yet shown little strength in Kansas. Even the *New York World,* which performed such valiant service against the Klan in the East, had not yet fired its first guns. At that time the Klan was fighting—and murdering—in the South on a not unpopular racial issue. In the North it played on the aversion of the more narrow-minded Protestants to Catholicism and, since editors are always chary of taking sides in any religious controversy, most newspapers held their peace. But on this subject Mr. White, with his great prestige, his popularity as a newspaperman's newspaperman, spoke out.

His first editorial reference to the Klan appeared on August 4, 1921, under the head "The *Beacon* Pans It," referring to the *Wichita Beacon,* published by his friend Henry J. Allen, then governor of Kansas, who for some time had been carrying on a courageous and effective fight against the Klan. The Klan organizer for Kansas, Mr. White reported, lived in Wichita. There followed in a few days a second editorial entitled "Enough of Ku Kluxism," and a third, "Nix on the Ku Klux Klan." In this one White wrote that there were of course bad foreigners and good ones, good Catholics and bad ones, and all kinds of Negroes; but "To make a case against a birthplace, a religion or a race, is wicked, un-American and cowardly."

By August 11, he had brought the subject home to Emporia. Reverting to his old style of a pioneer editor in a fight, he denounced "the pot-bellied pollywogs and the white-livered lizards of the Klan," and added:

"The Emporia lodge of the Klan so far has nothing but a lot of hot air and cold feet in their office on Fifth avenue, where the easily distinguishable typewriter of the most austere angle-worm of the Klan is having a sad time with an unsympathetic environing cosmos."

For a year he hammered it in:

The Ku Klux Klan is a curious example of the tyrannies of men in masses. Cowards who fear to lift even their voices in protest against what they deem unrighteousness, when they are massed in mobs are brave enough. . . . It is government or anarchy in this country in the fight against the Ku Klux Klan . . .

The Klan organizer tells the dupes whom he is trying to herd into the organization at so much per, that the Klan takes care of the cases which the law does not reach. And that is exactly the case. When a man is living within the law, no matter how disagreeable he may be, no matter how much his neighbors may dislike him, that man is living within his rights as an American citizen, and being within his rights as an American citizen should be protected in them, and not attacked and blackguarded and bullyragged because some fellows don't like him.

The whole trouble with the Klan is that it permits a lot of men under irresponsible leadership to do dastardly and un-American things under the guise of Americanism. Any dupe who would join the Klan, would be stupid enough to follow its wicked and cowardly leadership to a lawless and disgraceful act.

In June, 1922, the Emporia Klan offered to the *Gazette* an advertisement setting forth its noble aims. White accepted it with $7.56 in payment, and on the editorial page urged his subscribers to read it, and then ask one question:

If the Klan contains all the virtue, all the righteousness and all the patriotism that the oil stock salesmen claim for it, why hide all that virtue behind a mask and why not wear a button to show your pride in it? Imagine Christ chasing the Pharisees out of the temple behind a mask, and Lincoln riding around in his shirttail before signing·the Emancipation Proclamation.

He had begun to get action by now. Other courageous editors not only in Kansas, but even in the East, were falling in behind him. And his own wrath rose to such heat that he printed two editorials on the same subject the same day.

One reported that Governor Allen had asked the county officers of Cowley County to stop the invasion of the Klan, and then commented:

Yet in this town 150 suckers bought stock of the oily-tongued stranger who sold them memberships.

How would you like to belong to an outfit whom the President of the United States, the Governor of the State, the Masonic Grand Lodges and the best citizens of every town are denouncing?

And then on top of that, how would you like to belong to an outfit which requires members to lie to their wives and deny even to them that they belong to it?

The second editorial blasted a secret society formed in Missouri to combat the Klan. "Fight it in the open," advised White, because:

If the Klansmen would wear buttons and make their membership public no one could seriously object to their propaganda. For in this country anyone has the royal right to make of himself as big a fool as his brains make him, and if wearing shirttails and waving fiery crosses is the thing he likes, then let him go to it. But secrecy in membership begets tyranny and tyranny begets brutality, and so wherever the Klan thrives brutality and cowardly tyranny thrive.

And a society with a secret membership to fight the Klan would be as bad as the Klan.

When Mussolini's Fascists took over Italy, White linked them with the Klan.

The mask is but an incidence. Bigotry and intolerance of the various ultra-national organizations identify them with a common brotherhood. The details of what they believe are unimportant. What they do and would do is the bond between them. . . . Only the ignorant, stupid and the bigoted respond to rumors, denunciations and baseless propaganda. . . . Reason and truth and common sense, even in a minority, can overcome the powers of superstition and darkness. The world is sick of force, of guns, of parading, of bloodshed, and the terror that flies by night. . . . Only reason will heal the wounds that men have made tearing each other's hearts out.

He was fighting not only editorially, but, so far as he was able, in the news. He could not go very far there. A big newspaper like the *New York World* has hundreds of reporters and correspondents, and in a real fight can spend thousands of dollars on detectives and investigators; he had only the little staff of a country daily. Traditionally, the Klan was a hard nut to crack. All its operations were secret. The members were not only allowed to deny membership but usually commanded to do so. The news most wanted was the identity of its members and especially of its officers. White found to his own satisfaction who the Grand Cyclops of Kansas was, but had not proof enough to print the name. But he did score one hit which played its part in killing the Klan in Kansas.

The story in Frank Clough's book about White (Clough was city editor of the *Gazette* during the Klan fight) contains an intimate account of one Klan episode. White, through his own investigations and those of his reporters, learned three facts. The Kansas branch of the Klan was going to hold a "Grand Konklave" in Emporia, with its leading officers present. They would all stay at a certain hotel. That very night, an Italian musical organization was putting up at the same hotel. The two conventions would jam the place; the management was going to refuse accommodations to all other persons. White, who had tried and failed to learn the identity of the visiting Klansmen, chuckled to himself and sent a reporter to copy the names in the register. The management caught him at it, closed the book and locked it up, virtually threw the reporter out of the place. White, angry now, telephoned with burning words to one of the hotel company's directors. The director came over to the *Gazette* office with a protest. "If you don't let us copy those names," said White, "I'll throw your advertisement out of the paper, and never print the name of your hotel again." A quarter of an hour later, the manager reappeared, carrying the register.

Only one editor in a thousand would have had the restraint and subtlety to do what White did next. He refrained from editorializing. He simply printed on his front page a few lines to the effect that the Italian musicians and the Grand Konklave of the Ku Klux Klan had stayed at the Blank Hotel the night before, that there had been room for no other guests, and that the following persons had registered. Few readers of the *Gazette* were so stupid and incurious as not to cross out the palpably Italian names and read the list of the leading Kansas Klansmen. The career of many a promising young political crook was blasted then and there.

By the end of 1923, Mr. White found a ray of hope in the Klan situation, because "Emporia's Kluxer mayor has appointed a Catholic chief of police—and a dandy one too, and a colored man assistant chief, and he's a daisy. The world is in pretty bad shape. The Emporia end of it is all to the good."

For a while he merely skirmished with the local Klan, as when an anonymous letter writer told of a Klan gift to the Baptist Church in Emporia and asked sarcastically how much the *Gazette* gave. Mr. White replied in print that it was a fair question; the *Gazette* had given without charge 66 inches in the news columns, or a total of 528 lines which if sold as advertising would have cost $63.36. It wasn't much, he added, "but it was four and a half times more than the Kluxers gave the Baptist evangelist, and we didn't have to pull out our shirttail to do it."

But the situation in Kansas as a whole was growing alarming. In 1924, an election year, the Klan showed its power.

White charged that Paulen, the Republican nominee, had

Klan support, as also had Davis, the Democratic nominee. Others believed that one of these men was a member. Certainly neither of them was saying a word against the hooded order. White wrote:

"The *Gazette* feels that the endorsement of any oath-bound secret political society is a shameful thing for any candidate to have. . . . It is vastly more important to a man's glory as an American citizen to be defeated like a man, than to be elected by the endorsement of an oath-bound society, whatever it might be."

He was making, now, toward one of the great determinations of his life. The Klan already dominated Oregon. It was reaching for the control of Indiana and neighboring Colorado. Kansas might be next. This issue overshadowed all others in the state election. But with both parties virtually pledged to silence, the campaign would be a solemn farce. And late in August he dropped this hint of his own intentions in an editorial headed "Take the Curse Off":

"As sure as sunrise, independent Republican candidates will enter the field against these Klan candidates where the people of Kansas have no alternative but to vote for a Klan Republican or a Klan Democrat."

Calling upon the Republican party council to remove that alternative, he added:

"The voters are entitled to cast their ballots for a man who is not Klan-endorsed . . . They are not going to be left without the opportunity to cast a free-born American vote."

Two days laters, he turned loose in the old, free-wheeling Western style:

Well—there they are, the biggest of the invisible government, the trouble makers, nit-wits, the fourth-raters, who are denounced by every national party. In Kansas their votes are isolated. The segregated district in Kansas this year is around Ben Paulen [Republican candidate for governor] and his lieutenant governor. So take the shirttail rangers, Ben; let 'em romp around you with their fiery cross. A vote is a vote in this country and if the man behind the vote is a lame-brained hoot owl who is ashamed to show his face and afraid to declare his membership in an organization which no national party will accept—take him, Ben. A vote is a vote. . . .

So take 'em, Ben, and joy go with you. But spice 'em up with a jigger of sweet stinkum every now and then, for they certainly do smell.

And again, turning to national affairs, he remarked that whereas six months previously the politicians had been coddling and loving the Klan, stroking its nightie, patting its hood, and feeding it taffy, the Democratic National Convention two months earlier had given it a good, swift kick and it "didn't bite. It just whined." As a result, politicians who previously had taken the Kluxers to their bosoms were now busy getting away from the Klan.

In September, 1924, he went beyond hinting. Writing about "The Governorship," he noted that Emporia was manifesting some interest in the possible candidacy of the editor of the *Gazette* for governor, and announced flatly that if he got into the race it would not be because his man did not win the primary. Instead, it would be because the Klan was the enemy of our fundamental principles of government; that it stood for force instead of reason, terror instead of the due processes of law.

If the Reds of Russia had won in the primary, the editor of the *Gazette* should not feel bound by that primary, and when the Klan wins in the primary, and when Paulen, the winner, is beholden to the Klan, and when by his prestige he forces a resolution on the State Committee shutting off all debate on the subject of the Klan; and finally when he uses, in denying his membership in the Klan, the phrase "at this time" which all Kluxers use in denying their membership, then the editor of the *Gazette* is not bound by any primary to degrade his citizenship.

And he crossed the Rubicon. Someone must bring this issue vividly, personally, before the people—not only of Kansas but of the United States. Someone must run for governor as a focus for the protest vote. But no "Protestant, Gentile, native-born American" in Kansas was both willing to undertake the fight and capable of making it effective—except himself. Further, he knew that he was the most famous citizen of Kansas; and this affair was not a mere civil war in one state but a national issue. His fulminations and witticisms directed against the Klan had crowded into editorial pages all over the country. Now he proposed to break into the news columns.

In an age when self-advertising had become almost an industry, White had never exploited his own personality. His distaste for false renown at that price was doubtless one reason why he hesitated until the election was only six weeks away; that and his old "monastic vow" against running for public office. However, this would not be exploiting himself. "I am not running for governor; I am running for a principle," he said at the time.

So in mid-September he announced in the *Gazette* that he had filed his petition for governor "to free Kansas from the disgrace of the Ku Klux Klan."

. . . I want to offer a Kansas afraid of the Klan and ashamed of that disgrace, a candidate who shares her fear and shame. . . .

Kansas, with her intelligence and pure American blood, of all states should be free of this taint of bigotry and terror. I was born in Kansas and have lived my life in Kansas. I am proud of my state. And the thought that Kansas should have a government beholden to this hooded gang of masked fanatics, ignorant and tyrannical in their ruthless oppression, is what calls me out of the pleasant ways of my life into this distasteful but necessary task. I cannot sit idly and see Kansas become a byword among the states.

I call to my support least of all those who are oppressed by the Ku Klux Klan. We must have no class issue here. I call to my support rather all fair-minded citizens of every party, of every creed, to stop the oppression of this minority of our people. It is a nationwide menace, this klan. It knows no party. It knows no country. It knows only bigotry, malice and terror. Our national government is founded on reason and the Golden Rule. This klan is preaching and practicing terror and force. Its only prototype is the Soviet of Russia. So I feel that I am walking the path of duty in going into this race. I ask my fellow Kansans to come with me and to stand with me for free government and the righteous guarantees of our constitution, to all its citizens.

Starting late, with no organization, no campaign fund, nothing that a candidate needs except a good cause and his own personality, prevented his being elected—an outcome which he would have regarded as a calamity. He has himself told how, lying awake one night after an especially enthusiastic meet-

ing, the thought that he might win caused him to break into
a cold sweat. But in the morning, common sense resumed its
reign. However, he had to maintain that victory was certain.
In politics, that attitude is not considered lying. It is a fair and
allowable convention of the game, like bluffing in poker.

This item is from memory: In the course of a long interview
for the *Kansas City Star,* just before the election, he presented
his case at length. In answer to the reporter's last question,
which concerned his chances of victory, White replied that of
course he would win—no doubt about it. Then, his sense of
humor getting the better of him, he leaned toward the reporter
and whispered: "I'm Napoleon!"

So he started on a swing through the state by automobile to
"laugh the Klan out of Kansas." Supporters and admirers found
halls, parks, and pasture lots for meetings. Public speaking was
the least of his intellectual talents, and he did not try to orate.
He just talked as a man to his fellow townsmen, about the "cow-
pasture edicts" of a handful of cheap, ignorant "genii, whang-
doodles, wizards, willopsies-wallopsies, shirt-tail rangers," who
had scared the life out of Kansas politicians. From the day of
his first declaration, his news judgment was vindicated. In that,
a presidential year, with a third of the United States senator-
ships and a majority of the governorships under contest, he
drew more front-page notice throughout the United States than
any other candidate except the three who were running for
president. His biographer, Everett Rich, has noted that "he
set the stage for lower political propaganda than usually prevails in Kansas." Naturally, with the Klan inspiring most of it.
The low point was a purported letter of White's, given out by
his opposition, grossly insulting Catholics, Jews, and Negroes.
He simply laughed that off, and went on giving the liberal-
minded of Kansas and the country a good time. And even this
was good press for his cause.

A day before the election, under the title "The Prodigal's
Return," Mr. White reported to the readers that the White
family had reached home after a six weeks' "joyous journey in
Kansas." This trip had covered 2,783 miles. Young Bill was
chauffeur. Mrs. White went along to take care of him. During
that time Mr. White had made 104 speeches and estimated that

he addressed 100,000 people. Enormous crowds had attended meetings in the Kansas cities—the largest meetings, he said, "not only in this campaign but in any campaign since Roosevelt's day."

Summarizing the campaign and speaking of himself, he wrote that he was happy to be home and had no anxiety about tomorrow because his job was done. That was to get before the people the menace of the Klan and "to keep it before them for six weeks." By doing this, he had, he felt certain, "removed from scores of small towns the curse of silence which the Klan had put upon the issue." He was certain that he would get a decent vote of protest and added that one of his major fears was that he might win the election. Referring to the old suit of clothes he had worn to the office that day with flaming red necktie and an old brown hat, he said, "This rig is my fiercest protest against six weeks of circumspection, Sunday clothes, punctilious conduct and the public life. The goldfish has flopped out of the aquarium back into the puddle and is having a gay and festive time today."

He lost, of course; in fact, he ran third. But he polled about 150,000 votes—more than were cast that year in Kansas for John W. Davis, the Democratic party's candidate for president, and representing probably ten times as many citizens as there were Klansmen in Kansas. In a state notorious for its party loyalties, something like a quarter of the electors had jumped their tickets to register their indignation and their contempt for the "thriving and profitable hate-factory and bigatorium" which seemed to have taken over the old parties.

In a brief editorial entitled "A Personal Word," he closed the episode as far as he was concerned. He told how glad he was over having given his supporters a chance to vote for someone not tainted with the endorsement of the Klan; assured them that naturally he never wanted to be governor or "I should have gone about getting the job in the regular way." But he assured them, "With all my heart I desired to protest against the un-American influence of the Klan in politics. . . . I am proud that I could serve those who felt as I feel. They are good people. They deserved a better candidate." And being associated with such people for six weeks was the finest experience of his life, a beautiful adventure, which he always would treasure in his heart.

"As to the immediate result, it is unimportant. The seed is sown. The fight must be fought out. It will come up next year in the struggle for nomination. Then we shall finish what we started. The Republican party must not be mortgaged to the Ku Klux Klan. The war on that crowd is only well begun."

The *Encyclopedia Britannica,* in its article on the Klan, says that up to and including the elections of 1924 the organization was extremely successful in controlling local politicians, but that before 1928 "its power had waned appreciably and it had little effect on the elections of that year. This rapid disintegration is difficult to account for . . ." To one familiar with the political movements of that period the explanation is not hard to find. The real reason the Klan disintegrated rapidly following 1924 was that the local editor of a small-town Kansas newspaper had used his rich gifts and his rare wit to laugh it off the political map—off the earth.

In August, 1926, Mr. White could crow as follows:

The Ku Klux Klan in Kansas is a busted community. It went into the recent Kansas primary full of fight. It tried to control the Supreme Court. Instead the Klan was overwhelmingly defeated by the voters. The Klan selected candidates from the charter board, who were running for Attorney General and Secretary of State. The two candidates who openly denounced the Klan were nominated by good pluralities.

Two years earlier, the Klan was entrenched in Kansas, had endorsed both the winning candidates for Governor on the major party tickets, and was sitting on the moon with its toes in the stars. Now its endorsement is a liability and its friendship is a reflection upon a Kansas politician's patriotism and good sense. That much has been done in a two years' fight in Kansas. It can be done in any state where the decent elements exhibit courage and hard work. But anyway, thank Heaven, Kansas is free.

8. NATIONAL POLITICAL ACTIVITIES
1928–1943

WHITE'S SELF-IMPOSED MORATORIUM on national politics drew to a close in 1928. The shock and numbness caused by his daughter's death, his battle for free expression, his magnificent fight against the Ku Klux Klan and other intolerant movements, and his lack of spiritual sympathy with either the Harding or Coolidge administrations had combined to reduce his interest in the doings at Washington. But now Coolidge "did not choose to run," and when many Republican leaders were trying to soft-soap him into changing his decision, many others were looking for a candidate more sympathetic to liberal ideas.

So at the age of sixty, White returned full force to the political fray. Two factors contributed to this. One was his admiration for Herbert Hoover, who, when Coolidge stuck to his decision, simply walked away from all the other aspirants to the Republican nomination.

In 1915, when the Commission for Relief in Belgium was beginning to attract the attention of the world, I remember conversations with him about Hoover. White spoke with utmost admiration of this young man's ability, imagination, humanity, and resourcefulness. And later, when he had made his acquaintance, he was especially attracted by Hoover's spiritual quality.

The other inspiration to action was the fact that Hoover and the platform on which he was nominated supported the prohibition law, then on the statue books, called it "an experiment, noble in motive and lofty in purpose," while Governor Alfred E. Smith, Hoover's opponent, was a wet of wets. White himself was a prohibitionist of the first water. His few critics have called this a flaw in his armor of liberalism. Perhaps; "consistency is the hobgoblin of little minds." White was Kansas all through, and the state long has taken pride in its "peculiar institution." In one of his magazine articles, White argued the question out with himself. Kansas, he wrote, owed its low incidence of crime, its high standards of education, its comparative freedom from graft and gangdom in politics, to the fact that it did not have to wrestle with the saloon. On the other hand, might not there be some obscure link between alcohol and genius? What had Kansas ever done, of note, in the arts? What national leader of distinction had Kansas ever given the country? At that time White himself was an answer to the question, and at that exact moment a Kansas country-town boy named Eisenhower was preparing himself to become our greatest field general in our greatest war.

Prohibition prevailed with White. Probably his own experience tipped the balance. He had seen many fine, brilliant, promising young friends and associates take "the hell-west and crooked route" to its sad end with the help of hard liquor. He fought against repeal to the very end, preached through his editorial columns throughout the years for a law that would prohibit the sale of hard liquor.

Another thing: Smith was a Tammany man. Indeed, the West considered him the tiger's favorite son, its child. As White said in one *Gazette* editorial during the campaign:

"We shall progress as Americans after the American fashion, not after the Tammany fashion. We shall not pattern our economics nor our morals after the standards set by European visionaries, nor turn our moral and spiritual ideals toward a wide open America wherein license is confused with liberty and the righteousness of our fathers' God mocked by the cynical philosophy of a creed outworn, 'Eat, drink and be merry, for tomorrow we die.'"

And so, for a time, his part in the campaign consisted largely in pouring it into this supposed ally of the saloon and Tammany. He specialized on the Governor's voting record while a member of the New York assembly, which he had secured at his own expense and for his own use. He said that Smith's was a "curious political record." In a speech delivered in Kansas in July, 1928, he charged Smith with having supported saloons and prostitution through his votes. The publication of White's charges in New York City newspapers caused Smith to challenge their accuracy, and to pay his violent respects to the man he suspected as White's informant. As always in such controversies,

one word led to another and each hotter than the last. A few
weeks later, White started for Europe. He stopped off in New
York City to check and recheck his original information and to
write a reply. It mentioned that Governor Smith had done him
"the honor to wallop me over a preacher's shoulders, calling the
preacher, whom I never heard of, a liar and an 18-carat faker."

In these two weeks I have employed two experts, working inde-
pendently, and have gone into the New York assembly journal. I
am now ready to present his assembly record to Governor Smith,
not merely in broad, general terms, but to face him with his own
votes on questions affecting the saloon and its two parasites—the
gambler and the prostitute. . . .

He voted, or is so recorded, nearly a dozen times in the big controversial measures with the most notorious saloon men in the Tammany delegation.

No klansman in a boob legislature, cringing before a kleagle or a
wizard, was more subservient to the crack of the whip than was Al
Smith . . . in the legislature when it came to a vote to protect the
saloon, to shield the tout, and to help the scarlet women of Babylon,
whose tolls in those years always clinked regularly in the Tammany
till.

This record is, of course, an old record of a young man. But the
young man rose on this record. And today the issue is formed on the
elements that made this old record—the return of the saloon, which
Governor Smith as a young man defended so ably. But the Tammany system goes on today as it went on 100 years ago and, indeed,
as it will go in all of our American cities unless Governor Smith
and the sinister forces behind him are overthrown.

Up to this point White had been acting entirely on his own.
Now, however, the hurry of those last hours before sailing
caused a slip. Having no facilities in New York for releasing his
statement, he asked his friend Henry J. Allen, then chairman
of the Republican National Publicity Committee, to get it to
the newspapers for him. Allen gave it to an assistant, with ex-
plicit instructions to label it as a personal release from White.
The assistant, either careless, indifferent, or dumb, sent it to
the newspapers as a Republican Committee release.

The alert Democrats leaped into the opening. White was in-
vulnerable to any countercharges directed at his personal
record. Not so the Republican National Comittee. Plenty of

Republican politicians now supporting a bone-dry platform had voted wet in their time. Smith's publicity agents and newspaper friends tagged the Republican Committee with the authorship or inspiration of this document, and the fat was in the fire. To complicate the situation, some of Smith's friends caught White before he sailed and persuaded him that Smith's voting record was not so bad as the statistics indicated. Had they been acquainted, White probably would have esteemed the gallant Al for what he was, in spite of differences of opinion.

White, generous and fair as always, issued a statement saying in effect that he would suspend judgment until all of the evidence was in. The Democrats saw another opening. Their newspapers, inspired by their national committee, ran headlines and wrote leads which implied that White had withdrawn his charges. By now, he was on his way to Europe. The controversy, one of those side issues to a political campaign which burn up much energy and do not in the least affect the result, was still simmering when he returned. In late August, and again in October, he tried to straighten out what he had done and not done and why—"Mr. White never at any time retracted anything he ever said about Governor Smith's record . . . but he felt that such topics should have no part in the dignified discussion of a Presidential campaign . . . The word prostitution . . . would inflame people so that they would not think straight and this would confuse the paramount issues of the contest . . ."

What troubled him most was the feeling that he had put the Republican National Committee and the Republican candidate in an embarrassing position. When, returning from Europe in late summer, he found the political atmosphere still thick with charges and countercharges, he and I discussed the situation at length during a meal at the National Arts Club in New York City. As I was leaving he put his hands on my shoulders and said, "Son, if you love me, if you ever want to do anything for me that really counts, make Hoover understand that I stay put."

I promised. When next day I saw Hoover in Washington I repeated what White had said to me. He listened to the end and remarked, "Isn't he the sweetest man that ever lived?" He buzzed for his secretary and when she came he said, "Take a letter to William Allen White: 'Dear White: I am glad to learn that you are back home. Don't let your heart be troubled. Faithfully yours."

Following Hoover's election White wrote in the *Gazette* on those leaders such as Washington, Lincoln, Roosevelt—men who led America not in conquest over the material universe but upward toward spiritual ideals, "who have made the injustices of life repugnant." And: "Hoover can be a great spiritual leader of the world if he will. He has the idealism that is necessary. It is given to him to understand the equities of many situations and he has the courage of his convictions and intelligence. . . ."

He added that Hoover had a mandate to make the country really dry, that the Republican party was definitely the stronghold of prohibition.

Three months after Hoover's inauguration:

"President Hoover's Memorial Day speech was the utterance of a practical ideal. The way to peace is to reduce world armament. His speech will thrill the world. It is a new note from America, muted since Wilson's day. . . ."

This was the first time since Wilson's death that White enthused editorially over a president.

Then came the crash of October, 1929, the reaction from a fake prosperity to the deepest depression in a century, storm clouds over the administration, the mid-term congressional elections of 1930, decisively Democratic. Commenting on them, Mr. White wrote that it happened largely because the American people misunderstood Herbert Hoover, that he lacked the capacity to dramatize himself as the exponent of any cause; that as administrator he had every virtue of a splendid executive, but, alas, some of those virtues, a certain secrecy, reticence, an imperious determination to have his way, are not democratic virtues and will not help a democratic leader.

"So it was not what Hoover did . . . it was the way he failed to appeal to the popular imagination, that caused the Democratic landslide."

In early 1931, when the depression seemed to have sunk to its depths, he wrote:

"[Hoover] stutters, grumbles, fumbles, hesitates and is not

dramatically vocal in his leadership of the people in the controversies with Congress, but when a matter narrows down to an
administrative policy, Herbert Hoover is as right as rain . . ."

"The President, ladies and gentlemen—up everyone!" he
wrote when, later that year, Hoover arranged the moratorium
on war debts. "It took a wise, brave man to do this."

In October, 1931, Mr. White, scanning the political future,
pointed out that times and situations change quickly. For example, eighteen months ago the American people were excited,
divided, and bedeviled over prohibition. Now no one seriously
talked about it. Now, he said, it was more and more evident
that the issue of 1932 was to be economic, related to the depression, and added:

Unless a miracle sends us well out of the depression, the issue is
sure to concern two fundamental stabilities, the stability of investment and stability of employment. The invested dollar and the invested life in our civilization have suffered severe deflation through
financial maladjustment and industrial unemployment. If so-called
Christian civilization west of Russia is to survive Russia's challenge,
capitalism must in some way provide security for the man who saves
and the man who works. But the gambler can not ask security, nor
can the lazy man. The issue of the coming campaign will concern
these two, the worker and the careful investor. Some way in the next
decade the problem must be met.

Mr. White, in an editorial in mid-November, 1932, summarizing the campaign and Hoover's record, said that Hoover had
shrunk with almost physical revulsion at dramatizing himself
as a hero in the great play of forces with which he was struggling.

So he suppressed the drama which another man with a politician's
instinct for heroizing himself in any crisis might have turned to his
own advantage. If he had any illusions, and certainly the President
had few, about American politics, one was a blind faith that some
way democracy in the end would be able to see with its own eyes
the truth about the President. He believed that the people could
see it clearly and logically without a passion play, without drama,
without a hero in whose struggles they could see a story and so feel
their way to the truth. But alas the President was wrong in attribut-
ing a logical habit of mind to men in the mass. They must emo-

tionalize their thinking. They need a story. They learn the truth in parables and President Hoover rested in his democratic faith during August and September. By that time the bitterness of three years of hate sown in the soil of depression almost with mechanical deliberation, had rooted and bloomed and come to fruit. It was too late then, six weeks before the election, to overcome three years and a half of public suspicion which grew from animosity to wrath.

On March 9, 1933, Mr. White, writing of President Hoover, said that he had done what he could:

But the forces he fought were cosmic, beyond him, beyond government, beyond any human control. They engulfed our world. He had to stand by all but impotent in the face of disaster. He tried and tried to stop it, but of course he failed. . . . He will be known as the greatest innocent bystander in history. But history will also write him down an honest, earnest, intelligent man, full of courage and patriotism undaunted to the last.

Here is tragedy. The forces of evil working their havoc upon a brave man fighting valiantly, futilely to the end.

FRANKLIN D. ROOSEVELT

Mr. White's first editorial of commendation of Roosevelt appeared in August, 1932, in which he said he wanted to lift the flag of truce and present Roosevelt with a bouquet for the way he handled the Mayor Walker case.

In mid-May, 1933, Mr. White wrote of the President's candor:

"Last night the President talked to the American people and he spoke wisely and well from his viewpoint. He is obviously taking the people into his confidence. Clearly he is not afraid to make a mistake. Evidently he regards inaction, hesitancy and timidity as more dangerous than action, even though it is wrong action. He is right."

Mr. White went on to say that what the American people wanted was drama and action and something doing, because they were nervous and weary of the long battle of the great war called depression; that they were yearning for a dawn of peace and wanted someone as a national leader who would at least go through the motions of doing something. He added that this was probably unwise, but it was the national mood; that President Roosevelt, being a consummate politician, was giving the people what they wanted.

Mr. White, as a reporter for a newspaper syndicate, attended the London Economic Conference in July, 1933, and in one of his dispatches he wrote:

But one note was sounded in unison through all the long day's oratory: The note of recrimination—recrimination against the United States, specifically the President of the United States, for dealing the blow that made the conference finally futile. It was all most polite. The President's attitude was referred to as "an unfortunate circumstance" and as "entirely unforeseen," or as one of those regrettable circumstances made inevitable by the swiftly moving course of events.

Under the camouflage of circumlocution there lingers a certain bitterness toward the Americans and their President. The leadership which they might have taken was lost. Whatever leadership is left at the end of this conference is undoubtedly in the hands of the British.

In March, 1934, Mr. White wrote:

Roosevelt's great problem this year can be stated thus: Can government chain its dollars, harness them to the common good and still retain free men and free institutions? It has never been done before. Political liberties always go down when economic liberty is circumscribed. But this is a new world. Our Democracy for a hundred years has been a new order, but it is more deeply rooted here than in Europe. Probably America can do this new strange thing—establish a new revolution of free men with their dollars in shackles.

This summarization by Mr. White of Roosevelt's first year furnishes a hint of why Mr. White found it difficult to the end to accept Roosevelt completely.

In February, 1934, Mr. White quoted progressive Democrats as claiming that the different alphabetical agencies, "the NRA, the AAA, the PWA, etc., ad infinitum, constitute the second American revolution," that the changes are permanent, that they feel the old order is gone. Mr. White said, "Maybe it is," and added:

Far be it from the *Gazette* to carp. We are supporting the ad-

ministration and the whole alphabet thereunto appertaining. But
are the American people ready for the revolutionary change, the
fundamental break with their American past that is necessary if this
revolution takes hold permanently? Today it is a palace revolution.
It has captured Washington. How far and how deeply in the hearts
of the American people has it gone? . . . Again we say these questions are not asked by an impertinent enemy, but by a sincere friend
whose fond and fervent hope that the day he long has sought is
really here.

A hint of worry about the Roosevelt administration appeared
in another February, 1934, editorial concerning "Our Limited
Democracy." Mr. White expressed the belief that America had
hit a new low in democracy and that democracy itself was in a
depression. While he held that Roosevelt was a trustworthy,
benevolent dictator, made so by common representative consent, as things stood today America was becoming a limited democracy, working out a co-operative economic security for the
greatest number. He was worried because, he said, "here and
there the New Deal has extracted an idea from each of the
tyrannies, with the ideas modified"; thus "a limited democracy
is more than a possibility. It is here; but is it here to stay or
just visiting?"

Late in 1934 Mr. White referred to what he called the President's zigzag course to the left, after which he "zagged right-
ward by making a honey-mouth to American big business . . .
and bright and early this Monday morning he takes a short zig
to the left by commending the purely socialistic enterprise
TVA. . . . So the old boy takes a gay little zig to the left and
tomorrow will zag to the right, but always the curve bends left-
ward."

President Roosevelt's Supreme Court bill in 1937 prompted
an editorial called "Adroit" from Mr. White, who took Roosevelt to task for not being forthright, which aroused irritating
suspicion, and charged that Roosevelt had flouted the democratic process of open discussion by revealing in the previous
campaign no inkling of his plans; that his silence then in the
present light was little more than insincere. He concluded:

This presidential adroitness, this uncanny capacity to avoid the
direct joining of the issues in full, free and fair debate, the seem-

ingly instinctive lack of candor, this smiling assumption of courage while avoiding all danger, this elaborate stage play to flatter the people by a simulation of frankness while denying Americans their democratic rights and discussions by suave avoidance—these are not the traits of a democratic leader. These are tricks that have been played in the new game wherein other peoples have lost their democratic liberties in other lands.

How long will the people be fooled?

Following the President's fireside talk regarding his proposed changes for the Supreme Court, Mr. White asked:

By what right, human or divine, does the President demand a law to disqualify a member of the Supreme Court or give a judgment without a hearing upon the complaint that the Lord is slow in ordering the angel of death to strike down those with whom President Roosevelt disagrees? . . .

His power over Congress plus a change in the Court will make this a one-man government, a benevolent despotism if you please; but nonetheless a government submissive entirely to the will of one man.

That is the issue before the American people. . . . Democracy takes the middle way. Democracy holds to the rule of the people, by the people, for the people, that their liberties shall not perish from this land.

In June, 1938, Mr. White took issue with President Roosevelt's attempt to purge his party of those congressmen and senators who opposed him. He held Roosevelt didn't need to do it because he had a hundred times more power to punish his enemies, a hundred times more power to buy primary and election votes, than any other president had ever had; Roosevelt, he said, was almost as omnipotent as Hitler, Stalin, or Mussolini.

And because he loves the democracy which is the foundation of our liberties, he should use his power sparingly. . . . For him to assume that the presidential office gives him a mandate to befoul the wellsprings of democracy by substituting self-interest for reason in his appeal to the voters, is a cruel and terrible thing.

That is the new issue, the only issue before the American people today. A man as acute and as sensitive as Franklin Roosevelt should see the obligation of nobility in this hour and should rise to his duty. He has a vastly more imperative duty to preserve democracy than to help his friends or punish his political enemies. His economic program is important but not so important as the preservation of democracy. . . .

No man in a democracy has a right to play god.

In July, 1939, Mr. White wrote of the President that "Smart as he is, he has something which a politician should never keep in his baggage—a vindictive memory.

"No matter how many terms he has, this fault will follow him. Here is the flaw in his armament and he will be as impudent in this third term as he is today. His ears were knocked down yesterday but it will not housebreak him. He'll do the same trick again."

Three months later Mr. White was calling on the newspapers to quit pulling the deadly parallel on our beloved president. He said:

Three years ago he was clamoring for neutrality by the way of the embargo. Now he is demanding the repeal of the embargo and the right to sell on a cash and carry basis armaments and other goods and services to whomsoever may come. . . .

We have at times said harsh and maybe bitter things, even possibly untrue, in hasty inadvertence about our noble leader in the White House. At other times we have strung along with him, but always we have lifted up our humble pride for tolerance. He may be goofy, he may smile too much, and he may always be playing the game with his eye on the ball—the same being the main chance for F. D. R. . .

Mr. White now was beginning to veer toward support of President Roosevelt in his international program, changing from his previous critical attitude toward Roosevelt's domestic program, which appealed to White less and less.

In March, 1940, writing under the title "Seven Years," Mr. White said of Roosevelt's administration:

"History will write of him that he tried. History will say that he gave us reforms that were long past due, reforms based upon civilized ideals and justice. But history will also say in the great problem, the vital danger breeding problem of unemployment, President Roosevelt was a poor doctor. He doctored symptoms —not the disease. The things he tried were the wrong things, and the years, passing years, multiplied the danger until now we stand in the need of a new leader, a new solution of the problem which has been beating men down in despair."

By inference in 1939, Mr. White gave what perhaps was the basic reason for his failure to go all out for Franklin Roosevelt. His definition of a liberal in a *Gazette* editorial toward the end of Roosevelt's second term implied the fundamental differences between his and the President's social and economic philosophy. He defined a liberal as being:

A citizen who is proud of his country's progress in the past, who knows that the tempo of past progress cannot greatly be speeded up, who realizes that haste makes waste in a democracy and too much haste brings tyranny. A liberal is deeply grieved at the evils of his day and generation. He sees injustice in wrath. But also he is proud of his country's progress. He does not shrink from the battle against the evils of his day and time. He does not believe that he must destroy to build. His pride in the achievement of his fathers tempers his indignation at the injustice which he realizes must be overcome only through compromise in the orderly parliamentary democratic processes. But above all he never wearies of well-directed hell-raising. The militant liberal believes in his heart that if he is patient and persistent justice will come far more swiftly than if in rage and temper he strikes out blindly.

In September, 1940, writing about the two candidates, Roosevelt and Willkie, White revealed some other reasons for his inability to be an out-and-out Roosevelt man.

So man for man, stripped for the ring, the challenger and the champ, we are for Willkie. He has what it takes. And best of all he is fighting for the old hard way of American life, for a capitalism that stresses opportunity. Whereas Roosevelt is fighting for a capitalism that would over-use government as an agency of human welfare and make men soft.

We are for Willkie.

WILLKIE

Mr. White's first editorial mention of Wendell Willkie was made in early May, 1940, when in writing of a trip to New York he wrote:

Next to the World's Fair, I should say the newest, most interesting phenomenon in town is Wendell Willkie. . . . I met him last fall for the first time and liked him. He is a large, Newfoundland dog of a man, shaggy and cordial, friendly and politically photogenic—which means that he takes a good spiritual picture. I met him twice on this trip. I sat next to Wendell Willkie and introduced him once at a formal dinner, where he made an exceptionally good speech. His political photogeneity—if I may coin a word—consists largely of a certain radiant don't-give-a-damnativeness, which is rare in politics and which is called courage, though it may be a vast indifference. Anyway he says what he thinks, no matter how it affects his fortune. He makes a plutocrat shiver when he talks about civil liberties, and the right of labor to assemble and talk and say its say even in times of strife. His frankness is refreshing in American politics, where so many men are corrupted by the desire for votes . . .

It is easy to understand, because of Mr. White's great concern about the European situation and his lifelong interest in international relations, why he leaned toward Willkie.

In June, 1940, in answer to the query of a reader about why the *Gazette*, which had said many fine things about Willkie as a presidential candidate, "had not gone plunk, slap dash, slam bang for Willkie," Mr. White wrote that if the reader must know the reason it was that he hadn't met Mrs. Willkie.

"You don't know a man until you know his wife. She reveals two things; first the skill and wisdom of the picker, which is most important, second, by her own character, she points the way of his future course. . . . A man's wife is a revelation of his real self."

In June, 1940, Mr. White wrote an open letter to Mr. Willkie about a speech he had delivered.

Your courage is a precious gift, a divine inheritance, in truth. So cherish it, this royal American independence of yours. No matter where it takes you, up or down in the political world, if you hold fast to the truth and the courage to tell the truth, spit in the eye of the false gods who lure you to the path that holds on hell, you will be a happy useful citizen. Leadership is often much more powerful in the hands of an honest private citizen than in the hands of a self-seeking public servant.

One month after Willkie's nomination, Mr. White wrote that he had gone to see him in his office in New York and found him, as in a half a dozen other relations, easy-going, slow, but sure-moving, with a tremendous lot of personal reserve in his mien and manner:

A good listener and a wise talker, with few words. He is always earnest as well as considerate, but never pompous. There is less stuffed shirt in Wendell Willkie's spiritual cosmos than in any presidential candidate I have ever known. Which—and just for a moment let me glance backward for nearly fifty years—brings me to the curious fact that excepting Harding and Coolidge, I have known before he went into the White House with some degree of friendly association every President we have had since McKinley. . . . I should say that Wendell Willkie and Theodore Roosevelt impressed me more deeply and favorably by their sincerity, by their wide intelligence, and their robust deep sense of humor. . . . I should say that Willkie is more nearly a Theodore Rooseveltian than he is near any other type of modern statesman.

In the last sentence we find the real answer to White's enthusiasm for Willkie.

9. A MAN OF PEACE

PREVIOUS to the early days of August, 1914, when the bolt came from what to America seemed a blue sky and the First World War began, with Germany, Austria, Russia, and Britain as the principals, American public opinion was preponderantly against having any part of it. Although Mr. White had visited in Europe previous to this time and had gained a keen appreciation of the contributions European culture had made to civilization, he nevertheless remained aloof from that contest at the start. In one of his early comments about that war he commended the work of Mr. Hoover's Commission for Relief in Belgium, an undertaking which naturally interested his generous and humane spirit.

Early in 1915, he wrote of one by-product of the war, a French officer's murder of his wife.

"He mechanically dispatched her in a scientific and professional manner. War is murder and it will warp the moral fiber of the men of Europe as it did this young officer, who before the war was a kind, considerate and loving husband."

Later he wrote, "Before that [1914] no country editor of the midwest ever editorialized on anything east of Sandy Hook—except on the fourth of July . . . but now [1924] we all have a foreign policy out in the tall grass."

That war was a momentous incident in human history. It marked the end of an era. Therefore, it was too big an event for anyone to grasp in all its implications, least of all the editor of a Midwest, small-town newspaper. This particular editor even then had widened his sympathies and understanding until they had become nation-wide, but they had barely spread beyond the borders of his country.

A systematic study of White's editorial and magazine articles shows that he had an astonishingly high batting average as a prophet, but his prophet's eyes were blind in this case. For once he drifted with the crowd while he went through the process of

making up his mind. Like all of us, he saw one side of an un-
determined question on one day, another side on another. They
all went down on paper. No man who ever wrote revealed more
clearly and fully his intellectual and spiritual insides than Mr.
White, except Samuel Pepys, and he was writing to himself, not
to the public. So in the first month of World War I he had written, "The Germans are no worse than the rest of us," and let it
go at that for the time being.

In early 1915, Mr. White, a lifelong advocate of peace, wrote
that we were willing to go to war for peace, as was shown by the
way the devil's own row begins whenever two or three are gathered in any kind of organization for the purpose of propagating
peace.

"Until we peace advocates," he wrote, "get into a blessed
unity of mind, the outside world need not be worried much
over the arrival of the eternal mollycoddle. There is enough at
stake in the methods of peace to keep the pot boiling for some
time to come."

By June, 1915, ten months after the war started, Mr. White
was beginning to be disturbed by Germany's ruthlessness.

"Germany, time and again in this war, has killed Americans.
No other European nation has killed an American in this war.
The President properly can arbitrate matters concerning trade
that may submit to a calm discussion of the rights of property.
But Germany is trying to argue us into a Hague lawsuit over
deliberate, cowardly murder."

Man of peace that he was, Mr. White found it difficult to re-
sort to war until all avenues to peace had been explored. In
late 1915, he had reached the conclusion that:

"Certain matters are not arbitrable—direct premeditated in-
sults, acts of aggression, and the like. These are to be submitted
before war is declared to a board of conciliation, who is to investigate and publish the facts . . ."

Such a board, in his belief, could have averted that war; he
believed, he said, in the league to enforce peace, but he knew
we were not living in a chocolate-éclair world nor did he believe
that powder puffs and nose rags could sweeten the tempers of
mankind:

"But we do feel that we are presenting a workable plan for

peace and that in America at least some of the most patriotic citizens of the country have lent their influence and are giving their time and money putting this league in a position to begin work after the war is finished."

In November, 1915, he wrote realistically:

"War is abroad in Europe. To ignore it, to declare that we are protected by our geographical position is folly. Guns and powder, ships, men, and well trained officers will save us, and nothing else."

Peace should not come "to Europe until the victors themselves are sick of war and would be willing to enter into an international compact to disarm." Edging slowly toward accepting war he called it "a war between the democratic ideas . . . and the autocratic military ideas of the earth." This recognition of what was going on led him to add:

"War means horror and injustice and cruelty and barbarism. But a dishonorable peace, the mere laying down of arms to pick them up some other day, will be a disgraceful peace."

Even so, with his whole inner being opposed to war or cruelty in any form, he held that:

". . . to say how far we should go in aggression, how much we should do on foreign soil, what we should do to other nations to maintain our national honor, is also the job for experts, and not one to be solved while the printer howls for copy on a dull day."

His old world was falling to pieces about him, he was groping through the ruins, feeling his way. Arthur Bullard, liberal, said at this time, "Some days I feel like Bryan and some days like Bernhardi"—the latter being the popular symbol of Prussian militarism. So it was with White. He seemed wobbly to the superficial. He had, however, found one little foothold on truth. The western democracies—France, Belgium, Britain—with all their faults stood for the liberal world which was his earthly goal; the Central Powers, no matter how glittering their material progress, stood for spiritual reaction.

Following the sinking of the *Lusitania*, Mr. White reached the conclusion that "Force is the one word that German imperialism understands, and in the name of civilization, it may be necessary to use force."

His steps toward war by March, 1917, were longer, more firm than previously.

"We have," he wrote, "turned the other cheek until it is calloused with blows . . . we are at war . . . We should join the Allies so that our blows will count. We should not concern ourselves with European boundaries in the peace which shall come. But we should concern ourselves with human rights."

One week later, March 29, 1917, Mr. White called upon the nation to "Fight and Fight Hard."

To talk of hitting a wrist blow in this war is silly. We must go where our men and money and munitions will cost Germany most dearly. If that means fighting in Flanders—there we must go—if it means fighting on the high seas, there we must fight. . . . Let us make ourselves the champions of republican government in the beginning of the world's republic. . . .

"It is well that we waited, for now we know that the blood we shed shall be shed in a holy cause. If we were only prepared while we waited our patience would have been wholly virtuous. As it is— only time can say whether or not it was wise to let war come without preparing for war. And it may turn out that this also was right.

Hater of war as he was and supporting the President's declaration as he did, White continued to resist extremes, dared—for it took moral courage then—to register his disbelief in such falsehoods as that the German army systematically cut off the hands of Belgian children. He editorially denounced the suppression of Wagnerian operas and all other German music (demonstrating again that he was many years ahead of his country; this music was not suppressed in World War II). He also opposed ordinances and rulings which sought to prohibit teaching the German language in the public schools. He refused to indict a whole people or a whole people's culture. Even two decades later, when tyranny and miseducation had brought the Germans far nearer to our old popular idea of them, he continued to maintain that attitude.

Will White, the country editor who had come to know America so well because he knew Emporia so well, had for thirty years or more constantly sharpened his knowledge of the United States. His travels to Washington, New York, Chicago, to the political conventions—those spots where we were making current history—enabled him to bore deeper into the minds of his readers. It was natural, therefore, that he should go to Europe and see the war for himself. He was accompanied on a Red Cross assignment by his friend Henry J. Allen. His report to the nation appeared in the form of a book entitled *The Martial Adventures of Henry and Me.*

He had not planned to write a book about the trip, but upon his return Mrs. White, who had saved all of his letters from Europe, urged him to do so.

Since the book was so conceived, and further, since his notes for it consisted of material in his personal letters to Mrs. White, it was natural that he should not have discussed the big issues of the war. It was, taken all in all, a kind of military *Innocents Abroad.* Nevertheless, he gathered impressions on this trip, a glimpse here and a flash of intuition there, and clear understanding at all times, for his final opinion. It was all to crystallize before Armistice Day. This war, as probably most wars, was unnecessary. It was due almost entirely to cutthroat economic competition between nations. That he emphasized this point unduly at first indicates that he had not entirely fathomed the European mind, that he did not allow for the importance of tradition, of caste, of what they called honor, in the affairs of that truculent continent. He was to learn these things with further experience, but he did see that if we kept on with war it meant not only material destruction beyond imagination of the devil, but also the end of progress and human liberty for America as well as the rest of the world. "We cannot keep out of the next war," he wrote prophetically. These were also roughly Wilson's views before November 11, 1918, and when the guns were stilled he was in agreement with the President in all essentials.

Even before Wilson announced his great dream of a League of Nations, White had joined hands with that group of Republicans who founded the League to Enforce Peace and had become a director of that organization. In 1919 Mr. White attended the Versailles Peace Conference as a correspondent. There, stage by stage, he saw Wilson tricked here, traded into a corner there, saw him exchange point after point for support of his League of Nations plan. When the full text of the Ver-

sailles Treaty was given out, White, like every other informed
liberal at the conference, was appalled. It was a rickety structure, impossible of enforcement. But they consoled themselves
with the vain hope that the League would modify its unenforce-
able clauses. The conference had at least founded a parliament
of man where causes could be argued openly, where by judgment of the nations of the world, disputes with the danger of
war in them might be adjudged and compromised. White returned home dissatisfied, critical, but ready to go the limit to
get the League of Nations covenants through the Senate. At
first this probably looked like a comparatively easy job. He did
not know then that some able senators would from various motives make its approval difficult or that the returned soldiers and
their families, disgusted with the war, would be instinctively
against its adoption. Those opposed to the League also argued
—and they found great support for their timid folly—that the
way to keep the United States out of war was to have no dealings with those slick foreign diplomats. Perhaps the greatest
advantage of those opposed to the League of Nations was found
in President Wilson's breaking health, combined with his stub-
born refusal to make any changes in the treaty even when those
changes agreed with his own views.

Although Mr. White continued to urge through his writings
and hope for the creation of some kind of international machinery that would help make war less likely, he was by the
early 1920's beginning to realize even more clearly that the
task was an exceedingly difficult one.

In 1921 he expressed the conviction that the one way to stop
war was for the nations of the earth to get together and put
pressure on the imperialists, thereby making them stop dreaming of conquest. "Isolation," he held at that time, "will bring
nothing but another world-crushing war and the sooner we get
rid of the isolation hallucination the better it will be for civilization, which America is bound by her economic strength to
preserve."

A few years later, writing again on the subject of isolation, he
held that:

America's job is a world job. Our isolation is a fiction. We are in

Europe now no matter how we may feel that the Atlantic severs us. Great currents of human feelings sweeping across civilization, great waves of economic pressure rising with the rise in population all over the earth, breed wars, and we cannot keep out of wars if we remain a part of civilization. But doing our full duty as a neighbor among the nations of the earth, we may prevent war.

In 1923, writing on "The Ghastly Joke of It," of the claim that World War I was a war to end wars, he said:

"What a ghastly joke with all our fine idealism. How long will we go before we are fooled again?

"Is God to be mocked?"

In and out of season Mr. White encouraged with high commendation every serious proposal which sought to create steps that would make war less likely. In one editorial in 1926, "A Realizable Ideal," Mr. White wrote:

The Society of Friends, which means Quakers, are a wise, kind people whose patriotism could never be questioned, are tremendously interested in peace. One of the things the Quakers are asking is a National Peace Department, coordinated with the Army and Navy Department. The thing is a realizable ideal. There's no reason why America and all civilized countries should not spend as much in preparing for peace as they do in preparing for war.

Again he wrote that plans for world peace were available aplenty but men pick flaws in and reject them all, "And for what?" he asked:

"For war, for force, for the supremacy of the jingo. Is the human animal going to fight himself to extinction and leave a blood stained world to our wiser brothers, the monkeys and the donkeys?

"Why do we claim to be the lords of creation when we have less sense than the birds and the bees?"

To him war was "the great social disease of the planet and unless civilization can control it, civilization will succumb to the disease in another century. Any man who sneers at any peace is an enemy of humanity."

Writing in the *Gazette* in 1936 about Armistice Day in 1918, he pointed out that the sinister correspondence of American diplomats published during the previous decade made it plain

that before President Wilson reached his great decision to enter
the war the threat of a major panic rose, because of our heavy
loans to the Allies, which would have created a terrible financial catastrophe in the United States had the Allied powers lost.

What we really went to war for was:

To trade the lives of our boys for security against panic. The
same depression that eleven years afterwards met us in spite of the
blood we had shed.

It was a futile war. Democracy has been banished from most of
the continent of Europe. Liberty is threatened seriously all over the
world. Wars more terrible even than the World War seem hovering
inevitably upon the horizon of the immediate future. . . . No war
ever forced man further forward than he would have gone in the
time it took to wage the war and patch up the wounds.

One should hate war not because it is bloody and cruel, not because it is ruthless and terrible, not because it is always followed by
calamity worse than was threatened before the swords were drawn.
Those are more excuses for staying out of war. The real reason
why humanity should hate war and avoid it is that war is utterly
futile and useless. War settles nothing. It raises more wrath than it
allays; and in the end all that was to be adjudicated by the god of
battle still has to come before the court of reason finally before men
find the truth. Every sane man or woman should hate war, hate war
with all the energy of his nature, resist war propaganda, and remember always that wars are made by lies. The truth never could
get a nation into war. Hate war for what it is and its vast futility
and waste.

Hate war!

In May, 1938, Mr. White wrote again:

War is the most terrible affliction that can come upon man. No
nation, no region, no race ever wins a war. War is madness. And
madness when it runs its course and hands victory to one or the
other combatant, hands to the winner only a mockery. The peace
that follows war is made by madmen. The peace carries with it the
seeds of other wars and so through the ages the wars' seeds march
on. About all Americans can do is to hope for peace and hate war,
and hate it in all of its manifestations. Watch out for propaganda.
Keep the peace by curbing your emotions. There is no other way.
Hate creeps so quietly into the heart and hate breeds war. When
you find yourself hating another people or another race, remember

those are the seeds of war. Stamp them out. Uproot them. We Americans will have to find our own antiwar leadership. It is not in the White House—it never abides there in the nature of things. Every possible personal and political advantage for any President lies with the approach of war. Don't expect the White House seriously to preach peace or really to promote it. War's lure is more than human nature can stand. The impact of power and the overwhelming responsibility that goes with the presidency carries with it the eager, subconscious desire to stay there and war is one safe way. So, no presidency is consciously militant, no President realizes where he is going. The war gods are hypnotic. They paralyze reason, even in high places, to lead nations to war with the love of power in the dazed eyes of their leaders.

These are days, even though the present war scare blows over, when all men of good will should keep a hope and a prayer for peace in their hearts.

In January, 1940, in a hopeful mood Mr. White wrote:

. . . War will have to stop; sooner or later it will be apparent to the world that force is an impossible solution. And when that time comes—it shouldn't be long now—of necessity will come a time of deeper and less selfish understanding of the fundamentals of good neighborliness. Nations will be compelled for their own sakes to consider themselves a part of the international community. They will finally learn that peace and good will toward others is no more and no less than peace and good will to themselves.

They will learn this only at the end—but they will learn it. And that will be the day!

In a less hopeful mood in the middle 1930's, Mr. White wrote of World War I that it was "futile."

The social forces working outside of war for the last fifty years would have moved more swiftly toward social and industrial justice if they had not been impeded by the war and chained by debts that followed the war. Moreover, we would have been a better and nobler people if we had kept out of the war.

He now employed sarcasm, a device he seldom used, in an effort to high-light his point.

So let the eagle scream. Let the fifes blow and the drums beat as the marching soldiers symbolize the pomp and panoply of glory in war. Let them lure us into another slaughter that means nothing!

Until man cures himself of the war madness his life on this planet will be a nightmare. For from now on the devil has the machinery of war in his hands—terrible machinery, devastating machinery. War is the devil's own device. It means mass slaughter and agony, cruel and universal, not merely for the combatants but for civilians hundreds of miles from the battle line. So let's build more fighting ships, train more boys for the slaughterhouse, and bear more babies to be massacred with gaseous poisons and shrapnel dropped in bombs from the great vultures of war that will blacken the air when war comes.

So step lively! Listen to the fife and drum! Thank God you belong to a nation that will fight!

During the years leading up to World War I and through to our entry into World War II, Mr. White, with all of the instincts of a man who would not kill a rabbit, and whose precepts in life were the Golden Rule and the Sermon on the Mount, shrank always from supporting any move that would send our boys, or other nations' boys, into war's meatgrinder. War to him was "the most horrible material thing that can happen to a country."

In December, 1939, he wrote:

Men for thousands of years of slowly rising peace gradually have been enlarging the areas in which it pays to be decent and reasonably kind; from the family group where mutual help prospered the group, to the clan where they stood together and were considered neighborly, then to the tribe of many clans where kindness has its wider area and it paid men to tell the truth, to respect their neighbors' property and to set up the institution of marriage in its various forms. . . . So a morality was set up. Morality of altruism of sorts. Morality which grew out of the home, the clan, the tribe, the state, the nation. In these larger areas men accepted the fact by the millions that honesty was the best policy, that lying gets you into trouble. . . .

But in war, and particularly in modern war, the first thing that has to break down if a war is conducted competently is the standard of morals that make men happy in peace. Lying pays. Murder pays. Who cares for rapine—boys will be boys! Stealing is unmitigatedly profitable. And to hell—literally hell—goes all that man has built up for thousands of years.

The worst scar that this great flame of war will leave upon the world will not be the broken cities, not the maimed men and women. . . . It will be a fundamental belief seared in the hearts of millions and millions of people that force, used for any purpose —to lie, to rob, to murder—is altogether a good and profitable way of life. There is the hell of it, the deep, burning agonizing hell of war.

To Mr. White the European war boiled "down to a challenge of the Christian way of life."

Which doesn't mean piety and going to church and getting out of hell into Heaven. Nothing like that. It means living decently, the right of the strong man to be useful and the right of the ordinary man to be kind, neighborly and just to whom he pleases—black or white, Jew or atheist, rich or poor, weak or strong—when he pleases and where he pleases, and not to be channeled in his duties and limited in his right. . . . But instinctively because totalitarian governmen can not flourish where men are free to worship, to think, to vote, to read, and to speak; and where laws and institutions reflect this kind of free philosophy of Jesus of Nazareth, the philosophy of meekness, the philosophy of kindness, the philosophy of consideration for one's duties and one's neighbors' rights. This challenge to Christianity is at the heart of the world turmoil.

This man of peace, who could write on his sixty-fifth birthday, "So far as I know every friend of my childhood who is living is my friend today. I have never had a major quarrel with anyone, and I am not conscious of having an enemy," lived and worked for peace among all men. His remarkable understanding of man's higher purpose enabled him to see the futility of war. Then in the late 1930's and early '40's he came face to face with the challenge of civilization's most awful, most destructive war. He saw in the immediate offing the real possibility of his beloved country's being involved in the growing world cataclysm. He believed that he could see an honorable, effective, peaceful way by which our nation could avoid involvement. Even though the years had taken a heavy toll on his strength he entered the arena again. This turned out to be the greatest fight of his long career. It was to shorten his life, to leave him no ease but to bring him to the end in glory.

10. COMMITTEE TO DEFEND AMERICA BY AIDING THE ALLIES

UNLIKE MANY PEOPLE with the reforming spirit, White never "swallowed all formulas" nor took on more opponents than he could handle effectively. For him, one fight at a time was always enough. In the years between 1922 and 1925, during which Mussolini marched on Rome, took Italy over, and solidified his dictatorship, White was busy with his own fights for freedom of the press and against the Klan. Now and then he noted in the *Gazette* the close resemblance between the Knights of the Invisible Empire and the Fascist blackshirts, especially in matters pertaining to costume and manners; but he showed as yet slight apprehension over that new, sinister gangster motif in the concert of powers, that reversion to barbarism, which was to come so near to destroying civilization two decades later. It was not until 1926 that he wrote:

"The whole scheme is backed by force—not by reason. The Fascists enforce the decrees of the state. Government in Italy under Mussolini is what government in America would be if the Socialists had the government and turned it over to the Kluxers to run. . . ."

However, he perceived more than a year in advance Hitler's coming assassination of German liberties. In October, 1931, he noted editorially that the German cabinet, on the pretense of suppressing radicals, had suspended the Teutonic equivalent of the Bill of Rights and prohibited all meetings of "subversive groups." But—

Having muzzled the Communists, why do they permit the Nationalists to pop off? Yesterday Hitler's steel helmeters had a convention in the little town of Herzberg. To the government he said, "Get out or we will storm your ramparts." Several of the Kaiser's sons and all the old war party were there in the eagle's bloom with full regalia, declaring their intention of assuming power, by force if necessary, to tear up all of Germany's international obligations.

Here are utterances as violent as any threats made by Communists. They are far more disturbing to the peace of the world.

This was probably his first editorial mention of Hitler, but from then on he never stayed his hand from that battle. In January, 1933, Hitler came to full, absolute power in Germany. On November 11, the fifteenth Armistice Day, White printed one of those editorials in which all his powers seemed to come together full flood.

Fifteen years ago today came the Armistice, and we all thought it was to be a new world. It is! But a lot worse than it was before.

Ten million men were killed, as many more maimed, fifty billion dollars' worth of property destroyed, the world saddled with debts. And for what?

What was the good of it? Four years of peace would have made a better world.

Would it have been any worse if Germany had won? Ask yourself honestly. No one knows.

Is this old world as safe for democracy as it was before all these lives were lost?

There is no democracy east of the Rhine. Tyrants have risen where constitutional monarchs ruled twenty years ago. In America democracy is threatened by gunmen and racketeers. Big, greedy plutocrats are undermining democracy at the top, while dirty underworld rats are gnawing at the foundation below.

The boys who died just went out and died. To their own souls' glory of course—but what else?

The slacker who stayed at home is getting the jobs and piling up the rocks and ducats. About the largest haw-haw that the world has is for the poor patriotic plodder who did his bit. The goddess of liberty might well have cried "hello sucker!" to her devotees in the war. For liberty lost the war. No one won it.

Yet the next war will see the same hurrah and the same bow-wow of the big dogs to get the little dogs to go out and follow the blood scent and get their entrails entangled in the barbed wire.

And for what?

Look at Russia ruled by the proletarian tyrants!

Behold Germany governed by paranoiac sadists!

Italy has lost her liberties to fill her stomach and enthrone the rich!

Poland, the Balkans, and central Europe—a super powder magazine—waiting for the match to blow civilization back to the dark ages!

America?—read the newspapers!

What a glorious war! All wars are like that. The next one will be worse.

War is the devil's joke on humanity. So let's celebrate Armistice Day by laughing our heads off.

Then let us work and pray for peace, when man can break the devil's chains and nations realize their nobler dreams!

These white-hot paragraphs amounted to the platform which was to govern his attitude toward foreign affairs during the years when catastrophe drew nearer and nearer. At times he appeared wobbly; some of his editorials and articles almost endorsed that isolationist attitude which prevailed in the Middle West, others came nearer to supporting armed war on the dictatorships.

But one factor in his thinking remained constant. Never did he falter in his opposition to the Nazis. In January, 1934, writing under the ironic head "German Liberty," he recalled that under the new German law the worker could not complain of hours, wages, or shop conditions, suggest arbitration, or strike. "The boss is the absolute master." He quoted the comment of Goebbels:

"It is the most advanced labor legislation in the world."

"Crazy?" asked Mr. White, and answered his own question:

"No, just self-hypnotized. Mob mad. Beyond the realm of logic. Germany was that way in 1914. And look what happened."

These prophetic words of his pointed toward the terrible catastrophe which was to strike the world five years later.

When in September, 1939, the blow fell, White had oriented himself, perfected the policy which as a private citizen he maintained during the interval between the murder of Poland and Pearl Harbor. "We cannot keep out of the next war," the League of Nations partisans all said in 1920, even White himself. But there was still a slim chance; for all his sympathies with France and England he felt that it was his duty to take that chance. The Neutrality Act forbidding American merchants to sell munitions to a belligerent, American ships to sail for his harbors, American volunteers to enlist in his armies, American citizens, in effect, to visit his shores, had gone whooping through Congress in 1935 with the people, as public-opinion

polls showed, overwhelmingly behind it. President Roosevelt
was against it; probably he signed it because he saw that it
would be passed over his veto. But he remarked, "It may drag
us into war instead of keeping us out." Many of Roosevelt's
most eminent Republican opponents agreed with him. A state
of war is an atmosphere in which force alone counts. A neutral
has no rights that a belligerent respects, unless he shows clearly
that he may fight for them. People like the European and
Asiatic dictators and their war lords would interpret a neutral
attitude as a license to step on our toes. There would be "incidents"—the *Lusitania* affair in other terms—a quick overturn of
public opinion, a rush into a war for which we would be un-
prepared. White had supported the Neutrality Bill, a revision
of it in 1937 by which we virtually abandoned our old policy
of freedom of the seas, the Johnson Act, which in effect prohibited loans to belligerents. Now, however, he swung toward
the President's position.

There was another course open for us if we were to avoid
war, a course a little less promising than absolute, inert neutrality, yet offering a slim chance. It was the only one he saw.
Repeal or amend the Neutrality Act, put our infinite manufacturing resources practically at the disposal of the democratic
belligerents, let them fight while we supplied their needs for
war material. The British Navy held the seas; Germany could
not take advantage of our offer to sell goods to whoever might
come and get them, any more than she could from 1914 to 1917,
when American munitions enabled the Allies to hold out
against the German army in its flower. It had this further advantage: It might turn the balance in favor of democracy—be
the decisive factor in crushing Fascist and Nazi rule by criminal
gang.

He presented his case in the *Gazette:*

"As far as human ingenuity can go, this cash-and-carry bill
takes us out of war yet it is not without its dangers. The only
way to avoid danger absolutely is to draw a line around the
United States and tie all our ships at the docks. That would
cause panic and deeper depression. It might save us from war,
but plunge us into revolution. . . ."

On the eve of war Mr. White had joined the Union of Con-

certed Peace Efforts, a child of the now moribund League of
Nations Nonpartisan Association. In the very month when
Hitler struck Poland down, the directors of this society met in
New York, and, since implementing the national will for peace
was largely a job of creating public opinion and influencing
legislation, founded the Nonpartisan Committee for Peace
through revision of the Neutrality Law.

With thousands of the ablest and most influential men in the
country willing to give their lives for the cause, the leaders of
the new organization picked William Allen White, country
town editor, to serve as chairman. Honors were piling thick upon him in these, his later years; but none other proved what a
position he had reached.

Mr. White was reluctant to accept the job. On the personal
side, he was now nearly seventy-two years old, was already under
medical treatment, and had accepted with philosophical cheer-
fulness the fact that he could not last many years more. He still
edited the *Gazette* and wanted to devote his spare time to writing his long-promised autobiography. Then, too, although he
had of late increasingly given his name to committees for causes
in which he believed, he had never in his life done any administrative work more extensive than running a country newspaper. But on top of the invitation from Clark Eichelberger,
executive secretary of the union, came letters, telegrams, personal appeals from hundreds of friends and comrades in good
fights.

Mr. White thus began nearly two years of work as hard as
ever he did in the strenuous period when he was making his
name as a fictionist while putting the *Gazette* on its feet. Those
early years, however, were bright with hope; these, as he found
when he settled down to a desk at the New York office of the
committee, tortured with clash of nerves. War is madness, and
maddest of all in its preliminaries and its aftermath. All over
the country and especially in New York, isolationists and extreme interventionists were clawing at each other's throats.
Anti-Nazi societies, formed in the days when Hitler was working up to his climax, were bickering and skirmishing with
frankly fascist organizations or their practical equivalent,
founded by sincere pacifists but supported immediately by

secret agents of the Nazis and the Communists, which, so far as
the burning issue of the moment was concerned, meant practically the same thing. Such periods belonged to the extremists,
not to a true liberal advocating a moderate policy.

There followed the brief lull in hostilities which we called
hopefully "the phony war." Then in the spring of 1940, Hitler
launched the blitzkrieg in the entire world. Holland, Denmark,
Belgium, France, Norway fell like stalks to the scythe, and England, last rampart of European democracy, seemed doomed.
Never since 1775 had Britain been so popular in her one-time
colonies as in the dark but glorious hours of Dunkirk and the
great air battle over her skies. On this side of the water there
was a clamor of babbling tongues. Above them all rose the clear
voice of White, speaking from his remote pulpit, the editorial
pages of the *Emporia Gazette*. Never had reprints of his editorials so crowded the pages of the newspapers. Everywhere
speakers were repeating his telling phrases and sentences—"It
must be obvious now to the blindest citizen of the United States
that the war in Europe is a war of ideals"; "Hitler cementing
his German civilization by hate and extending it through seven
years of malicious concentration on military preparedness, is
the most powerful, terrible enemy [to] the philosophy and
religion of Jesus that the world has ever known"; "Like a spiritual cancer, that blight has covered central Europe"; "This is
no longer a battle of empires but a battle of ideals." At times,
the shock and horror in the day's news carried him further than
he intended to go in the beginning—and further than he went
in the end—as when he wrote in the fateful month of May that
this malignant growth was moving westward, that when Germany tried to take over those Caribbean islands which are the
key to Panama, "that day America is in the war."

"She must fight and fight not with mere economic sanctions
but with guns and men. If the democratic idea is to prevail, we
must quarantine this continent and the islands which control
this continent against . . . totalitarian government."

In the meantime, we should give help to the Allies, for they
were our hope now. "If and when that hope fails, we must,
despite all our noble ideals of freedom, fight gun with gun,
force with force. This world cannot endure half slave and half

free. . . . It is up to this country and up hard and soon. The fall of Holland is portentous. The spell of doom is tolling."

After Dunkirk and the fall of France, the organization changed its title to the Committee to Defend America by Aiding the Allies, but so long as White remained its chairman, its fundamental policy remained the same. Membership of this committee, within a month after White took the chairmanship, was large and influential enough to make an impression on legislation. It grew until there were 750 chapters. However, this strength had its flaw. Among the new members, to a certain extent among the old, there were people who wanted to go the whole way, to jump at once into the war, and who belonged to other societies created to encourage just that.

White once wrote in the *Gazette* at the beginning of his work with the committee, "I fear I am merely the rooster on the cow catcher." Never before in a life of modest self-deprecation did he so overdeprecate. Actually he was filling three jobs in one—four if one counts the *Gazette,* which he was managing intermittently and for which he was writing constantly. First, he was practically a propagandist on a large scale, writing much of the copy himself. Second, in the successive stages of getting the Neutrality Act revised and finally virtually repealed, he was a volunteer lobbyist, fighting for extension of the cash-and-carry act, arranging—this was the hardest struggle of all—for the loan of fifty of our overage destroyers to Britain in order to help fight off the German submarines which were attacking the convoys of merchant ships. Mr. White originated this idea. It was his child from the start, and he persuaded a reluctant Republican opposition in Congress to support it. Third, he was the committee's link with the White House. He seemed forever to be traveling a circuit from Emporia to New York to Washington and back to Emporia.

The liaison with the President was perhaps the most important part of his job. Presently he found himself a guest at the White House, where he had visited so many times before with other presidents, both Republican and Democrat. Franklin Roosevelt was another of the men whom he could oppose without forfeiting friendship.

He had opposed Franklin Roosevelt twice as a candidate. He

had written most favorably about many New Deal proposals, and in sharp criticism of many others.

But from the time when the European war seemed imminent, White had backed the President's European policy. As regarded the present critical stage of events, he felt that he and Roosevelt saw eye to eye in the program to give Britain, now fighting alone, every possible aid short of actual war. Whether or not this was the President's inner, secret purpose, or whether he was even then maturing plans for participation in the war, is immaterial. The important point is what White believed. Franklin Roosevelt had the political art of being able to run with the hare and hunt with the hounds. It was one of his working methods. Such technique would have destroyed most politicians, but Franklin Roosevelt, as skillful a political manipulator as ever lived, managed to make it one of his strengths. "Our frontier is the Rhine," he had said early in the war. There are those who believe that even before June, 1940, when France fell, Roosevelt expected and intended that we should get into it and finish off Germany as we had done in 1918, but he knew that the American public would not follow him as yet, and he kept his secret. We may never know exactly what was in the President's mind at this time; after we are all dead the records at Hyde Park may give the answer.

All the world loved William Allen White. Seldom has any man risen to the eminence which he achieved, ever enjoyed such affectionate good will. Thus, during the first stages of this most important of his undertakings, the opposition pulled its punches because of their acute fear of his popularity. True, Father Coughlin—remember him?—called White a "stuffed shirt," but by now no one who counted paid any attention to Coughlin. As the controversy waxed hotter, however, the six-shooters came out of their holsters and the opposition, all expert name-callers, began shooting epithets at him and his committee. "War-monger," "hick," "slave of Wall Street," "traitor," filled the air. The climax came when Mayor Fiorello H. La Guardia, of New York, one of the men who had most persistently urged White to undertake the job, called him "a Laval." In Kansas, still isolationist, he was as near to unpopularity as ever in his life. In the successive stages of his fight to get aid to

Britain, not a single member of the Kansas delegation in Congress voted for any of the measures which he was backing on behalf of the Administration. Even Landon, whom he had supported in the campaign for nomination and election to the presidency in 1936, opposed him.

White had his own inimitable way with opponents who got personal in controversy. A sensitive organism, he was never touchy about the dignity of William Allen White. Kansans, he once wrote, "don't care so much about the fictitious thing called honor . . . The Kansas man laughs too easily. Before his honor gets to hurting, he sees the joke on himself, and then it's all over. No man can fight laughing. Kansas laughs too easily to bother much about the points of honor. . . ." Usually he regarded these attacks with genuine amusement. When, as sometimes happened, the situation was such that he had to answer, he either admitted the accusation, added a few graphic details for good measure, and concluded in effect, "What has that to do with the point of issue, anyway?" or burned his adversary brown with a single witty quip. But when his present opposition, led by the Communists, charged that the international bankers, the munition makers, and sinister foreign factions were paying the expenses of his committee, he was forced to reply. And this time he spoke with all the seriousness of a United States senator talking for the record. He stated that he had accepted the chairmanship only on condition that the committee take no money from anyone having a direct pecuniary interest in the war, and that the average contribution was $25. This indication of a faint resentment of personal criticism was a proof of his weariness and a forecast of his approaching physical breakdown.

Once about this time he asked in a *Gazette* editorial what the Hitler conquest of Europe meant to the United States. It didn't mean much so far, he admitted, but it did give Hitler more power. What then could we do?

About all we can do is trust to the deep spirit of justice in man. Hitler at home and abroad is fighting against that spirit. His empire is built upon force, not upon justice. . . . But if there is anything in the aspiring soul of man, if there is anything in the wisdom of the ages that sounds in the morality of all religions, it gives us hope that democracy founded upon the faith of man in man, democracy founded upon the ancient yearning for justice in human relations, will prevail in this world. . . . We have a right to hope and deeply believe that Hitler's reliance upon force and his terrible tyranny that comes with unchecked power, will lead him eventually to his doom. . . . Alexander, Caesar, Napoleon, all the great conquering tyrants, have conquered armies only to be overthrown by the divine fire in the heart of man . . . a simple but unconquered menace that all tyrants face.

That most discouraging year of the war ended with the German tide still flowing over Europe unchecked and the German U-boats torpedoing cargo ships inside of our six-mile limit.

It began to seem possible that all our aid to the one ally which still stood firm would be in vain. The German element was exultant, the isolationists hesitant, the pro-ally coming to the unwelcome conclusion that the only hope was for us to convoy our own ships—which meant, in anyone's book, an act of war. More and more White's supporters and colleagues were leaning to that opinion, which brought on the crisis that was the occasion, although probably not the whole cause, of his resignation from the chairmanship of the committee.

An "interview" with White in the Scripps-Howard newspapers spilled the beans—an affair too complex and tangled for full relation here. Oversimplifying the story: In order to forestall an attack on the committee from the Scripps-Howard newspapers, Mr. White had written a personal letter to his friend Roy Howard, in which he refuted some of the expected charges. Howard replied by telegram to White at Emporia, asking for permission to publish the letter. After adding a hurried paragraph, White consented. To make it a little more acceptable as front-page copy, the Scripps-Howard staff changed the letter into an "interview." It appeared, accompanied by a laudatory editorial, on December 23, 1940, two days before the gloomiest Christmas the liberal world ever had known. Hell popped immediately.

If the overworked White had realized the full importance of this statement, he would have sat down and written it for the intended purpose as he wrote an editorial for the *Gazette*. It would have said, with that fine tact which was the summit of his literary skills, exactly what he meant. But written for one purpose, warped to serve another, revised without much thought, the interview was hazy and susceptible to double interpretation. One particular sentence in the hasty addition to the original letter raised a storm: "Any organization that is for war is certainly playing Hitler's game."

Some of the more moderate and judicious members and supporters of the White Committee deplored it. White, they felt, passed as a spokesman for President Roosevelt in matters concerning our aid to the Allies. A declaration which could be interpreted as a refusal to fight in any circumstances would have the same effect as the neutrality law. The President was fighting a power which recognized only force or the threat of it. This would tie his hands. Letters, telegrams, clippings from editorial pages rained on White's desk at Emporia. Many, it was true, were friendly, but these came mostly from individuals, organizations, and newspapers whose favor he did not seek. Ten days of this, and then on January 2, 1941, he resigned his chairmanship quietly, flatly, finally, and with no defense or explanation of the "interview," other than a "Purely Personal" editorial which appeared in the *Gazette* on the day of his resignation. In it he declared that Roy Howard and he had held friendly discussions concerning the danger of the United States getting into the war if she kept on aiding Britain.

In the end [White said] he asked me to put in writing what I thought about the position of our Committee to Defend America by Aiding the Allies in relation to war and the involvement of our committee. Here is my answer:

The only reason in God's world I am in this organization is to keep this country out of war. I don't go an inch further or faster than Wendell Willkie or the American Legion or the American Federation of Labor or the National Grange; nor an inch further or faster than you went this month in the Filipino magazine on the Eastern question. The story is floating around that our committee and I are in favor of sending convoys with the British ships or our own ships, a silly thing—for convoys, unless you shoot, are confetti; and it's not time to shoot now or ever. Another thing: Our loathed but highly esteemed adversaries keep insisting that we are in favor of repealing the Johnson Act, a stupid thing to do because it would not help Great Britain, and there are half a dozen other good legal ways to aid Great Britain.

Mr. White added that the President was following his own road, that if he were asked to write a short motto for the committee it would be: "The Yanks are not coming," that we had less than 200,000 men ready to fight, and that we needed them more at home on the assembly lines than in Europe.

War would defeat the first and last end for which our committee is organized—to defend America by aiding Great Britain . . .
I have no doubt that some members of our organization who are not officially representing us are martial minded. . . . I have sat in all our executive counsels, all our policy making committees, and I have never heard war as an alternative objective seriously discussed by an official group of our organization at any time. . . ."

Those whom his attitude puzzled, those who called him inconsistent, forgot the last sentences of that editorial on the arms embargo by which he announced that he had entered this fight:
"When war is abroad, it is an infectious, social, economic and political disease. . . . The serum that will stop war from spreading from nation to nation has never been discovered. The second World War is a menace to America. We must have the indomitable will to keep out of it."
He, who hated hate, cruelty, violence, unreason, could not bring himself to give full endorsement to war, even in a cause as righteous as the one which he was trying to support, by every means short of war, in 1941.
Despite all the confusion and differences of opinion, within and without the committee, which led up to Mr. White's resignation, the work he did in his capacity as chairman, the last public service of his life, was perhaps the most important of his services to his country. It was a complete success, aside from the unhappy ending. By his skill, his leadership, his public reputation, he had done what he started out to do—get the Neutrality Act revised, make it possible for Britain to obtain munitions here, help fight off the U-boat menace, clarify public opinion

in America on the grave issues which faced us. He prepared our minds for what was coming, so that on the fateful day of Pearl Harbor we had our factories converted to the making of munitions, our military plans advanced, our people resigned to the inevitable. Through this service, given for neither fame nor gain, we were able to get a running start and thereby save countless American lives.

11. LAST EDITORIALS

Mr. White's last *Gazette* editorials were written when he was seriously sick.

In one which appeared in the weekly *Gazette* of October 14, 1943, entitled "A Fourth Term Doubtful," he said that he was "one of those rare birds who believes Roosevelt may not run for a fourth term. He is certainly, however, giving a correct imitation of a fourth term candidate at this writing."

On October 21, 1943, in "His Draft Card Unchanged," Mr. White wrote: "The Topeka *Capital* calls the editor of the *Gazette* 'trusting' and one who has always been able to find more sunshine than sorrow in this vale of tears." He quoted the Topeka editor: "It may have been his optimistic viewpoint that leads him to conclude that Mr. Roosevelt is not a candidate for a fourth term."

White went on: "The other day the editor of the *Gazette* said editorially that the President is only giving a correct imitation of a fourth term candidate.

"But to the Topeka editor it appears that F.D.R. actually is giving an imitation of a candidate for a fourth term with the idea of convincing the public that it is only an imitation, thereby concealing the fact that it is the real thing."

In another of his final editorials in the weekly *Gazette,* October 21, 1943, "On Domestic Issues," he wrote:

The Republican campaign next year may be fought now on domestic issues. The Republican party has come close enough to the foreign policy of the Administration so that no grave question of difference between the two parties on the foreign policy need come into the campaign. . . .

This is as it should be and for the very good reason that there is a serious fundamental difference between the two parties, no matter who is the candidate of either party, no matter who makes the policies. The people of the United States have the right to vote for the continuation of the New Deal or for something better. The fundamental philosophy of the New Deal is challenged by the

Republicans. They will not get far abusing the President, but they will get a long way if they go definitely and fundamentally into the political philosophy back of his creed. They will go even further than that if they set up their own policy, if they offer something more substantial, more American, more self-respecting than the New Deal, which the President has offered to the American people.

There is a chance for an issue here. It is a great issue. If the Republicans are brave and wise they can win on it. But the foreign policy need not be cluttered up in any attack on the New Deal in this campaign.

In the same issue, writing under the title "Schoeppel and Labor," Mr. White said that union organizers were trying to unionize Kansas state employees under the merit system.

There is no sense or justification in unionizing state employes. The state represents the organized forces of society and it is supposed to protect all the citizens and functions in a going civilization. State employes are much like soldiers. Soldiers have no right to strike, no right to go clamoring for more pay while they are on duty, state employes have the same limitations. State employes take their jobs knowing what the salary is. They take the job knowing that they are protected in their jobs, which guarantees them vacations and social security.

The only thing that justifies the organization of state employes is the fee of the organizer. The organizers of the union can't do one blessed thing for the state employees except get them into trouble. . . . A union raises a confliction of double loyalty, loyalty to the union and loyalty to the state. There can be no double loyalty in the government of Kansas. Men employed on the roads, men employed in protecting the health services of this state, men employed in the educational institutions, all are soldiers, protecting the state. It is unthinkable and un-American for them to join the union.

White's open mind and understanding heart enabled him to see as early as 1910 that:

As men widen their sphere of knowledge they broaden their sensibilities. As the sensibilities of the millions broaden, society redistributes its rewards, changes its codes; evils multiply; sin increases. But it is not the number of evil deeds that grow, it is the public sense of evil that is widening.

It pays to be decent. That means only that the spiritual is dominant in a material world. . . . The good that a man may do is limited only by his talents. . . . We may as well make up our minds to all good intents and for all high purposes that this is not a material world. Whoever would achieve any worthy thing must found it upon the common law of kindness.

In life, man has his choice between the treadmill of the eternal grind, and the path of the eternal journey. It is his only choice in all the scheme of things. For on his choice depends his character; from his character, not from his environment, will come his happiness. . . . Happiness is usefulness; meanness is waste. . . .

Neighborly kindness, instinctive courtesy, gentleness, consideration for the rights of others, and yearning for a better social order were fed from the inexhaustible wellsprings of his warm heart. His interest, his efforts to serve the Commonwealth in a multitude of ways, never lagged. One of his major efforts was to interpret social, economic, and political problems in such manner as to enable all men to see how to improve and strengthen his beloved America.

In an editorial on this subject written not long before his death he set down the essence of his wisdom on public affairs:

Surely in private industry on this continent there is an adequate margin of operator's profit wide enough to keep American commerce afloat as a going concern, allowing for decent earnings, for living wages, for attractive prices to the consumer that will move the goods. And surely again America can produce brains in a free industry to solve this terrible problem somewhat outside of politics without too much government aid or control.

And how worthwhile it is to do this immediate job that lies before us! No other institution on earth has such a large survival value in human happiness as democracy. The free man, whether worker, investor, or consumer, lies at the foundation of the democratic scheme of things. The ballot box is the free man's weapon. Free speech, a free press, the writ of *habeas corpus,* the right of trial by jury and freedom of conscience are the American's royal privileges which he should guard sacredly from abuse. In a world where these privileges are denied, every other blessing which nourishes the spirit of man is soon denied.

It is easy to get out and fight a futile war to save democracy. But it will be hard for us, harder even than war for all of us, workers, investors, consumers, to make in peace those inevitable compromises that are needed to guarantee the maintenance of free institutions. We must all give a little. This hour has no time for the man who refuses to compromise even to his own hurt. Half of the civilized world today beyond our borders has surrendered the rights, privileges and blessings which democracy accords to free men. Should not the roaring waters of disaster, flooding ever nearer the feet of those who follow the tyrants, warn us to turn to the ways of peace with justice which are the only guarantees of freedom?

12. THE END OF THE STORY

THE LAST TIME I saw Will White for more than a mere glimpse was in the spring of 1943 in New York City. He and Mrs. White had invited me to have breakfast with them at their hotel. After a period of waiting in the lobby, unusual because he always was punctual, I saw him get off the elevator, slump to a near-by settee, and collapse. He said when I hurried over that he felt "a great deal like a minority report," but would be all right soon. Then he explained that he had spent a half hour getting dressed and that Mrs. White was not feeling well and would not come down. A bellboy brought some aromatic spirits of ammonia I had ordered, and Mr. White took a few whiffs from the bottle, remarking as he did so that it likely might do him more good if he were to drink it. He asked for hot milk, in place of the whisky I had suggested. The doctor, who had been summoned, arrived and we moved Mr. White to a more comfortable, less conspicuous settee. Then he insisted that I eat breakfast. "Sign my name to the check—you are my guest."

Meanwhile his son and daughter-in-law reached the hotel and quickly got the senior Whites on their way to a hospital. There they spent their fiftieth wedding anniversary, Mr. White getting over an attack of pnuemonia and Mrs. White one of influenza.

They left for Emporia as soon as the doctor permitted, and spent the spring there and the summer in Estes Park, where Mr. White worked at his forthcoming autobiography. Letters from him reported that his health was greatly improved. In one he said he was doing the best writing of his life. He continued his Book-of-the-Month Club work, carried on a heavy correspondence, and performed innumerable friendly services.

His last letter to me, written in October from Emporia, was only a note to say that he and Mrs. White were scheduled to reach New York City on a given date for a visit of two or three weeks, and to express the hope that I would be in the city.

Shortly after his letter reached me newspaper stories reported that he had gone to the Mayo Clinic at Rochester, Minnesota, for a checkup. Later reports from members of the White family told of the gravity of his condition. In time they revealed that he never would recover.

During the interval between his return to Emporia on November 18 and his death, he made four or five visits to the *Gazette* office. The first of these, according to a *Gazette* story, occurred within a few days after he and Mrs. White had returned home. Probably the weather on that bright, warm, late November Saturday afternoon had encouraged Mrs. White to take him for a ride about town. Only a few members of the staff were at the office. They expressed surprise at seeing him back so soon. "Yeah," he replied, and his eyes had that old twinkle, "I'm here. They thought they'd take me off the front end of the train at Kansas City but I fooled them and got off the back end."

Two or three days before his death the Whites' housekeeper for over twenty years, Bertha Colglaizer, more a family friend than servant, visited Mr. White after having been kept away from him for several days because of a bad cold.

He asked her: "Do you think I'm going to get well, Bertha?"

She replied that she believed he would because he was looking so much better than when she had last seen him. He answered with a smile: "You are going to have to spend a long time in purgatory for that lie, Bertha."

His condition grew steadily worse, and he died on the morning of January 29, 1944.

The thoughts he expressed in a *Gazette* editorial when T.R. left the White House on March 4, 1909, held true in his own case. He had written then that the chief, the most important part of the heritage Theodore Roosevelt had given was himself.

[T.R.] went into office a strong, virile, frank, honest, fearless man —full of youth, full of faith in man and God, full of ideals. And for seven years and a half he has lived and worked before the people, and has come out—not a broken, jaded, worn-out, disillusioned man —but the same high, clean, unbending, youthful man that he went in.

One's ideals are gauged by his conduct. The reason Roosevelt has faith is because he has kept faith himself. The pessimist is the man who has compromised with life, who has lowered his flag for expediency, who has surrendered. Theodore Roosevelt has made mistakes, but he has not surrendered. He has lived up to his ideals. He has played an honest hand, and he is leaving eight years of great service as he came—unconquered and unbowed. That is a great achievement—perhaps his greatest achievement. For he has given an example of what a decent man may do. The example he has left probably is worth more to the nation than the laws he has forced through Congress and the policies he has promulgated.

The weather the winter day of Mr. White's funeral was mild, so mild that seemingly God Himself had taken charge. Kansas days in midwinter can be atrocious with blustery winds, ice, snow, and zero or subzero temperatures, but on Monday, January 31, 1944, the sun smiled a benediction on Emporia.

A flood of messages from friends and admirers swept into Emporia the day following his death.

The late President Roosevelt called him one of the

. . . wisest and most beloved editors. . . . As a writer of truth, forcible and vigorous prose he was unsurpassed . . . He ennobled the profession of journalism. . . .

Herbert Hoover wired:

I greatly grieve the loss of one of the greatest of American citizens . . .

Anthony Eden's message read:

We in Britain remember with gratitude the friendship he showed us in times of great anxiety and peril . . .

Lord Halifax said:

The cause of Anglo-American co-operation owes an unpayable debt to him for his generous and unsparing efforts to bring a better understanding between our peoples . . .

Cordell Hull wrote in his telegram:

[Mr. White] exercised the very finest influence on American journalism . . . the community and the country have lost one of their finest citizens.

Old friends from as far away as both the west and the east coasts, from Washington, Chicago, from the Missouri Valley states and from all over Kansas, began to arrive in Emporia that morning. By noon all schools, stores, and public offices had closed for the day.

Solemnity rather than grief was the spirit of Mr. White's fellow townsmen that day. They seemed, in those hushed hours, to have caught a glimpse of the rich blessing of the true nobility and greatness they had enjoyed for so many years. Some of them knew that Emporia had lost a spiritual giant, that a glory which long had hovered over the town was gone.

Luncheon at the White home, presided over by Mrs. White and young Bill, was not an unhappy occasion. At times it was nearly festive as one or another of our small group would recall some act or quote some quip of Mr. White's. Shortly after luncheon old friends began coming to the house. Soon the great living room was filled and remained so until we began the trip to the chapel of the College of Emporia, where the funeral service was held.

Utmost simplicity marked the services both at the chapel and at the cemetery. The casket was covered only by a wreath of pine needles and cones. There were no other floral decorations. The minister recited two scriptural selections: the Thirteenth Chapter of First Corinthians and the Twenty-third Psalm—read at the services of Mary White in 1921. In fact, the funeral services of the father duplicated those held twenty-three years earlier at the daughter's, which the father had planned. Mrs. White had given the minister who was to officiate at Mr. White's funeral a copy of the sermon delivered at Mary's, and told him that practically everything that had been said of the daughter could well be said of the father.

After a brief prayer by the minister the chapel filled with the chords of Tschaikovsky's *Symphonie Pathétique*. Henry J. Haskell, editor of the *Kansas City Star* and an intimate friend of Mr. White's, talked simply but with great feeling about his friend and dulled some of the sadness of the occasion by recalling the contagious exuberance of Mr. White's writings. Mr. Haskell went on:

It was in keeping with the pattern of his life that he gave himself to arousing his apathetic countrymen to their danger by organizing the Committee to Defend America by Aiding the Allies. The sentiment that he mobilized contributed powerfully to changing the neutrality laws so we could sell arms to the democracies. And finally it was on his suggestion that the superb trade was made that gave hard-pressed England the fifty over-age destroyers in return for the Atlantic bases.

Englishmen have expressed to me their surprise that a man from far off Kansas should have been such a factor in the salvation of the British commonwealth and the cause of civilization itself. They could not know the long years of work that had brought this Kansas editor to his position of influence in American life.

Behind all his work was the personality of the man. He was a great human being—great in intelligence, in understanding, in courage, in zest. Life to him always was a glorious adventure. "I never have been bored an hour in my life," he wrote on the occasion of his sixty-fifth birthday. "I get up every morning now wondering what new, strange, gorgeous thing is going to happen, and it always happens at fairly reasonable intervals. Lady Luck has been good to me. I fancy she is good to everyone only some people are dour, and when she gives them the come hither with her eyes, they look down or turn away and lift an eyebrow. But me, I give her the wink and away we go!"

On our way to the cemetery young Bill expressed pleasure that such a large number of Kansas newspaper editors had come to be with them, to which his mother replied, "Newspapermen are the finest on earth. I always said even before I met Will that I would marry only a newspaperman."

It was not until we reached the grave that we realized how great the attendance was. Mrs. White suggested that we wait in the car until everyone was there, "Because," she explained, "Will never liked the final services to begin until everyone was present." So we waited for perhaps fifteen minutes while one automobile after another, a seemingly endless procession of them, hurried down the lane between the trees.

The ceremony at the grave, in keeping with Mr. White's life, was without ostentation but dignified. After a brief prayer a chorus of Welsh singers from Emporia's big Welsh population sang their unimaginably moving resurrection hymn, "Byyd Myrrh O Rhyffeddodan," which most movingly blends a dirge for the dead with exultant joy over the promise of the resurrection.

The sun had nearly set when we left the cemetery. Mr. White, who had "feared life much more than death," but was "ready to take greedily whichever comes," who was "not afraid of to-morrow for I have seen yesterday and live today," had started on the greatest of all adventures at the full tide of his powers, with such a multitude of expressions of affectionate good will from the great and the lowly of the earth as few men ever deserve or get.

His place in this and the next world is secure if, as he once said in a *Gazette* editorial, "what we are in the next world depends not on what we make here but what we take from here —what of kindness, what of strength, what of wisdom."

At the time of William Gladstone's death in 1898, Mr. White wrote in a *Gazette* editorial:

He was a man of culture . . . He kept abreast of the best thought of the civilized world on all lines of knowledge—economics, social science, natural science, general literature, psychology, ethics . . . . It was because Gladstone translated the best things of great minds into the common sense of the people that he was grand. He was grand because he was cultured—because he acted upon the best wisdom of the best minds of all time. . . . He was grand because he knew the best and strove for it.

Following John Hay's death in 1905, Mr. White said:

He was a strong man who never blustered, a shrewd man who was never cunning, an honest man who never shook hands with him-self in congratulation. He had become a power in the world during eight years of public life, and his power has made America a power. We climb by our representative men . . .

It is men like Hay who make America—men of ideals, men who live in practice what they preach. It is so easy to talk; so hard to live up to it, but John Hay preached truth in the first part of his life, and in the last part of it stood a world monument for truth. Nations are only as great as the honest men. . . .

When Briand died in 1931, Mr. White prophesied in a *Ga-zette* editorial:

The world will miss him but missing him out of its yearnings for peace, mankind will follow the workings of some mysterious spirit-ual alchemy and will produce another of his kind, for leadership in any cause is the flower of human aspiration and causes make men, not men, causes.

The qualities Mr. White found in Gladstone when he was thirty years old, in Hay when he was thirty-seven, and in Briand when he was sixty-three all were to be found in his own mind and heart, with one additional quality, uniquely his: that of knowing the best hearts of his time, the men and women in every grade and walk of life who believed beyond all doubt that spiritual qualities in our material world are alone above price and enduring.

With that quality added, the characteristics of Gladstone, Hay, and Briand as he estimated them epitomized the life of William Allen White.

*   *   *   *   *

The evening after the funeral, two of Mr. White's old friends visited the cemetery. As they were standing near his grave, two boys rode up on their bicycles, boys about ten or twelve years old, one white, the other Negro, whose parents, perhaps even their grandparents, had been blessed in a multitude of ways by Mr. White's ministrations to the people of Emporia.

The friends heard one boy exclaim about the great mountain of flowers over the grave. "Just look at all them flowers!" he said. "Why are there so many?"

His companion replied: "You know why; it's because he was the greatest man in all the whole world."

Index